Wisdom's Friendly Heart

Wisdom's Friendly Heart

Augustinian Hope for Skeptics and Conspiracy Theorists

Jennifer Hockenbery

CASCADE *Books* · Eugene, Oregon

WISDOM'S FRIENDLY HEART
Augustinian Hope for Skeptics and Conspiracy Theorists

Cascade Books
An Imprint of Wipf and Stock Publishers
199 W. 8th Ave., Suite 3
Eugene, OR 97401

www.wipfandstock.com

PAPERBACK ISBN: 978-1-5326-9084-6
HARDCOVER ISBN: 978-1-5326-9085-3
EBOOK ISBN: 978-1-5326-9086-0

Cataloguing-in-Publication data:

Names: Dragseth, Jennifer Hockenbery, author.

Title: Wisdom's friendly heart : Augustinian hope for skeptics and conspiracy theorists / by Jennifer Hockenbery.

Description: Eugene, OR : Cascade Books, 2020 | Includes bibliographical references and index.

Identifiers: ISBN 978-1-5326-9084-6 (paperback) | ISBN 978-1-5326-9085-3 (hardcover) | ISBN 978-1-5326-9086-0 (ebook)

Subjects: LCSH: Augustine, of Hippo, Saint, 354–430. | Truthfulness and falsehood—Religious aspects—Christianity. | Truthfulness and falsehood. | Relativity. | Gnosticism.

Classification: BR65.A9 H57 2020 (print) | BR65.A9 H57 (ebook)

Manufactured in the U.S.A.   09/22/20

For my Adeodati

Luke, Phoebe, and Hope

You are my gifts from God and the surest signs
of God's friendly heart.

Thank you for all you have taught me.

Contents

A Note on Translation and Citations

I HAVE USED ONLY my own translations for all non-English quotes in the body of the text, attempting to be as literal as understandable English allows. In particular, I have paid close attention to the pronouns used by each author for God, using the masculine, feminine, or neuter in English when the author has done so in Greek, Latin, French, or German. Importantly, all four of those languages use the feminine pronoun for Truth and Wisdom. In addition, I have tried to translate other terms for God as close to its cultural context as possible. For example, the term *dominus* in the late antique Roman empire was a regularly used term of respect for a male who was a citizen and the most prominent member of his household. Sometimes, Augustine was implying a familiar relationship when he addressed God as *dominus,* as if God were a fellow citizen. In such instances, I use the term "Sir." At other times, Augustine is clearly using the term to denote the person in charge of a household, a household in which Augustine was considering himself a child or, at times, a servant. At such times, I use "master of the house." Augustine would have understood that "dominus" was the Latin translation of "adonai" in Hebrew and "kyrie" in Greek, terms that are also forms of address for human men with wealth and property, although not in a feudal context. The medieval English term "Lord" conveys a meaning that would have been foreign to Augustine's context. Of course, the term is appropriate to Hildegard, Thomas, and Luther's medieval feudal contexts. So for those authors, I do use the word "Lord" for *dominus.*

I always have included the passage in its original language (if other than English) in the footnotes. The sources of the original language quotes appear in the bibliography as do quality English versions of most of the books cited in the original language. I use the English translations of the titles of all works I cite in the body of the text but include the original titles in the footnotes and the bibliography. Augustine's works are cited in the footnotes with an abbreviation of the Latin title and the book, chapter, and paragraph number. For those works that only have one book, only the chapter and paragraph number appear, and in the rare instances where there are no chapters, only the paragraph number is cited. For the quotes from the Confessions, I use J. J. O'Donnell's edition of the Latin. Quotes from the other texts of Augustine are from Latin texts from J. P. Migne's *Patrologia Latina*, published online.[1] Other ancient sources are similarly cited using standard pages or book, chapter, and/or paragraph numbers. When available, I also have provided an online location for the original language text. My hope is that those who want to check these quotes for accuracy or for the purpose of their own research will be able to do so easily, while those who simply want a general understanding of the ideas will get a taste of the rhetoric and style of each of the philosophers and other writers I quote.

1. See Augustine, *Opera Omnia.*

Abbreviations for Augustine's Works

All quotations from the *Confessions* are from J. J. O'Donnell's edition. See Augustine, *Confessiones*. All quotations of Augustine's other works are from J. P. Migne's *Patologia Latina* and can also be accessed online. See Augustine, *Opera Omnia*.

BV	*de Beata Vita* (*On the Happy Life*) (386)
CA	*Contra Academicos* (*Against the Academic Skeptics*) (386)
CD	*de Civitate Dei* (*The City of God*) (413–427)
CJ	*Contra Secundam Iulianam responsionem imperfectum opus* (*Against Julian*) (421)
Conf.	*Confessiones* (*Confessions*) (397–401)
DGM	*de Genesis contra Manichaeos* (*On Genesis against the Manicheans in Two Books*) (388–389)
DG	*de Genesi ad litteram imperfectus liber* (*On the Literal Meaning of Genesis: An Unfinished Book*) (401–415)
DG12	*de Genesi ad litteram libri duodecim* (*On the Literal Meaning of Genesis in Twelve Books*) (401–415)
Doct.	*de Doctrina Christiana* (*On Christian Doctrine*) (396–426)
DM	*de Magistro* (*On the Teacher*) (389)
DME	*de Moribus Ecclesiae Catholicae et de Moribus Manichaeorum* (*On the Morals of the Catholic Church and the Morals of the Manicheans*) (387–389)
DSD	*de Sermone Domini in Monte* (*On the Sermon on the Mount*) (393)
Ench	*Enchiridion de Laurentium de Fide, Spe, et Charitate* (*Handbook on Faith, Hope, and Love*) (421–422)
Enn. Ps.	*Enarrationes in Psalmos* (*Narrations on the Psalms*) (396–420)

Epis.   *Epistolae (Letters)* (386–430)

LA   *de Libero Arbitrio (On the Freedom of the Will)* (388–395)

NB   *de Natura Boni (On the Nature of the Good)* (399)

Ord.   *de Ordine (On Order)* (386)

Ret.   *Retractiones (Retractions)* (426–427)

Sermon   *Sermones (Sermons)* (393–430)

Sol.   *Soliloquia (Soliloquies)* (386–387)

SL   *de Spiritu et Littera (On the Spirit and the Letter)* (412)

TJ   *Tractatus in Evangelium Iohannis (Tractate on The Gospel of John)* (406–430)

Trin.   *de Trinitate (On the Trinity)* (399–419)

VR   *de Vera Religione (On True Religion)* (389–391)

UC   *de Utilitate Credenda (On the Usefulness of Belief)* (391)

Timeline of Augustine's Life

November 13, 354   Augustine is born in Thagaste, in the province of Numidia.

371   Augustine begins his studies in Carthage.

Augustine begins his long-term relationship with his concubine.

371–73   Augustine's concubine gives birth to their son, Adeodatus.

Augustine reads the *Hortensius* and is converted to philosophy.

Augustine joins the Manicheans.

375   Augustine teaches rhetoric in Thagaste.

376   Augustine teaches rhetoric in Carthage.

383   Augustine goes to Rome to teach rhetoric, taking his concubine and son with him.

384   Augustine becomes professor of rhetoric in Milan.

385   Augustine divorces his concubine and becomes engaged to a woman of his mother's choosing. His concubine returns to Africa. Adeodatus remains with Augustine.

386–87   Augustine converts to catholic Christianity. He breaks off his engagement and pledges celibacy. Augustine is baptized with his son Adeodatus. Augustine is forced by illness to leave his academic post and retreats to Cassiciacum to discuss and write philosophy.

387   Augustine's mother, Monica, dies.

388–90	Augustine goes to Rome and then Carthage before returning to Thagaste.
390	Adeodatus dies.
391	Augustine is forced into ordination as a priest in Hippo.
392	Augustine publicly debates Fortunatus the Manichean.
396	Augustine is forced into ordination as Bishop of Hippo.
403–12	Augustine debates the Donatists.
408–10	The Visigoths attack and sack Rome.
410	Pelagius comes to Africa to escape the Visigoths.
412	Rome bans Donatism by imperial decree.
412–21	Augustine debates the Pelagians.
418	Carthage bans Pelagianism as heresy. Augustine warns Rome to do likewise.
429–30	Vandals invade Africa from Spain.
August 28, 430	Augustine dies.

Acknowledgments

A BOOK ON THE relational nature of truth seeking must certainly pay homage to the relationships that forged the thinking of the author. Let me begin by acknowledging three professors—Remi Brague, Margaret Miles, and the late Matthew Lamb—who introduced me to Augustine as a philosopher in graduate school. Biking through the rain from class with Miles on Harvard's campus to Lamb's Latin reading group at Boston College gave me time to think about their different approaches to the African doctor and their common clarity about Augustine's delight in the pursuit of truth. I am especially grateful for Miles and Brague's continued, friendly-hearted support throughout my last two decades as I have continued to grow and learn, enriching my understanding from my graduate school days to something somewhat more mature. I also want to acknowledge and thank Robert Neville, who served as the advisor for my dissertation on Augustine back in 1998, for his gentle but constant prodding that I ought to update my thinking for the current age.

My ability to read and admire Augustine's original language owes almost everything to my wonderful high school Latin teacher, Alan Corn, who in four years gave me a firm foundation in Latin grammar and vocabulary along with a passion for the ancient and late antique world that set me on the path to become a lifelong student of classics and philosophy. I must thank, too, my college classics professors, John Ambrose and Stephen Hall, who encouraged my passion for Latin and Greek language, assuring me that such knowledge was relevant for the current age. For access to many Latin and Greek Loeb Classical texts, I want to thank my predecessor at Mount Mary University, the late John Carmichael, whose family gifted me his classical library after his death. For access to Luther's works and almost the entire corpus of Augustine, I must thank the Reverend Ray Stubbe, who has donated hundreds of books to our family's personal library.

I am deeply grateful for my community at Mount Mary University. I want to acknowledge the gift of the sabbatical that allowed me the time to read, translate, write, and talk about these ideas. I especially want to thank my students who have taught me so much through their questions and insights. I am particularly grateful to Danielle Burdick, who worked as my research assistant and personal librarian. I also must acknowledge the wonderful Ryan Parker, master of interlibrary loan at Mount Mary, as well as the many librarians at the Milwaukee County library system who all worked to get me quickly whatever text I suddenly decided I required. Special appreciation goes to my colleagues in the theology and philosophy department, Austin Reece, Katie Homan, Helga Kisler, Donald Rappé, and Shawnee Daniels-Sykes. Our work together has taught me much not only about philosophy and theology but also about the best ways to teach passionate students who are vulnerable to radical skepticism and gullible to conspiracy theory. I am grateful for these friendly-hearted colleagues and for our relationship in which we pursue truth together.

Outside of the academy, I want to give thanks to and for Yael Stein, who taught me the Hebrew original for many of Augustine's Latin terms for Old Testament words. In addition, I am particularly grateful for the *misericordia* (*chesid*) she has given me this year especially.

Augustine's first teacher was his mother, and I, too, owe my parents for both life and learning. Thank you to my mother, who reads everything I send her, helping with editing and always offering encouragement. Thank you to my father, who tells me when I am misunderstanding Luther but mostly just praises my efforts. Your support has been invaluable this year.

Finally, I believe that Augustine learned the most about God's love from his experience of holding his own child. To feel such overwhelming love for a child allows a parent to understand a little of what God's overwhelming love must be for us. Luke, Phoebe, and Hope, you are truly God's gifts, and I love every aspect of your being and your becoming. Thank you for bearing with all the times I made you listen to stories of Augustine's fascination with dragons, for all the times you waited patiently when I wanted to write just one more paragraph, and for all the times you gave me helpful advice about a better of way of thinking and a better way of writing. You have taught me far more than I have taught you.

Chapter 1

Introduction

Is There Really a Place for Augustine in the "Post-Truth Era"?

IN 2005 ON HIS satirical show "The Colbert Report," Stephen Colbert invented a new word, "truthiness," to describe how a statement feels to a person who wishes the statement to be true even if there are no facts to support their feeling. Colbert joked that people should stop worrying about the truth of positions and instead rely on the "truthiness" of them. As always with satire, there was some truth—or at least truthiness—in his discussion of how contemporary people decide what to believe. In 2016, the Oxford English Dictionary named the adjective "post-truth" as the word of the year, a word that refers to the tendency of people in the twenty-first century to prefer opinion to fact or to be unable to differentiate between opinion and fact. By 2019, the expression "post-truth era" had become a mainstream term for the current age, an epoch in which people do not agree on any common criteria by which different people might judge the truthfulness of a statement. In the post-truth era, public opinion claims that the difference between ethics and aesthetics, between social good and social bias, and between science and conspiracy theory lies only in the heart, or the gut, of the person evaluating the claim.

This is in contrast to the era of the founding of the United States, an era commonly called "the Enlightenment," when Thomas Paine announced that certain arguments are "common sense" and Thomas Jefferson claimed that certain truths are "self-evident." And yet, if they were able to witness the present era, Enlightenment thinkers might be surprised to find so much skepticism about the possibility of objective knowledge even as the majority of American citizens have access to vaccines that have wiped out small pox, antibiotics that have radically reduced fears of scarlet fever and tuberculosis, and tiny computers that fit in their pockets that provide access to books, articles, and ideas from around the world. On one hand, contemporary thinkers are right to have a humility that Enlightenment thinkers all too

1

often seemed to lack. Of course, human beings, even those who are intellectual giants, see the world through the lenses of their biases. On the other hand, contemporary thinkers seem to be blind to how much knowledge the human community has gained. Indeed, the very fact that contemporary thinkers can see the racist bias of an intellectual giant like Thomas Jefferson could be cause for hope in the progress of knowledge rather than despair that nothing can be known.

And yet, the despair that nothing can be known seems to be getting more press than the evidence for hope in acquiring new knowledge. Headlines that disparage other headlines as "fake news" are the norm as are those that decry the lack of civil conversation. In many cases, it seems that people simply do not trust anyone to be able to see correctly. In some cases, it seems that people do not even trust themselves to see correctly. Such a lack of trust leads to a lack of earnest engagement by the public in inquiry and dialogue just at that point in time when human beings have so many technological tools that allow inquiry into the smallest and farthest corners of the cosmos and that encourage dialogue with people all around the globe.

There are many hypotheses about the root of this lack of trust. Perhaps it began in university philosophy departments. Western philosophers have been arguing that people should be more careful about making assumptions since the era of the Enlightenment. Philosophers in the last century especially have been deconstructing the systems of belief that were once considered common knowledge and admonishing people to be aware of bias and hegemony. At the turn of the millennium, however, the philosophical academy realized that it might have a new battle to fight. Not naïve realism but radical skepticism seemed to have become the norm in society. Those who made their living advocating for the love of wisdom started to recognize the danger to their profession if people stopped believing in wisdom. Worse, for those philosophers who believe that Carl Linneaus aptly coined the term *homo sapiens* (literally "wisdom knowing hominoids"), the crisis of "truthiness" endangers not just academic departments but also the ability of people to live truly human lives.

Indeed, the crisis is not merely academic but critical to every day human life. People who do not believe that humans beings are capable of arriving at truth through sense experience, reason, and conversation are more likely to advocate for obedience rather than education, force rather than dialogue, and totalitarianism rather than democracy. In contrast, hope that human beings can find wisdom is a hope that inspires literacy rather than punishment, debate rather than violence, and freedom rather than dictatorship.

This book proposes that Augustine, the fourth-century African Doctor of Grace, might inspire such hope. In this post-truth era, it might seem naïve to expect that the advice of a fourth-century African bishop might be of any real use. Some readers might expect that such a book will be nostalgic at best and dangerously conservative at worst, advocating a view that readers ignore the last 1,500 years of scholarship in order to return to a simpler time. That is not the intention of this book. Rather, this book introduces—or re-introduces—Augustine to the contemporary reader as a figure who lived in an era when popular opinion was skeptical about the possibility of wisdom, when orators argued for verisimilitude (truthiness) rather than truth, when elitist cults gained members by advancing conspiracy theories, and when academics scoffed at the idea that knowledge could be advanced beyond bias. Augustine not only lived in such an era but he himself was tossed about on the waves of this culture. As a young man, he joined an elitist cult. When he escaped, he shrugged his shoulders at the possibility of truth and decided to use his rhetoric skills to serve the highest bidder. But then, at the peak of professional success but in the pit of personal despair, he discovered hope that he could know truth after all. This is a hope worth sharing.

This book presents Augustine as a sojourner towards truth who discovered that he alone could not become wise. Augustine came to advocate that the journey towards truth is always done in relationship—in relationship with nature, in relationship with community, and in relationship with the Truth who befriends the philosopher. As such, this book does not advocate a return to the study of Augustine's specific views about the world as much as it advocates a future of study in which thinkers have hope that Truth is not beyond their grasp but is already in relationship with them. In short, Augustine believed that Truth has a friendly heart (*misericordia*) and that philosophy is the recognition of human friendship with wisdom. This belief was the foundation for his hope that human beings could inquire into nature, debate ethics and politics, and find ways to live happy, flourishing lives. This book evangelizes for Augustine's hope in order that readers might be inspired to engage earnestly in inquiry, dialogue, and debate about the nature of themselves, their world, and the possibility of the happy life.

Who Was Augustine?

For the reader who is new to Augustine, the following section serves to present the African doctor in his historical time and place. Born in 354 in Thagaste, a small town in Northern Africa, Augustine was the child of a

Christian mother and a polytheist father. While Western European Christians have been quick to consider him one of their own, Augustine was proud to be an African by birthright and by culture.[1] This was well-noted by his Italian contemporaries who insulted him for using "Punic logic"[2] and having "Numidian stubbornness,"[3] although Augustine did not seem at all ashamed of his African origins or his African accent.[4] Of course, Augustine also was cosmopolitan in orientation and scorned provincialism and nativism among both Africans and Italians. Perhaps this is why his *Confessions* has had such universal appeal to people in various cultural contexts throughout the last 1,600 years.

Augustine, often lauded as the first autobiographer, provided his readers with many details of his life in the *Confessions*. Writing for readers in his own time who might be Africans or Europeans, he assumed his audience would include catholic Christians as well as Donatists, gnostics, polytheists, Platonists, and academic skeptics. To all of these, Augustine, the master of rhetoric, gave an autobiography that is personal and intimate yet universal and inclusive.

Beginning with infancy, Augustine gave a portrait that was sympathetic to his childhood self and to children generally. He wrote about his mother, Monica, whom he adored, and his father, Patricius, who made life difficult for his mother. He barely mentioned his siblings, but it is known that he had a brother, Navigius, and a sister whom he does not name but whom tradition has called "Perpetua," perhaps after the Carthaginian martyr. About himself,

---

1. See Frend, *Donatist Church*, 230: "Augustine was first and foremost an African, and was influenced throughout his life by the Berber background of his upbringing. The researches of French archaeologists have shown that Thagaste, his birthplace, was one of the centres of Libyan or proto-Berber culture. . . . Augustine's Berber descent shows itself in numerous small ways, in the name of his mother Monnica, a Berber name perhaps derived from the Libyan deity, Mon, worshipped in the neighbouring town of Thibilis. . . . The rather odd name which he gave his own son, 'Adeodatus,' is intelligible only with reference to the Berber usage of naming children with a name connected with the worship of Baal—Adeodatus=Iatanbaal." See also Wilhite, "Augustine the African"; *Ancient African Christianity*.

2. CJ I.72: "Punicae dialexeos"

3. CJ I.16: "Numidae induruisse" For more discussion on the use of these insults, see Wilhite, *Ancient African Christianity*, 252–54.

4. For example, see Epis. 17, "Letter to Maximus of Madaura" (390), where Augustine chastised Maximus for being ashamed of his African language and African names. Also, note that Augustine asserted that both he and Monica spoke Latin with an African accent that the Italians mocked (Ord II.xvii.45). See also DM xiii.44, where Augustine talks about the difficulties of translating Punic to Latin, suggesting that both he and Adeodatus know at least some Punic. Wilhite proposed that they both learned the indigenous language from their mothers. See Wilhite, "Augustine the African," 18.

he explained that he liked to play ball more than he liked to do math and he liked to listen to Latin stories of Aeneas much more than do school work about the Greek epics of Odysseus, which his teachers demanded he read. He noted that he was often punished for fighting about who was best at ball on the playground, even though the same adults who punished him were rewarded for fighting amongst themselves in the academic arena. Generally, throughout the *Confessions*, he argued that there was very little difference between children and adults, and probably very little difference between himself and the reader.

His stories of adolescence were also in this vein, although he provided more particular details as his memories were sharper. He was an excellent student, and his parents decided to use their money to send him to Carthage to study for the law. In Carthage, he fell in love twice—with a young woman and with philosophy. He described his carnal love affair with shame, not so much because of its carnality as because of his ineptitude at loving well. Some scholars have decried Augustine for not naming his concubine in the text, but whatever her given name, she was clearly Augustine's Dido, the African Queen whom Aeneas loved and left in Virgil's great epic, *The Aeneid*. Augustine recalled and denounced the way he wept at the theater for the fictional Dido while failing to mourn for the real people he hurt with his own behavior. He claimed his own behavior was that of a foolish adolescent who loved the concept of love but did not know how to engage in loving his lover for her own sake. He claimed to have spoken about the pleasures of the marital bed with such eloquence that celibate friends forgot their vows. But his conjugal joys, he worried later, were selfish rather than self-giving. He blamed himself for engaging in lovemaking with his concubine without a desire to create children but only out of desire to find pleasure in the moment. Overall, Augustine's account of his love affair with his concubine is confessional; he portrayed his role in the relationship as thoroughly corrupt. And yet, in the narrative of his failure to love purely, the reader must recognize an authentic love for this woman whom Augustine knew he had wounded. Perhaps the memory of this love, despite his own ineptitude at it, helped him praise Christian marriage in his later writings as he did.

In contrast to his shame in loving his concubine, it is striking how he spoke of the love of his son, whom he named Adeodatus (Iatanbaal or Hannibal in Carthaginian Punic), literally "the gift of God."[5] The love

---

5. See footnote 1. For more discussion of Adeodatus's name, see Brown, *Augustine of Hippo*, 62–63. About the popularity of this name in fourth-century Carthage, see Kajanto, *Onomastic Studies*, 102–15. Interestingly, Wilhite noted that the other form of Iatanbaal is Hannibal, Rome's most famous conqueror. For Wilhite, this makes Augustine's son's name a significant choice, perhaps showing Augustine's early resistance to

he professed for his son is all the more striking given the secular culture which smiled upon both concubines and marriage but rarely suggested the responsibility of the father to love his child as more than a possession. Indeed, under the law of the Roman Empire, the father had the right to determine the life or death of his child and, in some cases, his grandchild. Thus, the midwife would turn to the father of the house rather than place the newborn infant in the arms of the mother, for the father had the right to turn his back on the baby. If he did so, the midwife was to expose the child, a practice that led to many infants being left for death or slave traders. In contrast to the behavior of many fathers of unplanned children, Augustine immediately took his son in his arms and cherished him for his entire life. Augustine was not unaware of the cruelty of the laws. He alluded in his discussion of original sin that having "to turn to your man"[6] after labor is a far greater punishment for the the the daughters of Eve than the pains during labor which all animals experience.[7]

In addition, Augustine was well aware of the cruelty men showed wives and concubines in marriage and divorce. He knew when he divorced his concubine that the choice was his not hers. He said in the *Confessions* that his heart was torn in two, focusing on his own grief in the moment of the divorce. But attention to her grief is shown in later works. As a priest and bishop, he admonished the newly baptized not to divorce their wives in order to become chaste unless the decision was fully mutual; he told newly converted husbands to continue to honor their commitments to their wives.[8] And he demonstrated heartfelt empathy for concubines who were faithfully monogamous while he denounced men who took a concubine and a wife.[9] All in all, even a casual reader of Augustine's writings must

---

the Roman Empire. See Wilhite, *Ancient African Christianity,* 251. Wilhite noted that Augustine was insulted at least twice, once by Jerome and once by Secundinus, first by being called "Hannibal" and then reminded that Hannibal lost to the Romans. See Wilhite, *Ancient African Christianity,* 252; "Augustine the African," 18–19.

6. DG12 XI.xxxvii.50: "ad virum tuum conversio tua"

7. See DGM II.xix.29; DG12 XI.xxxvii.50.

8. See DSM I.xiv.39: "Dominus dimitti coniugem vetat" (The Lord forbids dismissing a wife). See also Sermon 132; 260.

9. See Sermon 224.3: "Sed servat tibi forsitan fidem, et non novit nisi te unum, et non disponit nosse alium. Cum ergo illa sit casta, tu quare fornicaris? Si illa unum, tu quare duas? Non licet, non licet, non licet. In gehennam eunt. Vel hinc sim liber. Vel hinc liceat mihi dicere quod verum est." (But perhaps she serves you faithfully, and she knows no one but you, and she is not disposed to know another. Therefore, if she is chaste, why are you fornicating? If she has one, why do you seek two? This is not allowed, this is not allowed, this is not allowed. To hell they go. Here I am free. Here it is allowed for me to say what is true.)

acknowledge that Augustine loved his concubine, his African queen, whom he, like Aeneas, abandoned out of a desire to fulfil what he believed was a divine plan. Importantly, Augustine refused to absolve himself of the sinfulness of his cruelty. In his *Confessions,* he admitted that he had used his lover selfishly and thus failed to love her well. In his *Sermons,* he beseeched men to do better towards the women in their lives.

Augustine felt no shame in describing his second love affair, however, which came on the heels of his carnal love and existed simultaneously with it for a long time. This was his blazing desire for wisdom and his conversion to philosophy. While the reader does not learn the name of Augustine's concubine or the particulars of their courtship, the reader is given every detail of Augustine's first encounter with philosophy. Augustine was nineteen, reading Cicero's *Hortensius* as part of the prepared curriculum for his studies in law, when suddenly his heart was inflamed with a bewildering passion for eternal wisdom. Suddenly, he changed all his prayers to God and begged for Wisdom. Indeed, whenever Augustine wrote in his works of holding a lover, lying naked under the bedcovers, or fondling the breasts of his beloved, he was always referring to his relationship with Wisdom. The reader can only imagine that his concubine may have agreed with his final assertion that he had never loved her truly, for his heart was on fire for philosophy and the quest for wisdom became his primary concern. Yet the passionate and tender description of his love of wisdom requires the reader to assume that his relationship with his human beloved likely was also ardent and sweet.

Augustine described his late adolescence, that period of youth from the age of nineteen to twenty-nine, as a time of bumbling love. He was faithful to his concubine and a doting father but concerned that he was loving the wrong kind of thing entirely. This concern was encouraged by the doctrines of Manicheism, a gnostic cult that claimed to be Christian but not catholic in the sense of being universally available to all people. Augustine joined the Manicheans shortly after his conversion to philosophy in part because of their elitism. Manicheism claimed to be a type of Christianity for intellectuals and more spiritually minded people. Their code of ethics criticized all bodily delights as diabolical and prohibited sex along with the eating of meat and the drinking of alcohol. On one hand, Augustine was clear that he never actually gave up any of these activities. On the other hand, he claimed he found it admirable that the Manicheans were so pure. This confused him; he wondered why he desired and delighted in activities that he considered shameful. A prime example of this confusion is his famous reflection on the incident involving the pear tree. Remembering a time in his younger days, Augustine wondered why he once joined a group of boys who were in the process of raiding a pear tree. He painted a vivid picture of himself with a group of older children climbing a tree, laughing and calling, as they plucked fruit that they did not want to eat, throwing it to the farmer's pigs for sport. The shame of having willfully committed robbery was compounded by the older Augustine's Manichean shame that plucking fruit harmed the tree, causing it to weep milky tears over the loss of her child. Even after renouncing Manicheism, Augustine was dismayed to acknowledge that the pleasure he experienced in robbing the tree was in the wrongdoing of the act. The question of why a person—why he himself—would knowingly delight in wrongdoing remained a central question for the philosophical Augustine who hoped to find in Wisdom's arms a path to becoming a better man.

At the end of his twenties, Augustine found Manicheism intellectually unsatisfying and ethically bankrupt. He left the sect intending to live a life of academic success and philosophical humility. Having left Carthage for Rome, he decided to embrace a life without the expectation of being able to find wisdom. Instead, however, he found himself in despair. He found a cure to this despair in the sermons of Ambrose, the bishop of Milan and a noted rhetorician. Ambrose introduced Augustine to the possibility of Christian philosophy which differed from the gnosticism of the Manicheans and the biblically literalist Christianity of his mother's church. Augustine decided this universally accessible, catholic form of Christianity was the most plausible choice available. Importantly, Augustine used the term catholic Christianity to refer to a universal church in opposition to gnostic Christian sects who followed esoteric teachings and in opposition to provincial Christian sects who grounded their faith in a specific place (such as Africa for the Donatists or Rome for certain Roman Christians).

While embracing catholic Christian faith, Augustine continued to struggle with questions concerning good or right living. Dedicated to finding a wife in his own social class whom he would love rightly, he sent his concubine back to Africa, feeling that he could only love her selfishly. Their son, Adeodatus, remained with Augustine. But right relationship proved difficult to obtain for Augustine. With his heart still in pain from having been ripped in two after the divorce of his concubine, Augustine became engaged to a girl who was not yet of marriageable age but was considered an excellent match by his mother and the dominant culture. Unable, or unwilling, to remain celibate while he waited for her maturity, he took a new concubine. This relationship is recounted only briefly and with shame, without any of the tenderness described in his first love affair. The reader of Augustine's *Confessions* is torn between feeling angry at Augustine's cruel impulsiveness and feeling sympathetic to this young man who in so desperately wanting to be perfect failed to be simply good.

Giving all the credit to a graceful God, Augustine explained his later moral conversion as the new ability to live by the morals that he believed to be right. Augustine never described his own immorality as an understandable product of ignorance. Rather, he labeled immorality as action the actor considers wrong. Recounting a precise moment when he heard a child's voice in a garden telling him to "Take and read,"[10] Augustine confessed that he opened up his Scriptures to the letters of Paul where he found an admonition to cling to the graceful promise of God rather than to his own wealth, success, or desires for physical pleasure. This revelation changed his will; he divorced his second concubine, ended his engagement to the wealthy child bride, told his mother that he would never marry, and pledged lifelong celibacy. Augustine stated clearly in treatises and sermons that he did not believe celibacy to be a purer or better path than marriage. He often praised those men and women who loved their partners completely. But he was convinced that he could not love a woman carnally without selfish cruelty, so he decided to forego sexual passion and the stability and prestige an honorable marriage would bestow on him in the secular culture. This decision and the ability to abide by it, he credited to God.

Ending his sexual relationships with human women, Augustine then committed himself fully and completely to his relationship with Wisdom. Having been forced earlier to retire from his professorship because of respiratory problems, Augustine hoped to live quietly with his son, his mother, and his friends while reading, discussing, and writing dialogues about the search for truth and the happy life. During this period, Augustine wrote several philosophical dialogues in which he praised the life of philosophy and argued for an epistemology grounded in the graceful illumination of Christ.

After his mother's death in 387, Augustine returned to Thagaste in North Africa, hoping to continue a quiet, philosophical life. However, Augustine would not have a quiet philosophical life. African catholic Christians wanted educated priests who could evangelize and apologize for their faith. They found and seized Augustine, who was forced to take vows of ordination by the violent crowd. When he realized how strong the desire was for educated leaders, Augustine became nervous about preserving time for his own private study. For a time, he refused to travel to any province that was in need of a bishop. However, in 396, while Augustine was visiting Hippo, the bishop there unexpectedly announced his retirement, and Augustine was forced into the position.

---

10. Conf. VIII.xii.29: "Tolle, lege."

Embracing his call, Augustine used his position to inspire the priests and laity not only to believe but also to seek greater understanding of their faith. Amongst his flock he had not only Africans but also many Roman Italians who fled to North Africa seeking stability after the Visigoths sacked Rome in 410. In his hundreds of books, letters, sermons, and treatises, Augustine continued to write philosophically about Christian theology and to advocate for dialogue in communities of diverse people. He raised and answered questions while exegeting Scripture and studying human history. He fought especially hard against elitism. As a young man, he had found ethical problems with the Manichean view that the poor should be ignored while an overabundance of food was brought to those with the highest ranking in the cult. As a catholic Christian priest and bishop, he argued against the pronouncements of Donatists, who claimed that African Christians were purer than Roman Christians. Augustine was especially concerned by the heresy of Pelagius, who suggested that certain people could earn their own salvation. He, in a letter written with several African bishops privately to Bishop Innocent of Rome, warned that Pelagius was enjoying favor among some in Rome. His letter reminded Innocent of the need for all the bishops to converse and work together as both African and Roman Christians drew from one common source, the grace of Christ.[11] He must have been quite surprised when Innocent, the Bishop of Rome, replied to the council of Carthaginians thanking them for petitioning the Roman See, as Rome was the source and final authority of the church not a co-recipient with Carthage of the grace and authority of God.[12] It is notable that Augustine, against

11. See Epis. 177.19, "Augustine, Alypius, Aurelius, Evodius and Possidius to Innocent" (416): "Dabit sane nobis veniam suavitas mitissima cordis tui, quod prolixiorem epistolam fortassis quam velles tuae misimus Sanctitati. Non enim rivulum nostrum tuo largo fonti augendo refundimus. . . . utrum etiam noster, licet exiguus, ex eodem quo etiam tuus abundans, emanet capite fluentorum, hoc a te probari volumus tuisque rescriptis de communi participatione unius gratiae consolari." (May the most mild sweetness of your heart sanely allow that we sent to your Holiness a letter perhaps more long winded than you would have wished. Indeed, we do not funnel our rivulet to your large fountain to increase it. . . . Indeed, our little stream emanates from the same fountainhead as your abundant stream, and we want proof and consolation from you that your writings are drawn from our common participation in the unity of grace.)

12. See Epis. 181.1, "Innocent to the Bishops Who Took Part in the Council of Cathage" (417): "In requirendis divinis rebus . . . antiquae traditionis exempla servantes, et ecclesiasticae memores disciplinae, nostrae religionis vigorem non minus nunc in consulendo, quam antea cum pronuntiaretis, vera ratione firmastis, qui ad nostrum referendum approbastis esse iudicium, scientes quid apostolicae Sedi, cum omnes hoc loco positi ipsum sequi desideremus apostolum, debeatur, a quo ipse episcopatus et tota auctoritas nominis huius emersit. . . . quod illi non humana, sed divina decrevere sententia, ut quidquid quamvis in disiunctis remotisque provinciis ageretur, non prius ducerent finiendum, nisi ad huius Sedis notitiam perveniret: ut tota huius auctoritate

Pelagius's claims that some people merited God's salvific love, against the Donatists' claims that faithful Africans were the most pure Christians, and against the Roman bishop's claim of absolute authority, consistently calmly insisted on the catholic nature of Christianity and the equality of all Christians. Augustine proclaimed that Christian truths are available to all because Truth, not a single human person, is the rock,[13] and Truth has a friendly and gracious heart, open and loving to all.

Augustine's resistance to exclusivity fueled his passion for education. Although as a professor, he openly criticized certain aspects of the academic arena, he was a staunch supporter of the liberal arts. In old age he watched with fear and horror as mobs burned down libraries and schools in North Africa. Certain members of the Roman elite had continually stirred up anti-intellectualism and made strange alliances in order to maintain power and quiet certain factions. In 429 and 430, Governor Count Boniface, faced with accusations of treason made by the Roman Emperor's own mother, allied with the Vandals of northern Europe, inviting them into Africa to help strengthen his military position in case he needed to fight against Italy. When the crisis with Italy subsided, these Vandals did not honor the agreement as Boniface had planned. They refused to leave Africa when he asked. They burned schools, libraries, and churches and eventually took all of Carthage for themselves. In response, the Roman emperor Valentinian simply

---

iusta quae fuerit pronuntiatio firmaretur." (In inquiring into divine things . . . serving the example of ancient tradition and remembering proper ecclesiastic discipline you have added strength to our religion not only now in this consultation, but also before when you pronounced with truly firm reason to refer this matter to our judgment, knowing what is owed to the apostolic Seat, since we all who are put in this place desire to follow the Apostle, from whom the episcopate and its whole authority takes its name. . . . This is not human but divine decree, that anything that must be acted upon in any of the provinces, however distant or remote, should not be be brought to a conclusion unless it comes to the notice of this Seat, so that every pronouncement may be affirmed as just by our total authority.)

13. See Ret. I.xxi.1, where Augustine explained that neither Rome nor Africa was chosen to be above the other: "Sed scio me postea saepissime sic exposuisse quod a Domino dictum est: Tu es Petrus, et super hanc petram aedificabo Ecclesiam meam, ut super hunc intelligeretur quem confessus est Petrus dicens: Tu es Christus filius Dei vivi, ac sic Petrus ab hac petra appellatus personam Ecclesiae figuraret, quae super hanc petram aedificatur et accepit claves regni caelorum. Non enim dictum illi est: 'Tu es petra,' sed: 'Tue es Petrus.' Petra autem erat Christus." (But I know that afterwards I explained most often that this was said by the Master of the House, "You are Peter [Petrus] and above this rock [petram] will build my church," so that it was understood that he was building on the one whom Peter confessed when he said "You are Christ, the Son of the living God." And so Peter, named by this rock, represented the person of the Church which is built on this rock and received the keys of the kingdom of heaven. Not indeed was he told "You are the rock [petra]" but that "You are Peter [Petrus]." Christ, however, was the rock [petra].) See also Matt 16:16–19; 1 Cor 10:4.

signed a new treaty and conceded all of the western African provinces to the Vandals in return for their support as his allies. But later, the Vandals defied Valentinian's treaty as well. They pushed past all agreed upon borders. Perhaps with the help of Africans who were angry with Roman rule, they eventually conquered all of North Africa.[14]

At the end of his life, Augustine, who had preached at every opportunity about the importance of each individual using reason to ask, seek, and knock on the door of Truth, feared that the age of inquiry was ending in his homeland at the hands of the Vandals and those Romans and Africans who had allied with them in hopes of various political gains. It seemed to Augustine that not enough people trusted education and debate, so they relied on the dangerous and uncontrollable might of arms. Indeed, Augustine's death and the defeat of Carthage does mark the end of late antiquity and the beginning of the dark ages, according to many Western historians.

How Did Augustine Influence the History of Ideas?

Of course, inquiry did not come to an end with Augustine's death or even with the Vandal's triumph in North Africa. Indeed, by most accounts, general literacy as well as philosophy, theology, and science flourished in North Africa far better than in Europe during the Middle Ages. Despite Augustine's fears at the end of his life, Augustine's advocacy for philosophy survived. Carthage was ruled by Vandals for less than a century before being peacefully conquered by Greek Byzantines who ruled for another century. In the middle of the sixth century, the African church rose as a powerful theological and philosophical counter to the imperial Christianity that reigned in Rome; the African church used arguments from Tertullian and Augustine to advocate for a church free from the use of force and secular power. By the end of the seventh century, however, Arabs conquered Carthage and many residents converted to Islam. After this, the African Christian church ceased to effect a serious political challenge to the Roman church's theological, philosophical, and political views, but Christianity and Augustine's legacy remained active in North Africa.[15] Certainly, science and philosophy continued to thrive under Muslim Arab rule in Africa. Interestingly, in the nineteenth century, American Catholics of African descent had "a singular pride in being able to

---

14. For a detailed account of the fall of Carthage and North Africa to the Vandals, see Wilhite, *Ancient African Christianity*, 22–29.

15. In 1619, a Flemish explorer found an active church named for Augustine in Hippo that held writings of his. See Konig, "Augustine and Islam," 144.

point to Augustine as one of their own."[16] In 1841, free people of color established St. Augustine Church in New Orleans, the first black Catholic church
in the United States, and in 1858, emancipated black Catholics chose Augustine as the patron saint of the first black Catholic church in Washington
DC. Generally, Augustine's view of a friendly hearted Wisdom that lovingly
seeks out all people has had an important place in theology and philosophy
in Africa and for people of African descent.

Of course, the African doctor of grace was also a major influence
in Rome and Europe. Indeed, Augustine's work became the most significant influence in Western European theology and philosophy for the next
millennium. Perhaps for this reason, some Europeans began to paint Augustine's portrait with a Roman nose.[17] Possidius, Augustine's friend and
biographer, fled Africa for Italy after Augustine's death, bringing the whole
of Augustine's library with him. Certainly, Italy, like North Africa, was irre-
versibly changed by various attacks in the fifth century, and Roman culture
transformed into a hybrid of Roman elitism and Gothic rule. Nevertheless,
throughout this period, Augustine was read widely by scholars in Italy
and all across Europe—from Iberia to Gaul to Britain.[18] Indeed, his epistemological hope, which relied on the light of Christ for insight, was the
foundational hope that encouraged philosophical thinking throughout the
European middle ages. Moreover, his work was considered authoritative on
matters of both Christian theology and philosophy by nearly every Latin
speaking philosopher and theologian in Europe.

16. Davis, "History of Black Catholics," 12.

17. It is important to note, however, that many Europeans, even in the most racist
periods of European history, continued to recognize Augustine as a native African. See,
for example, the preface to the dissertation of Anthony William Amo, a Ghanian who
received his PhD in philosophy from the University of Wittenberg in 1734. In justify-
ing the genius of Amo and in confronting the racism of Enlightenment Europe, John
Godrey Kraus, Rector of the University of Wittenberg, wrote in a prefatory address to
the reader, "Great once was the dignity of Africa, whether one considers natural talents
of mind or the study of letters, or the very institutions for safeguarding religion. For
she has given birth to several men of the greatest pre-eminence by whose talents and
efforts the whole of human knowledge, no less than divine knowledge has been built
up. . . . In Christian teaching, too, how great are the men who have come out of Africa.
Of the more distinguished it is enough to mention Tertullian, Cyprian, Arnobius, Op-
tatus Milevitanus, Augustine, all of whose sanctity of soul rivals the learning of every
race. . . . Those who say that the African Church has always merely been a receiver
of instruction, do her immeasurable wrong" (Krause, "Rector and Public Assembly of
Wittenberg University," 77–79).

18. To see the remarkable scope of Augustine's influence, see the whole of the three
volumes of *The Oxford Guide to the Historical Reception of Augustine*. While there are
marked lacunas in this encyclopedia, it is a grand testament to the incredible effect of
Augustine's work on all of those who read him.

The European admiration for Augustine continued without pause into the middle ages and early modernity. Augustine's epistemology of grace was the foundation for liberal arts curricula in grammar schools and universities. His views encouraged women to read and study, even in times when the church condemned them for this. Moreover, his views encouraged many philosophers, such as Thomas Aquinas, who were interested in widening the canon of philosophical texts beyond the confines of previously accepted church teachings. As the middle ages drew to a close, Augustine's writings continued to be significantly important. When Martin Luther unknowingly began the Reformation by the posting of his ninety-five theses against indulgences, he did so as an Augustinian monk who found comfort in Augustine's words. Rival reformers Ulrich Zwingli and John Calvin both invoked Augustine as they explained their understanding of Christian faith. And Augustine was the theologian whom John Wesley studied most fervently. Thus, because Augustine influenced the founders of the mainline Protestant denominations as well as Roman Catholic thought, his work continues to be foundational for all Nicene Christian theology in Western Europe, even after the Reformation.

Importantly, Descartes, the father of modern philosophy, styled his *Meditations* similarly to Augustine's *Soliloquies* and grounded his new method on the Augustinian foundation that philosophy's hope depends on a God who is not a deceiver. Therefore, even as philosophy began to conceive of itself as a secular discipline, the influence of Augustine remained. Certainly, philosophers from Thomist, Calvinist, and Lutheran traditions continued to read and expound on the African doctor. But so did many Enlightenment thinkers who considered themselves deists. As a result, Augustine's influence extended into the modern European academy. Indeed, while perhaps too few secular philosophers today are aware of Augustine's views and their contemporary applications, the mark of his influence remains on virtually every Western thinker in the contemporary canon.

What Is Augustine's Relevance for People Today?

There are plenty of books and articles explaining Augustine's influence in the history of ideas. The purpose of this book is to suggest the possibilities of Augustine's hope for contemporary people who seek wisdom and meaning. While Augustine has interested readers in every era between his own and the present time, there are particular moments in which readers find themselves in a context more or less similar to Augustine's. The current era is one that shares a number of surprisingly common elements with Augustine's late antiquity.

First, fourth-century people saw themselves as part of a multicultural world, much as those who live in the twenty-first century do today. Augustine studied with and taught people of diverse cultural traditions, religious backgrounds, and theological beliefs. Augustine, like scholars today, expected to meet people who lived in a variety of places, and he expected to travel. His professional path from Carthage to Rome to Milan and back to North Africa was not unusual, and he did not consider it unusual. He did not expect everyone to share the same ideas or traditions. He wrote for a variety of different audiences. Yet he was aware that cosmopolitanism had its critics, who clung together in parochial communities preaching provincial and nativist ideas. Augustine, throughout his life, was aware of and troubled by African hostility towards Romans and Roman disdain for Africans. Such nativism and parochialism is very much alive today in the global marketplace of ideas.

Second, the fourth century was a time of clashing empires. As is true in the current era, various world leaders made unusual alliances, some even flirting with extremists and populists, in order to solidify or grow their power as they battled for political and economic control of various provinces and colonies. Internally, too, some leaders formed alliances with insurgent or external groups in order to quiet and to unseat political rivals.

Third, underlying this type of political behavior was, and is, a marked lack of trust in the accessibility and communicability of truth about justice. This lack of trust resulted, and is resulting, in a lack of honest and open debate. Interestingly, the academic skepticism of Cicero first gained popularity during the transition from the Roman Republic to the Roman Empire. Cicero proclaimed that the wisest human sought the truth but knew he would not find it. This philosophical viewpoint became synonymous with the Roman academic point of view for the next several centuries. These academic skeptics ran the schools that educated both lawyers and politicians whom they taught to persuade audiences to "verisimilitude" or "truthiness" rather than to objective truth. Today, the post-modern contemporary academy advocates for epistemological (if not intellectual) humility as the key element in the search for truth. Scholars on the threshing floor of the academic conference look very much like those described in Augustine's *Confessions*, working hard to score points by knocking down the arguments of their opponents while vainly claiming victory without ever proclaiming, or even seeking, truth. Their students, who become lawyers and politicians, seek to win cases and elections by making arguments that appeal to their listener's biases rather than appeals to empirical facts and reason.

Fourth, such skepticism fueled fanaticism as it seeped into the general culture of Rome. Today, many declare the impossibility of consensus, the impracticality of facts, and the death of truth, all the while reading conspiracy theories, embracing extreme positions, and joining elitist groups. Cult leaders in Augustine's era, too, relied on listeners' skepticism towards mainstream scientific, political, and theological views in order to promote their own teachings, which were often extreme.

Thus, in many ways, Augustine, in writing for people in his age, wrote for a contemporary audience as well. He appreciated people's differences but also believed that truth is universally accessible. He knew that many people seem to want power, wealth, and prestige, but deep inside they really want love, security, and the knowledge of true things. He knew that human beings need and desire to be in a relationship with their world, with each other, and with the Truth. To help people in this pursuit, he encouraged his readers to keep conversations open with people who disagreed with them so that they might avoid the trap of their own error. He also wrote to encourage people to trust their experiences and the testimony of other people so that they might avoid the traps of nihilism and apathy. Most of all, he wrote to evangelize the idea that Truth, which he believed all human beings desired, was not "out there" but rather in relationship with human beings as they moved and acted in the world.

What Is the Argument and Structure of This Book?

The argument of this book is that contemporary readers can benefit from Augustine's encouragement and hope for philosophy. Having introduced Augustine, the next chapter will explain Augustine's understanding of what philosophy is and how Augustine insisted that all people have a desire to know. The following chapter will explain how Augustine navigated some particular dangers in the path of the knowledge seeker—the dangers of elitist cults and of conspiracy theories that promise to teach secret knowledge and discourage open dialogue and inquiry. Then, the fourth chapter follows Augustine's journey into and out of skepticism and apathy, analyzing the danger of the fear of bias that leads to a refusal to assent to any position or belief. These sections show Augustine as a thinker who is surprisingly relevant to the contemporary lived experience of people who are trying to decide who to trust and what to believe.

In the second half of the book, Augustine's hope and redeemed view of philosophy is explained. As a convert to Christianity, Augustine came to believe that Truth was not the object of philosophy but a participant in it. Philosophy became what it literally means, a friendship with Wisdom.[19] As a philosopher, Augustine did not apologize for his faith by using Scripture and church doctrine; rather, he testified to his lived experience of a graceful God, who is Wisdom, who promised friendship to him. In Augustine's view, he did not choose Christian faith. Rather, Wisdom gave Augustine the faith he needed to continue his quest for understanding. Contemporary Christians who hold this same foundational faith in a God of Truth may find this hope of Augustine to be particularly relevant to them, encouraging them to study, to inquire, and to dialogue with others in order to seek a full understanding of truth beyond parochial belief. But Augustine also wrote for those outside of catholic Christianity that while they might not be converted to the Nicene creed they might be persuaded that recognition of truth is possible. This book makes Augustine's argument for hope in philosophy for as broad an audience as Augustine himself sought. Indeed, the canon of thinkers who have been inspired by his hope is immense. Two chapters, towards the end, thus concentrate on Augustine's influence on medieval, modern, and contemporary philosophy. This canon is a testament to the hope that through reading and writing, talking and listening, looking and touching, human beings grow in their relationship to Wisdom and to each other.

In the final chapter, the reader is invited to enter into her own relationship with wisdom, to create or discover her own philosophy. Augustinian hope announces that there is no era that is "post-Truth" and there is no need to settle for "truthiness," for whether recognized or not Truth is always in relationship with human beings, waiting for them to ask, to seek, and knock at her door. Human beings, whether in the fourth century or the twenty-first century, are socially bound wisdom seekers. There are dangers inherent to such a nature. People are easily misled both by those who intentionally deceive and by their own simple mistakes. When students seek and do not find immediately, they often fall into despair and distrust of others and themselves. Yet when a person examines her own life path she will surely find moments of enlightenment or, at the very least, moments when she discovered she had erred. Such moments suggest that truth seeking is not in vain. Such moments suggest that Truth has a friendly heart and reaches out to those who wish to know truths. Such moments inspire human beings to rely on their minds, hearts, friends, and even enemies to guide them as they pursue ideas, modes of thought, and ways of acting that improve their own flourishing and that of their neighbors.

---

19. Φιλια (*philia*) is the Greek word for friendly love. Σοφια (*sophia*) is the Greek word for wisdom.

Chapter 2

On Fire for Truth

Philosophy and Human Desire

Augustine's Conversion to Philosophy

WHEN AUGUSTINE WAS NINETEEN years old, he claimed he had a conversion experience, a moment when his ambitions and life goals changed, a moment when his heart was set on fire with a new passion: the passion for truth. Augustine's conversion to philosophy marked a turning point in his life. He confessed that before the moment of conversion, he was like the other "imbeciles"[1] with whom he studied. He simply "desired to be distinguished for the damned end and windy joy of human vanity."[2] But after he read a dialogue by Cicero called the *Hortensius*, he was changed. He wrote:

> Suddenly all my empty hopes lost their value to me and I desired immortal wisdom with an incredible burning in my heart. And I began to arise so that I might turn to you. Indeed, I did not act for a sharper tongue, which is what I was seen to buy with my mother's allowance in my nineteenth year, as my father had died two years earlier. No, therefore, I did not ascribe to this book because it sharpened my tongue, nor made me a better speaker. But I ascribed to it because the matter it spoke about persuaded me. How I burned, my God, how I burned to turn from earthly things to you, even though I did not know what you would do with me! With you is indeed wisdom. The love of wisdom is named in Greek philosophy, and to philosophy these letters encouraged me.[3]

1. Conf. III.iv.7: "Inbecilla."

2. Conf. III.iv.7: "Inter hos ego inbecilla tunc aetate discebam libros eloquentiae, in qua eminere cupiebam fine damnabili et ventoso per gaudia vanitatis humanae." (Among imbeciles I learned the eloquent books of the age, in that I desired to be distinguished for the damned end and windy joy of human vanity.)

3. Conf. III.iv.7–8: "viluit mihi repente omnis vana spes, et immortalitatem sapientiae concupiscebam aestu cordis incredibili, et surgere coeperam ut ad te redirem. non

Augustine had begun reading Cicero as a rhetoric student hoping to improve his public speaking skills so that he could get fine grades and have a prestigious career. When he finished reading Cicero, he had become a philosopher.

Such a story is not completely uncommon amongst the accounts of philosophy majors at liberal arts colleges today. Reading philosophy has this effect on certain young people, and they, like Augustine, often expect others to be converted as they were, even as those who fund their education might be wary of the enterprise. While many philosophy majors do not become professional philosophers, the philosophical desire for wisdom often marks the rest of their lives.

By all of his own accounts, this was true of Augustine. While he certainly wandered in his search for truth, and while he had a number of different professions throughout his life, including professor, orator, priest and bishop, it was as a philosopher that he searched, taught, and preached. For Augustine, hope in the philosophical quest for truth was linked to his hope for a productive and happy life. Moreover, he insisted, like many a new philosophy student home on winter break, that this is true for all human beings, whether they know it or not.

Augustine's Understanding of Philosophy

The first key to understanding Augustine's hope for philosophy is uncovering what he understood philosophy to be and why he understood philosophy to be central to the happy human life. Embedded in Augustine's description of his conversion is a definition of philosophy that, while perhaps not mainstream in its use today, was conventional in Augustine's time. This was the view that Augustine later preached as a bishop:

> In general, there is a common study among all philosophers. In this study that they share in common, they have divisions and they make different sentences and propositions. But in common all philosophers study, query, dispute, and live because they have an appetite for apprehending the happy life.[4]

enim ad acuendam linguam, quod videbar emere maternis mercedibus, cum agerem annum aestatis undevicensimum iam defuncto patre ante biennium, non ergo ad acuendam linguam referebam illum librum, neque mihi locution sed quod loquebatur persuaserat. Quomodo ardebam, deus meus, quomodo ardebam revolare a terrenis ad te, et nesciebam quid ageres mecum! apud te est enim sapientia. amor autem sapientiae nomen graecum habet philosophiam, quo me accendebant illae litterae."

4. Sermon 150.3.4: "Primo generaliter audite omnium philosophorum commune studium, in quo studio communi habuerunt quinque divisiones et differentias

Augustine was clear in this sermon that this goal is common for *all* philosophers that he knew: Stoics, Epicureans, Platonists, and skeptics. He insisted that this is the common goal for materialists and for idealists, for professional academics and for those who live in quiet solitude. For most ancient and late antique Greek, African, and Roman philosophers, philosophy was considered to be the pursuit of wisdom that leads to well-being. They would, indeed, have agreed with Augustine's assertion in the *Confessions* that "the happy life is to rejoice in truth. . . . Everyone wants this happy life, this life which is the only happy life. Everyone wants this; everyone wants to rejoice in truth."[5]

In Augustine's era, and in the ancient world generally, philosophers considered their discipline to pertain to the goal of *every* human life. Thus, while Augustine spoke of his particular conversion to philosophy, he also claimed that every human heart longs for wisdom. The philosopher is not differently constituted than any other human being. She merely recognizes what her authentic desire is, while others sublimate their true desire into the pursuit of worldly possessions and honors. Importantly, Augustine used the verb *concupiscebam* to describe his passion for wisdom after his conversion.[6] This Latin verb is usually reserved for carnal longing; perhaps *lust* is not an improper translation. Augustine made explicit that the passion for wisdom is not a different type of passion than carnal longing but rather the authentic passion of the human heart, a heart that can be confused about the object of its real desire. Thus, when he exhorted his friends and readers to study philosophy, Augustine did not try to abate or even moderate the desire of the hedonist, the aesthete, or the Casanova. Augustine did not think the aesthete should be changed into a philosopher, but the aesthete simply needed to be introduced to the object of his true desire. As Augustine said:

> The love of beauty (*philocalia*) is said to be vulgar: don't condemn the name because of the vulgar use of it: for the love of beauty (*philocalia*) and the love of wisdom (*philosophia*) share a similar name. . . . Indeed, what is philosophy? The love of wisdom. What is philocaly? Love of beauty. Ask the Greeks. What therefore is wisdom? Is it not truly beauty? Therefore, these are

---

sententiarum propriarum. Communiter omnes philosophi studendo, quaerendo, disputando, vivendo appetiverunt apprehendere vitam beatam. Haec una fuit causa philosophandi; sed puto quod etiam hoc philosophi nobiscum commune habent."

5. Conf. X.xxiii.33: "beata quippe vita est gaudium de veritate. . . . hanc vitam beatam omnes volunt, hanc vitam, quae sola beata est, omnes volunt, gaudium de veritate omnes volunt."

6. See Conf. III.vii.4: "et immortalitatem sapientiae concupiscebam aestu cordis incredibili." (I desired immortal wisdom with an incredible burning in my heart.)

sisters, procreated by the same parent. But this one was dragged from her heights through the filth of the libido and kept in a cage of the people. . . . Indeed the love of beauty does not know to which genus she belongs without philosophy.[7]

Philosophy helps the aesthete understand what his real goal is. To make this point clear, Augustine often used the language of lust and concupiscence to explain philosophical longing. In *On Order*, the character Licentius proclaims, "More beautiful is philosophy, I affirm, than Thisbe, than Pyramus, than Venus, herself, and Cupid, and all such types of love."[8] In *On the Freedom of the Will*, Augustine wrote:

> Truly, people shout that they are happy when they embrace the beautiful bodies they deeply desire, the bodies of their wives or even the bodies of prostitutes. And should we doubt that we are happy in the embrace of truth? People shout that they are happy when, burning with thirst, they come upon a fountain flowing with abundant healthy water or, being hungry, find a copious meal prepared. And should we deny that we are happy when we are watered and fed by truth?[9]

And in *The Soliloquies,* Augustine explained to himself his relationship with wisdom in the language of a corporeal love affair. His reason asked of him, "Now, we ask, what type of lover of wisdom are you, who with the most pure view and embrace, desire to see and hold her as if nude, without the imposition of clothes?"[10]

---

7. CA II.iii.7: "Philocalia ista vulgo dicitur: ne contemnas nomen hoc ex vulgi nomine: nam philocalia et philosophia prope similiter cognominatae sunt, et quasi gentiles inter se videri volunt, et sunt. Quid est enim philosophia? Amor sapientiae. Quid philocalia? Amor pulchritudinis. Quaere de Graecis. Quid ergo sapientia? nonne ipsa vera est pulchritudo? Germanae igitur istae sunt prorsus, et eodem parente procreatae: sed illa visco libidinis detracta coelo suo, et inclusa cavea populari . . . non enim philocalia ista unde genus ducat agnoscit, nisi philosophia."

8. Ord. I viii.21: "Pulchrior est philosophia, fateor, quam Thysbe, quam Pyramus, quam illa Venus et Cupido talesque omnimodi amores."

9. LA II.1xiii.35: "An vero clamant homines beatos se esse, cum pulchra corpora magno desiderio concupita, sive coniugum, sive etiam meretricum amplexantur; et nos in amplexu veritatis beatos esse dubitabimus? Clamant homines se beatos esse, cum aestu aridis faucibus ad fontem abundantem salubremque perveniunt, aut esurientes prandium coenamve ornatam copiosamque reperiunt; et nos negabimus beatos esse, cum irrigamur pascimurque veritate?"

10. Sol. I.xiii.22: "Nunc illud quaerimus, qualis sis amator sapientiae, quam castissimo conspectu atque amplexu, nullo interposito velamento quasi nudam videre ac tenere desideras."

In Augustine's view, human beings are erotic creatures by nature. In order to satisfy their longing, human beings seek to fill themselves with food, drink, physical pleasure, and sexual activity, among other things. Human life is a constant quest for satisfaction. But the philosophers of the ancient world agreed with each other that what human beings really need is wisdom. Thus, philosophy, in Augustine's view, is about the hunger, thirst, and lust for wisdom.

But what is the "wisdom" that the philosopher seeks? In the ancient world, just as in the contemporary world, philosophers sought wisdom about the workings of the universe, the elements of logic, the structure of the human mind and its relationship to the body, and an understanding of how and why the world exists. Different schools of philosophy held different propositions as true, but all believed that the pursuit of wisdom was the natural human vocation.

For example, materialists like the Epicureans claimed that "philosophy is an activity which secures the happy life by words and dialogues."[11] The materialists were not looking for a metaphysical being called Truth, as Augustine seemed to be; they might have insisted they did not know what a "metaphysical being" was. Yet they believed that discussion and debate were activities that soothed the human soul that ached to know true things. Epicurus once said, "Empty is the word of that philosopher by which no human suffering is healed. For just as medicine is not useful if it does not heal the diseases of bodies, neither is philosophy if it does not cast out the suffering of the soul."[12] He was clear that the process of philosophy is not empty, philosophy provides the fullness of human joy. He explained, "To say that the hour to study philosophy has not yet arrived or that it is past is similar to saying that the hour for happiness is not yet at hand or is no longer present."[13]

As another example, Stoics and skeptics fundamentally agreed with the Epicureans about the role of philosophy in the happy life. On the one hand, Stoics did proclaim the existence of a truth that transcended and guided the material world. But on the other hand, by Augustine's era, Roman Stoics

11. Epicurus quoted in Sextus Empiricus, *Against the Ethicists* VI.169: "καὶ διὰ τοῦτο Ἐπίκοθρος μὲν ἔλεγε τὴν φιλοσοφίαν ἐνέργειαν ἔιναι, λόγοις καὶ διαλογισμοῖς τὸν ἐυδαίμονια βίον μεριποϊοῦσαν."

12. Epicurus quoted in Porphery, "Πρὸς Μαρκελλαν" 31: "κενὸς ἐκείνου φιλοσόφου λόγος ὑφ'ου μηδὲν πάθος ἀνθρωπου θεραπεύεται. ὥσπερ γὰρ ἰατρικῆς ὀυδέν ὄφελος ἤ μὴ τὰς νόσους τῶν σωμάτων θεραπεύει ὀυτῶς ουδε φιλοσοφίας, εἰ μὴ τὸ τῆς ψυχῆς ἐκβάλλει πάθος."

13. Epicurus, "Letter to Menoikos" 122: "ὁ δέ λέγων ἤ μήπω τοῦ φιλοσοφειν ὑπάρχειν ἤ παρεληλυθέναι τήν ὥραν ὅμοιός ἐστι τῶ λέγοντι πρὸς ἐυδαιμονίαν ἤ μήπω παρειναι τήν ὥραν ἤ μηκέτ᾽εἶναι."

were mostly skeptics who did not expect that the human mind was capable of grasping real understanding of that truth. Yet, Cicero wrote, despite his skepticism about the possibility of obtaining truth, "Certainly, there is medicine for the soul: philosophy."[14] Cicero insisted that philosophy can be trusted as the path to the happy life. "Be assured of this, unless the soul becomes healthy, which without philosophy it cannot be, there will be no end to misery. Therefore, as we begin let us give ourselves to this cure, we shall be made healthy if we will."[15] The Roman Stoics claimed that while the human philosopher might never have complete understanding of truth, she can obtain through prudence "a knowledge of things good and evil and neither," "an art of life," and virtue that will give her life "great value."[16] Such a view is echoed in contemporary philosopher Martha Nussbaum's exhortation to philosophy: "The Hellenistic philosophical schools in Greece and Rome—Epicureans, Skeptics and Stoics, all conceived of philosophy as a way of addressing the most painful problems of human life."[17] Nussbaum praises these ancient thinkers in contrast to contemporary professional philosophers. She says, "They practiced philosophy not as a detached intellectual technique dedicated to the display of cleverness but as a . . . worldly art of grappling with human misery."[18]

Yet, of course, detached intellectual activity was considered to be an important part of the happy life of philosophy for many Epicureans, Stoics, and Peripatetics (followers of Aristotle). Aristotle famously began his difficult and dense work *The Metaphysics* with the simple phrase, "All humans, by nature, desire to know."[19] He also insisted in the *Nicomachean Ethics*, a work dedicated to addressing the concerns of human life in community,

14. Cicero, *Tusculan Disputations* 3.3.6: "Est profecto animi medicina, philosophia."

15. Cicero, *Tusculan Disputations* 3.6.13: "Illud quidem sic habeto, nisi sanatus animus sit, quod sine philosophia fieri non potest, finem miseriarum nullum fore. Quam ob rem, quoniam coepimus, tradamus nos ei curandos: sanabimur, si volemus."

16. See Sextus Empericus, *Against the Ethicists* VI.170: "Οἱ δὲ στωικοὶ καὶ ἄντικρύς φασι, τὴν φρόνησιν, ἐπιστήμην οὖσαν ἀγαθῶν καὶ κακῶν καὶ οὐδετέρων, τέκνην ʽθπάρχειν περὶ τὸν βίον, ἥν οἱ προσλαβόντες μόνοι γίνονται καλὸι, μόνοι πλόυσιοι, σοφοὶ μόνοι. ὁ γὰρ πολλοῦ ἄξια κεκτημένος πλούσιύς ἐστιν, ἡ δὲ ἀρετὴ πολλοῦ ἔστιν ἄξια, καὶ μόνος ταύτην ὁ σοφὸς κέκτεται, μόνος ἄρα ὁ σοφός ἐστι πλούσιος." (Stoics say outright that prudence, which is the science of things good and evil and neither, is an art of life, and only those receiving this become beautiful, only they become wealthy, only they become wise. For he is wealthy who possesses things of great value, and virtue is of great value, and only the wise man possesses this; therefore, only the wise man is wealthy.)

17. Nussbaum, *Therapy of Desire*, 18.

18. Nussbaum, *Therapy of Desire*, 19.

19. Aristotle, *Metaphysics* I.I [980a]: "πάντες ἄνθρωποι τοῦ εἰδέναι ὀρέγονται φύσει."

that complete human happiness includes detached intellectual contemplation, which in Greek is θεωρητική (*theoretike*):

> It has been said that this is the activity of contemplative study.
> This seems to agree with what has been said before, and with
> the truth. For this is the supreme activity (for the understanding
> mind is that which is supreme in us and that which is under-
> stood is supreme of all objects of knowledge).[20]

For Aristotle, Cicero, and other professional philosophers, the processes of
empirical research, logical analysis, dialogue, debate, and contemplation
helped humans in practical matters but also were in themselves necessary
and joyful parts of the happy human life.

Yet prefiguring Nussbaum's complaint about her own contemporaries,
Augustine found that many professional philosophers in his day did teach
and lecture with such intellectual detachment that they seemed only to be
interested in appearing clever and winning worldly honors, apparently unconcerned with the suffering of their students' or even their own souls. Like
many a young graduate student in philosophy, Augustine was annoyed that
his fellow intellectuals were not interested in the matters he deemed to be
most important. Furthermore, he warned wisdom seekers that too often

> people go and wonder at the height of the mountains, the flow
> of the sea, the widest reaches of rivers, the circling of the ocean,
> and the courses of the stars, but they relinquish wondering
> about themselves and they do not wonder how I can talk about
> these things when I am not seeing them in front of my eyes but
> nevertheless can talk about them.[21]

Augustine's point was that philosophers must wonder how it is that the human mind is able to know what it knows. This is a central question, yet
no materialist account could answer this question to Augustine's satisfaction. For this reason, Augustine came later to prefer the philosophers who
called themselves Platonists, for they looked not only for empirical facts,
valid propositions, and useful ethical codes but for the Truth, an ontological reality that allows all things to be what they are and allows the mind to

---

20. Aristotle, *Nicomachean Ethics* X [1177a15–25]: "ὅτι δ᾽ ἐστὶ θεωρητική, εἴρηται.
ὁμολογούμενον δὲ τοῦτ᾽ ἀνδόξειεν εἶναι καὶ τοῖς πρότερον καὶ τῷ ἀληθεῖ. κρατίστη
τε γὰρ αὕτη ἐστὶν ἡ ἐνέργεια (καὶ γὰρ ὁ νοῦς τῶνἐν ἡμῖν, καὶ τῶν γνωστῶν, περὶ ἃ ὁ
νοῦς)."

21. Conf. X.viii.15: "et eunt homines mirari alta montium et ingentes fluctus maris
et latissimus lapsus fluminum et oceani ambitum et gyros siderum, et relinquunt se
ipos, nec mirantur quod haec omnia, cum dicerem, non ea videbam oculis, nec tamen
dicerem."

recognize objects and facts.[22] In the writings of these Platonists, Truth was considered the foundation of both knowledge and being. They claimed that to seek Truth is to seek illumination of the soul and to rest in the fullness of Being itself. As Augustine confessed his philosophical journey, he claimed that he had always been looking for this type of truth, even as he wandered from sect to sect.

It was this understanding of philosophy, the pursuit of the Truth that makes the philosopher whole and at peace, which Augustine retained for his whole life. Ironically, he came to believe that his academic post was at odds with the philosophical lifestyle as he defined it. As a professional teacher, he said that he and his friends dreamed of quitting their jobs and living together in a philosophical community dedicated to pursuing Truth.[23] Later, having been forced to leave his professional position because of ill health, he wrote a letter to those of his friends who remained in academic posts beseeching them to join him on retreat to enjoy the pleasures of philosophy unfettered by professional obligations:

> Believe me, you will be very glad that the world has given you little of the prosperity and bland gifts that hold the uncautious. These things would have captured me, myself, as I was singing about them everyday, if I had not had some ache in my chest that coerced me to abdicate my profession of windy rhetoric and flee to the lap of philosophy. Now, in the leisure which we had vehemently wanted, she nourishes and cares for me.[24]

As is revealed in this passage, Augustine's definition of philosophy was not of an academic discipline that taught good reading, speaking, and critical thinking skills that would help a student get a job in law or politics. Philosophy for

22. See, for example, Conf. VIII.ii.3: "ubi autem commemoravi legisse me quosdam libros platonicorum, . . . gratulatus est mihi quod non in aliorum philosophorum scripta incidissem plena fallaciarum et deceptionum secundum elementa huius mundi." (However, when I talked about reading those books of the Platonists . . . he congratulated me that I had not happened on the writings of other philosophers full of fallacies and deceptions which followed the elements of this world.)

23. See Conf. VI.xiv.24: "Et multi amici agitaveramus animo et conloquentes ac detestantes turbulentas humanae vitae molestias paene iam firmaveramus remote a turbis otiose vivere." (We many friends were agitated in our soul and speaking together about the detestable turbulence of the molestations of human life, we were almost ready to live in leisure in a remote place away from the crowd.)

24. CA I.i.3–4: "mihi crede, gratulaberis quod pene nullis prosperitatibus quibus tenentur incauti, mundi huius tibi dona blandita sunt: quae meipsum capere moliebantur quotidie ista cantantem, nisi me pectoris dolor ventosam professionem abicere et in philosophiae gremium confugere coegisset. Ipsa me nunc in otio, quod vehementer optavimus, nutrit ac fovet."

Augustine was about leaving worldly concerns behind and gathering friends together to deepen their relationship with Truth.

While Augustine's later understanding of the Truth as a personally interested lover of the philosopher is uniquely Christian, many non-Christian philosophers in the ancient world held the idea that Truth and God are synonymous and that true philosophy and right religion were united. Indeed, this view of philosophy was common among Christians and Jews as well as Pythagoreans, Platonists, and many members of mystery cults.[25] Indeed, Augustine's view of philosophy already had religious overtones from the moment of his teenage conversion. This is revealed in his immediate decision to look into the Christian scriptures after reading Cicero to see if he could find the Truth there. While Augustine did not embrace catholic Christianity at that time, he refused to look into any philosophical schools that did not offer the total health and salvation of the soul. In *On the City of God,* he asserted that such salvation is the goal of philosophy and reminded readers not to be satisfied with a philosophy that does not offer a path to this goal.

> When Porphyry says near the end of his first book about the return of the soul that not yet has one sect found a universal way of liberation for the soul . . . without doubt he is confessing that there is another way but it has not yet come to his attention. . . . When, however, he said that even the truest philosophy did not bring to his attention a sect that held the universal way of the liberation of the soul, I think, he shows that this philosophy, which is his philosophy, is not the truest or that it does not contain this type of way. And in what way can that be the truest that does not contain this way?[26]

25. See the discussion of religion and philosophy in the ancient world in Nygren, *Agape and Eros,* 166–67. See also Brown, *Augustine of Hippo,* 40–41: "The exhortation to love 'Wisdom' had always been couched in such strongly religious streams. It is not surprising that by the fourth century it had come to act as the bridgehead in traditional culture both for the idea of a religious conversation and even of a conversion to a monastic life."

26. CD X.32: "Cum autem dicit Porphyrius in primo iuxta finem de regress animae libro nondum receptum in unam quondam sectam quod universalem contineat viat viam animae liberandae, . . . procul dubio confitetur esse aliquam, sed nondum in suam venisse notitiam. . . . Cum autem dicit vel a philosophia verissima aliqua nondum in suam notitiam pervenisse sectam quae universalem contineat viam animae liberandae, satis, quantum arbitror, ostendit vel eam philosophiam in qua ipse philosophatus est non esse verissimam, vel ea non contineri talem viam. Et quo modo iam potest esse verissima qua non continetur haec via?"

For Augustine, philosophers seek the liberation of the soul. His hope for philosophy was that a path to such liberation is possible. Throughout his life, he made no distinction between philosophical and religious paths towards this liberation. And in this way, his understanding of philosophy might be different than that of even the most ardent contemporary student of philosophy.

Augustine's Exhortation to Philosophy

While the first key to understanding Augustine's hope for philosophy is to understand his concept of philosophy, the second key is to recognize the erotic pull of the love of wisdom. To really understand Augustine, the reader cannot view his philosophical pursuit with academic disinterest. In his earliest philosophical dialogues, Augustine passionately encouraged the reader to join him in his search for wisdom in the same way that Cicero's book incited him as an adolescent. In *Against the Academics,* he urged:

> Wake up! Wake up! I beseech you. . . . It is indeed philosophy, from whose breasts no age may complain that it is excluded. I will incite you to be more eager to cling to her and to drink from her—I know well of your thirst for her—I have the desire to send to you a taste that for you will be most sweet, and therefore I hope this will lead to your induction, and I petition lest I hope in vain.[27]

Augustine was a gifted user of language, and he used the power of his pen to ignite the latent desire of his reader. Knowing the potency of rhetoric, Augustine committed his discipline to arousing only authentic passion. He explained, "It is certain that the use of eloquent rhetoric in teaching is for the purpose that in the process of speaking what which is hidden will be made clear. It is not to be used so that one will desire what one finds horrible or so that one commits to do what one resisted."[28] Augustine was not interested in using his pen to create false desires with clever speech, like a false advertiser, but hoped to make clear to the reader the true needs and desires of the human soul. Augustine was a philosophical evangelist.

---

27. CA I.i.3–4: "Evigila, evigila, oro te; . . . Philosophia est enim, a cuius uberibus se nulla aetas queretur excludi; ad quam avidius retinendam et hauriendam quo te incitarem, quamvis tuam sitim bene noverim, gustum tamen mittere volui, quem tibi suavissimum, et, ut ita dicam, inductorium fore, peto ne frustra speraverim."

28. Doct. IV.xi.26: "Prorsus haec est in docendo eloquentia, qua fit dicendo, non ut libeat quod horrebat aut ut fiat quod pigebat, sed ut appareat quod latebat."

In general, Augustine succeeded. His books forbid the reader to read disinterestedly. Every step of the way, the reader encounters passages beautifully extolling the pleasures of growing closer to wisdom and the horrors of turning one's back on the pursuit of truth. Augustine did not use the academic jargon of his day in his dialogues and treatises, but he did add plenty of rhetorical flourishes in order to arouse and convert. Throughout his works, Augustine asserted that Wisdom is that Good, that Feast, that Fragrance, that Truth, that God, that Mother, that Lover whom all humans need and desire. Augustine the rhetorician appealed to every sort of hedonist. For the reader who loves fine food, he evoked the flavors of a feast to explain the pleasures of finding truth. For the reader who wishes for absence of pain and disease, he spoke of fitness and health and the Truth who is a doctor of souls. For the reader who loves women, he invoked the images of full breasts and soft lips. For the reader who simply wants a quiet space to rest, Augustine asserted that all human beings are weary until they rest in Truth.

The Psychology of the Confessions

The third key to understanding Augustine's hope for philosophy is considering his psychology and his argument for the erotically philosophical nature of human beings. While this argument is given in several of his later works, including *On the Trinity* and *On the City of God*, it is in the *Confessions* that Augustine gave the most personal account of this argument. Indeed, the *Confessions* is both an autobiography and an apology for philosophy. Augustine rhetorically structured the *Confessions* to make philosophers out of his readers.[29] He explained, "Why do I narrate all of these things to you? It is not so that you will know about them through me, but so that I might excite those who read this with my affection for you."[30] In the *Confessions*, Augustine gave an account of human lived experience

---

29. See Miles, *Desire and Delight*, 68: "His own reading experiences, as well as those of his friends, led him to understand that reading—whether philosophical treatises like Cicero's *Hortensius*, or narratives of conversions, or Scripture—could transform life.... Augustine hopes that the *Confessions* will be one of those books that points the way to truth. Yet in order to point effectively, not merely to intellectual truth but to the truth that has the power to alter our lives, his text must first create in the reader an intense, energetic engrossing engagement." See also O'Connell, *St. Augustine's Confessions*, 16: "From this point of view the *Confessions* in its entirety represents one extended *exercitatio*, designed to reawaken the soul to knowledge of both itself and God."

30. Conf. XI.i.1: "cur ergo tibi tot rerum narrations digero? non utique ut per me noveris ea, sed affectum meum excite in te, et eorum qui haec legunt."

that reveals what he believed is the true nature of human desire in order to rightly order the desire of the reader.

Augustine began the work, as he began every work, with praise for God and God's wisdom. Then, Augustine commenced his narration of his own life experiences, beginning with his infancy. These first books, as is true for all the books of the *Confessions*, are not just about Augustine in particular but also about the human condition. Indeed, Augustine admitted that he did not even remember his infancy; he came to his knowledge about the first years of his life by listening to his mother and by observing other babies. In this way, the reader is invited to see Augustine as a person like any other person with a common childhood.

Augustine, like every infant, was an erotic creature. By nature, before the desires of their culture have been incorporated into their hearts, babies have desire. They cry for milk, for security, for care. They are needy, dependent creatures who can only exist in relationship with their care givers. Moreover, in Augustine's account, infants are not blessed, happy innocents easily sated by what is healthy and good. Augustine recounted stories of babies who scream to be given harmful things and jealous babies who would snatch food from their siblings even when they had themselves just been fed.[31] Straight from the womb, human beings are born wanting something they cannot explain or understand. Augustine's study of infants suggests that simple hedonism does not satisfy even little children. No baby is satisfied totally with the breast. They cry with a greater need.

After infancy comes childhood, an age in which material goods and simple pleasures still do not satisfy. As evidence, Augustine discussed play. He insisted that children do not desire to play in pursuit of physical pleasure; Augustine recounted that he played even when he knew he would be spanked for playing because he preferred playing, friendship, and victory more than the absence of pain.[32] This is equally true of children and adults, insisted Augustine:

> Is this childlike innocence? It is not, Sir, it is not. . . . It is all the same as the ages pass and we cross into adulthood from obeying and being punished by tutors and teachers and playing with nuts and marbles and sparrows to obeying and being more harshly punished by prefects and kings and seeking gold, presents, and mansions.[33]

31. See Conf. I.vii.11.

32. See Conf. I.ix–x.

33. Conf. I.xix.30: "istane est innocentia puerilis? Non est, domine, non est. . . . nam haec ipsa sunt quae a paedagogis et magistris, a nucibus et pilulis et passeribus, ad

While he understood why a child might prefer competing for prizes to studying and an adult might prefer gaining worldly riches to obeying the law, Augustine was confused by other desires he found in his heart. Most confusing to Augustine was his desire to do what he knew to be wrong and harmful. He found no philosopher who could suitably explain this phenomenon, who could explain to him why, for example, he would have ever robbed a neighbor's pear tree. He claimed that far beyond the physical pleasure of eating pears and even the emotional pleasure of pleasing his friends lay the pleasure of doing something wrong. Why would human beings get pleasure from doing what is wrong? Ultimately, Augustine decided that this desire for sin, which can be seen in babies and old men, points to the fact that human beings have a desire they do not understand and simply do not know how to satisfy themselves.

As Augustine described his later childhood and adolescence, he noted the "maturation" of human desire. No longer questing after the thrill of stealing pears or the joy of victory at ball games, the teenage Augustine was sent to Carthage to study rhetoric in order to obtain a well-paying career and to pursue the pleasures of a loving relationship, theatrical emotions, and prestigious honors. Augustine recounted, "I came to Carthage and saw all about me a sizzling skillet of loves."[34] Despite the caricature sometimes painted of Augustine's adolescence, his passions were traditionally admirable. Augustine experienced sexual passion in a monogamous relationship with a young woman he loved. He had a large group of friends with whom he enjoyed going to the theater and having discussions. He excelled in his studies. While he deprecated his lifestyle choices and his love of academic success, his parents might have been proud of his behavior. By Roman standards, he was a virtuous young man, a good student who used prudence to feed his appetites with moderation. And yet, Augustine declared that this life was empty. Physical love, friendship, theater, and academic respect were empty dreams compared to the bewildering passion he began to feel for the wisdom of eternal truth.[35]

Augustine's account of his conversion to philosophy follows a careful recounting of his normal human desires and aspirations. He wanted what most people wanted. Indeed, he had obtained what most people hoped to obtain. But the language used to describe his balanced life pales in comparison to the language he used for his pursuit of wisdom. The message to his reader

---

praefectos et reges aurum, praedia, mancipia, haec ipsa omnino succedentibus majoribus aetatibus transeunt, sicuti ferulis majora supplicia succedunt."

34. Conf. III.i.1: "Veni Carthaginem, et circumstrepebat me undique sarago flagitiosorum amorum."

35. See Conf. III.iv.7.

is clear. Nothing will really satisfy the hungry mind except wisdom. Compared to wisdom, the objects of all other desires are but shadows and fantasies. Throughout the *Confessions*, Augustine rejected a materialist account of human desire. Children cry for milk but also for affection, for victory, for good stories; adults seek physical pleasure but also emotional gratification, intellectual victory, and honor. Human desire cannot be understood simply in terms of bodily desire. Yet Augustine insisted that not even affection, victory, or prestige will satisfy the human heart ultimately. Augustine developed a psychology that claims what human beings really want is truth, real truth, not just pragmatic ideas that lead to worldly success.

Even after Augustine became a Christian theologian, he remained a dedicated philosopher. While he certainly connected his view of true philosophy to his view of right religion, it is important to note that Augustine never advocated that his reader simply join the church. Inside or outside of the church, Augustine insisted, the human person must pursue a philosophical life. As a priest and bishop, he insisted to his congregation:

> God gave you eyes in your body, reason in your heart. Arouse the reason in the heart, wake up the inner inhabitant behind the inner eyes, let it gather at the window, let it inspect God's creation. There is indeed something inside which sees through the eyes. . . . Awaken this, excite this. This is not denied to you. . . . God made you a rational animal. . . . Ought you just be using your eyes like cattle, so that you see only what you can put in your belly, not in your intellect? Therefore, wake up your rational observation, use your eyes like a human being, pay attention to the sky and earth, the ornaments of the sky, the fertility of the earth, the flying of birds, the swimming of fishes, the quantity of seeds, the order of time. Pay attention to facts and seek facts. Pay attention to what you see and seek what you do not see.[36]

Human beings, unlike cattle, cannot be satisfied with only material goods. Human beings need to seek facts, truth, and understanding.

---

36. Sermon 126.3: "Dedit tibi Deus oculos in corpore, rationem in corde. Excita rationem cordis, erige interiorem habitatorem interiorum oculorum tuorum, assumat fenestras suas, inspiciat creaturam Dei. Est enim aliquis intus qui per oculos videat. . . . Erige illum, excita illum. Non enim denegatus est tibi. Rationale animal te Deus fecit, . . . Siccine uti oculis debes ut pecus, tantum ut videas quid addas ventri, non menti? Erige ergo rationalem aspectum, utere oculis ut homo, intende caelum et terram, ornamenta caeli, fecunditatem terrae, volatus avium, natatus piscium, vim seminum, ordinem temporum. Intende facta, et quaere factorem. Aspice quae vides, et quaere quod non vides."

Twenty-First-Century Conceptions
of Philosophy and Human Nature

There is an unfortunate prevailing view in contemporary society that doing philosophy is no longer synonymous with the happy life. Although some people blame this on professional philosophers who changed the goal of philosophy in modernity from happiness to certainty,[37] no one has decried this change in attitude more than the philosophers themselves. The late nineteenth-century German philosopher Friedrich Nietzsche, for example, engaged Augustine's erotic language for the love of Truth as he chastised his fellows in philosophy in his preface to *Beyond Good and Evil*:

> Suppose that Truth is a woman—what then? Are there not grounds for the suspicion that all philosophers, insofar as they are dogmatists have been very bad at understanding women? That the horrible earnestness, the awkward advances, with which they are used to approaching Truth so far have been clumsy and improper methods for going straight into a woman's room? What is certain is that she has not allowed herself to be taken.[38]

The Austrian Ludwig Wittgenstein, who denounced much of the philosophical work of his contemporaries as nonsense, wrote in a work published posthumously, "Peace in their thinking, this is what someone who philosophizes yearns for."[39] Martha Nussbaum's numerous books have urged the public to read and discuss philosophy in order that they might have more fulfilled, flourishing human lives, even as she has denounced her colleagues for writing with too much jargon and too little concern for regular human life. All in all, philosophers, especially in this current age where many worry that the study of the humanities is in jeopardy, often invoke the language and the goals of the ancient and late antique

---

37. See Edmund Hill's note for Sermon 150 in his translation of Augustine's *Sermons*: "Could this be said to be the common concern of modern philosophers? I doubt it. But it was true of the ancient world, where philosophy really was concerned with ultimate causes, meanings, and values."

38. Nietzsche, *Jenseits von Gut und Bose*, 1: "Vorausgesetzt, dass die Wahrheit ein Weib ist—wie? ist der Verdacht nicht gegründer, dass alle Philosophen, sofern sie Dogmatiker waren, sich schlecht auf Weiber verstanden? dass der schauerliche Ernst, die linkische Zudringlichkeit, mit der sie bisher auf die Wahrheit zuzugehen pflegten, ungeschickte und unschickliche Mittel waren, um gerade ein Frauenzimmer für sich einzunehmen? Gewiss ist, dass sie sich nicht hat einnehmen lassen."

39. Wittgenstein, *Culture and Value*, 43: "Friede in den Gedanken. Das ist das ersehnte Ziel dessen, der philosophiert."

philosophers who sought in philosophy a path to reduce human suffering and to help humans live more livable lives.

Of course, in the twenty-first-century academic institution, the study of human nature and its well-being is considered the purview of biology, neurobiology, psychology, and sociology departments as well as philosophy departments. Interestingly, the findings of natural and social scientists correlate with the philosophers' consensus that all people desire to know. Why are both children and adults attracted to the internet—to Facebook, Wikipedia, Instagram, Snapchat, and Insider? In *Psychology Today*, Susan Weinschenk offered the most recent scientific explanation:

> Dopamine causes you to want, desire, seek out, and search. It increases your general level of arousal and your goal-directed behavior. From an evolutionary stand-point this is critical. The dopamine seeking system keeps you motivated to move through your world, learn, and survive. It's not just about physical needs such as food, or sex, but also about abstract concepts. Dopamine makes you curious about ideas and fuels your searching for information.[40]

Human biology is such that the human being is blasted with dopamine whenever he discovers a new fact. Many evolutionary biologists claim that this makes sense because there are so many evolutionary benefits for the human species when individuals are rewarded for seeking knowledge and sharing that knowledge in community. Some psychologists insist that this means that humans are neurologically wired to click on websites that promise new and exciting facts or information.

In general, many scientists who study the human mind today agree with Augustine, Aristotle, Epicurus, and Cicero, not to mention Nietzsche, Wittgenstein, and Nussbaum. All humans have a passionate desire to know. Augustine was right, the human heart burns for wisdom. Unfortunately, that passion is not always accompanied with the ability to discern truth from error. Thus, this very desire that makes humans *homo sapiens*, this very desire that helps human beings thrive, can also lead to marked danger and destruction. Indeed, this was Augustine's experience as an adolescent. His very desire for the truth that would help him thrive led him into a cult that truncated his authentic desires and ability to seek a happy life.

40. Weinschenk, "Why We're All Addicted."

Chapter 3

Everybody Loves a Secret

The Dangerous Lure of Gnosticism, Supremacist Cults,
and Conspiracy Theories

The Seduction of the Manicheans

Then I fell among people who were deliriously proud, so carnal
and so loquacious. In their mouths were diabolical traps. . . .
Yet they said, "Truth and Truth," and they said it many times
to me. Yet nothing was in these words, but false things were
spoken, not only about you, who truly are the Truth, but indeed
also about elements of the world, your creation. . . . O Truth,
Truth, deep inside me, the marrow of my soul panted for you.
. . . And these were the dishes they gave to me who was so hungry. . . . And on these dishes, they placed splendid phantasms
before me. . . . I chewed . . . but I did not receive nutrition from
these, rather I was more exhausted. Food in sleep is like the
food of those awake, yet nevertheless in sleeping they are not
nourished; indeed, they sleep. . . . In this way I was fed inane
things and I was not fed.[1]

AT AGE NINETEEN, AUGUSTINE was on fire for the truth. He was convinced
that his academic success, his friendships, and even his relationship with
his concubine and their beloved infant son were not enough for his full
flourishing. He was certain that the happy life required knowing the truth.

---

1. Conf. III.vi.10: "Itaque incidi in homines superbe delirantes, carnales nimis et
loquaces, in quorum ore laquei diaboli. . . . et dicebant, 'veritas et veritas,' et multum
eam dicebant mihi, et nusquam erat in eis, sed falsa loquebantur, non de te tantum, qui
vere veritas es, sed etiam de istis elementis huius mundi, creatura tua . . . o veritas, veritas, quam intime etiam tum medullae animi suspirabant tibi, cum te illi sonarent mihi
frequenter et multipliciter voce sola et libris multis et ingentibus! et illa errant fercula
in quibus mihi esuriente. . . . et apponebantur adhuc mii in illis ferculis phantasmata
splendida. . . . manducabam, . . . nec nutriebar eis, sed exhauriebar magis. cibus in
somnis simillimus est cibis vigilantium, quo tamen dorminetes non aluntur; dormiunt
enim. . . . qualibus ego tunc pascebar inanibus, et non pascebar."

34

He eschewed the simple faith of his mother's Christianity as he hoped to find a more mature way of thinking.[2] Still, he retained the warning of Paul to the Colossians: "See that no one deceives you through philosophy and empty seduction."[3] He vowed to be careful lest he adopt faulty positions. He was wary of what he read and to whom he listened.

Given all of this, how could it be that such a brilliant young thinker who had pledged to focus his attention on rooting out the truth would so quickly and easily be seduced into a sect like the Manicheans for almost a decade? This question has bothered no small number of Augustine's biographers and troubled Augustine himself after he left the group.[4] Indeed, this question concerns anyone who hopes for a possibility of sorting out truth from error and living a philosophical life.

Augustine's experiences with the Manicheans reveal a very particular danger to any seeker of truth: gnosticism or occult knowledge. Gnostic cults in the ancient world were conveyors of secret teachings, teachings that by definition could only be understood by an elite group of "knowers."[5] Their teachings gained authority by virtue of being different than mainstream knowledge. Their teachings mocked the doctrines of more common religions and often contradicted leading opinions in natural science. Gnosticism, in general, denounces the physical world, including the physical body, as evil and a source of deception for the pure mind or spirit of the elite knower. While many catholic Christians and Platonists made pointed arguments against the methods and foundational doctrines of gnosticism,[6] their adherents were inoculated against these arguments with the advice to

2. See Conf. III.v.9: "non enim sicut modo loquor, ita sensi, cum attendi ad illam scripturam, sed visa est mihi indigna quam tullianae dignitati compararem. . . . sed ego dedignabar esse parvulus et turgidus fastu mihi grandis videbar." (No, indeed, I did not experience Scripture in the manner that I now speak, but rather, first when I attended to Scripture it was seen as lacking dignity when I compared it to the dignity of Tullius. . . . But I disdained to be a little one. I, swollen with pride, saw myself as a grown up person.)

3. Col 2:8 quoted in Conf. III.iv.8: "videte, ne quis vos decipiat per philosophiam et inanem seductionem."

4. For example, Maria Boulding said, "It may surprise us that a man of Augustine's intellectual caliber could have been seduced even for a moment, let alone for nine years, by what we might consider nowadays to be a farrago of nonsense" (Boulding, Introduction, 15). Similarly, William Mallard asked, "After his encounter with Cicero and his new found love for truth, Augustine surprisingly became for nine years a follower of the Manichean religion. . . . The very passages he quoted from Cicero had warned him against just such a sectarian group. Why then did he almost immediately turn to them?" (Mallard, Language and Love, 52).

5. From the Greek word for knowledge, γνῶσις.

6. See Irenaeas, Scandal of the Incarnation; Plotinus, Enneads II.9.

refrain from discussing the core of their knowledge with those outside the sect. Thus, Augustine later came to believe that their type of false teachings was especially dangerous as were all teachings whose adherents proudly refused to question their own foundations or examine other competing theories. As Augustine recounted the nine years he spent believing and preaching the doctrines of the Manicheans, he demonstrated a very real danger for every human truth seeker—no matter how educated, how clever, or how passionate for truth. Indeed, the contemporary reader who studies Augustine's account of his time with the Manicheans realizes that the most passionate philosopher may have the greatest vulnerability to the seductive power of gnostic-type teachings.

While Manicheanism is extinct today, there are many contemporary sects and cults that contain similar elements of gnosticism. Furthermore, there are many conspiracy theorists that use gnostic tactics and strategies to recruit believers. Indeed, the difference between a conspiracy theory and simply a new theory lies in the use of gnostic strategies. Any new theory may contradict formerly believed knowledge; a conspiracy theory promises secret knowledge. A new theory appeals to empirical evidence; a conspiracy theory denounces empirical evidence. Interestingly, conspiracy theories are flourishing in the twenty-first century. Thus, an examination of Augustine's experience with the Manicheans is especially relevant to those who wish to seek truth in the contemporary world.

Manichean Teachings

On the surface, Manicheism appears to offer teachings of the same type as many other religious sects. The teachings of Mani, a third-century Persian prophet, included a theory of metaphysics and physics that attempted to explain the origin and nature of the cosmos. These teachings also included a strict rule of conduct and a doctrine of salvation. In all, the Manicheans promised to give knowledge of the soul, its place in the cosmos, and its path to the blessed life. As such, the Manicheans promised to teach the very wisdom that the ancient philosopher was seeking. However, their theories were founded on a metaphysics that justified an elitism among its members and denied the possibility of a universal path to truth for all people. As a result, Manichean teachings were insulated from critiques made by those outside the sect and even from the empirical evidence and reason of those who questioned within the sect.

Specifically, the Manicheans taught that there were two fundamental substances: light and darkness. The world that humans inhabit was considered to be the product of a battle between the forces of light and darkness, of good and evil, with the result that some fragments of the light were imprisoned in the dark matter. Augustine explained,

> They say indeed that certain souls, which they claim are part of the substance of God and of his same nature, have not spontaneously sinned, but at the command of the the Father, and not of their own will, they descended into battle against the race of darkness, which they call the evil nature. They were conquered and were taken captive, imprisoned within the horrible globe of darkness.[7]

This metaphysics thus asserted that the souls of the elite were of a different nature than all the other things in the earthly sphere, "the horrible globe of darkness."

Augustine admitted that the creation story of the Manicheans was easy to grasp by his teenage mind that was used to thinking only in terms of material substance. Both the forces of light and the forces of darkness were considered to be physical substances of some sort. Augustine imagined the light to be substantial in the manner of air—a thin and subtle corporeal body. The darkness was considered to be the type of substance that is the dirt of the earth and the flesh of bodies, a heavy and vulgar type of matter. Moreover, the Manicheans taught that the battle between light and darkness was exhibited in the material movements of the heavens. The books of the Manicheans included predictions and calculations concerning the movement of the stars and planets, which they provided to the listener as evidence of their scientific validity.

However, when Augustine discovered that most of the astronomical predictions and calculations failed to be as empirically adequate as those made by more mainstream natural scientists, he was "commanded to believe many most absurd and fabulous things because they could not be demonstrated."[8] The sect's fundamental metaphysics demanded this. The adherents proclaimed that the nature of the divine soul of the elect was of a radically different substance than the bodies of scientists outside the sect and even radically different than the Manichean believer's own corporeal body. This meant that scientific studies could be discounted if they

---

7. NB xlii: "Dicunt enim etiam nonnullas animas, quas volunt esse de substantia Dei et eiusdem omnino naturae, quae non sponte peccaverint, sed a gente tenebrarum, quam mali naturam dicunt, ad quam debellandam non ultro, sed patris imperio descenderunt, superatae et oppressae sint, affigi in aeternum globo horribili tenebrarum."

8. Conf. VI.v.7: "postea tam multa fabulosissima et absurdissima, quia demonstrari non poterant, credenda imperari."

contradicted the teachings of Mani. Even the empirical evidence witnessed by the Manichean believer himself could be dismissed. Thus, Manichean teachings were protected by their own doctrines. They were impervious to questioning and debate as any evidence against them was considered, by virtue of being against them, diabolical in nature.

In order to fight the diabolical darkness, the members of the sect followed a strict code of conduct. They were strict vegetarians who considered the flesh of animals to be a product of dark matter. They abstained from alcohol and sexual contact because both pulled the soul towards delight in the material flesh rather than towards the ethereal pleasures of the liberated soul. Elite members of the cult could not pick fruit, for they believed that this caused pain to the tree, who wept milky tears at the site of the injury. Thus, the picking of fruit was done by slaves who were not members of the sect and, being evil already, could not be further contaminated by the crime of picking fruit.

Indeed, the elitism of the sect required that the elect must treat other humans not as equals but according to their elect or non-elect nature. The elect members were supposed to abstain from all sexual contact, but hearers and new initiates to the cult were told that if they were unable to control the dark forces of lust in their own bodies they should not blame themselves but the diabolical will of their flesh. The sect provided manuals on birth control for these incontinent hearers as the conception of a Manichean child was believed to be the entrapping of a fragment of the divine into the dark matter of the flesh, a terrible crime. There were also separate ethical codes regarding those who were entirely outside of the sect. For example, the elect members were commanded to eat large quantities of food in order that, through chewing and digesting, the interior divine souls of fruits and vegetables might be released back to God. Yet Manicheans were forbidden to share food with the hungry or to offer sustenance to beggars lest those vegetative angels that slept in bread become imprisoned in the heavy flesh of the non-elect. Augustine explained,

> I believed a fig, when it was plucked, cried with the milky tears of its mother tree. Nonetheless if this same fig were to be devoured by a saint, especially plucked by another, of course, so as not to pollute the saint himself, then the fig would mingle in the bowels of the saint, and thereby be breathed out as angels when the saint groaned in prayer, belching out particles of God. Particles of the highest true god were left in this fruit, unless the teeth and belly of the holy elect freed them. Yes, miserable as I was, I believed that more friendly hearted empathy was to be given towards these fruits of the Earth than to human

beings for which these fruits were created. Indeed, if some person was begging in hunger who was not a Manichean, it was seen as if the fruit would be damned to a capital punishment if it was given to him to eat.[9]

Yet both adherence or failure to adhere to the Manichean codes of conduct only confirmed Manichean teachings. Augustine, for the duration of nine years, remained outside the inner circle, mainly because of his desire and love for his concubine. This love was explained by the Manichean psychology as simply an overpowering of his true will by the dark desires of his flesh. His sympathy for beggars might have been similarly explained. The Manichean sect required no confession of sins and no serious investigation of the usefulness of their own moral code for they claimed that any failure to obey the codes of conduct were caused by the evil forces in the flesh and irrelevant to the soul's own struggle for goodness.

Later, looking back, Augustine found his own nearly decade-long commitment to the Manicheans to be laughable. Manicheism was an occult sect, a secret society with rituals that were considered strange according to the reason and culture of North Africa and the larger Roman Empire. Their beliefs ran contrary to the theories of most of the scientific and academic community. The very things that should have repelled him as a philosopher attracted him. The promise of secret knowledge, the naïve materialism, and the supremacist elitism were all elements against which both Cicero and Paul had warned. But Augustine had been attracted to the gnostic group precisely because of their occultism, their materialism, and their elitism. Precisely because the ideas were not held by common people, he believed that he was discovering an important truth. Precisely because their doctrines did not require abstract thinking, he grasped them easily. Precisely because only the elite were considered worthy, he was flattered to be amongst the hearers. Like many who find themselves caught in cult doctrines, supremacist ideology, or simply the lure of a conspiracy theory, Augustine was led to false belief because of his very passion for truth. The recruiters of the group preyed on his naïveté and pride as they introduced their gnostic doctrines, which, taken as a whole, were protected against dissent and free inquiry.

9. See Conf. III.x.18: "crederem ficum plorare cum decerpitur et matrem eius arborem lacrimis lacteis? quam tamen ficum si comedisset aliquis sanctus, alieno sane non suo scelere decerptam misceret visceribus et anhelerat de illa angelos, immo vero particulas dei gemendo in oratione atque ructando. quae particulae summi et veri dei ligatae fuissent in illo pomo, nisi electi sancti dente ac ventre solverentur. et credidi miser magis esse misericordiam praestandam fructibus terrae quam hominibus propter quos nascerentur. si quis enim esuriens peteret qui manichaeus non esset, quasi capitali supplicio damnanda bucella videretur si ei daretur."

The Danger of Philosophical Desire

Ironically, the very drive in the human psyche that pushes the mind to seek truth is the same force that can lead the philosopher into error. Such is a risk for philosophers and students of all kinds. Perhaps as a warning to those new to philosophy, Plato placed this issue as the central concern in his rendition of one of Socrates earliest public dialogues. In his *Protagoras*, Plato portrayed the young Socrates's interactions with a teenage boy who was passionately on fire to gain wisdom from a traveling sophist, Protagoras. A lusty and impetuous young man, Hippocrates was so eager to start his educational journey that he beat upon Socrates's door in the middle of the night seeking a recommendation to study with the man who was the "only one who is wise."[10] Socrates, recognizing the young man's excitement, saw the youth was especially vulnerable. Socrates warned Hippocrates that while true teachings nourish the soul, false teachings can make the soul sick. Thus, it is of the utmost importance to choose the right teachers. Socrates said,

> Do you see what kind of danger you are about to put your soul in? On one hand, if you had to trust your body with some-one and risk its becoming healthy or sick, you would consider carefully whether you should entrust it or not, and you would talk together with your friends and all in your household for many days. On the other hand, when it comes to something more valuable than your body, namely your soul, and when everything concerning whether it goes well or badly depends on whether it becomes worthy or worthless, I don't see you together with your father or brother or a single one of your companions to consider whether or not to entrust your soul to this recently arrived foreigner.[11]

Plato gave important advice to his reader through the character of Socrates. Rather than consulting an esoteric teacher, who teaches in the basements of wealthy men and whose teachings are unknown in the wider community, a new seeker of truth should begin by talking to family and

---

10. Plato, *Protagoras* 310d: "μόνος ἐστὶ σοφός."

11. Plato, *Protagoras*, 313a–b: "οἶσθα εἰς οἷόν τινα κίνδυνον ἔρχῃ ὑποθήσων τὴν ψυχήν; ἢ εἰ μὲν τὸ σῶμα ἐπιτρέπειν σε ἔδει τω, διακινδυνεύοντα ἢ χρηστὸν αὐτὸ γενέσθαι ἢ πονηρόν, πολλὰ ἂν περιεσκέψω, εἴτ' ἐπιτρεπτέον εἴτε οὔ, καὶ εἰς συμβουλὴν τούς τε φίλοθς ἂν παρεκάλεις καὶ τοὺς οἰκείους, σκοπούμενος ἡμέρας συχνάς. ὃ δὲ περὶ πλείνος τοῦ σώματος ἡγεῖ, τὴν ψυχήν, καὶ ἐν ᾧ πάντ'ἐστὶ τὰ σὰ ἢ εὖ ἢ κακῶς πράττειν, χρηστοῦ ἢ πονηροῦ αὐτοῦ γενομένου, περὶ δὲ τούτου οὔτε τῳ πατρὶ οὔτε τῳ ἀδελφῷ ἐπεκοινώσω οὔτε ἡμῶν τῶν ἑταίρων οὐδενί, εἴτ'ἐπιτρεπτέον εἴτε καὶ οὐ τῳ ἀφικομένῳ τούτῳ ξένῳ τὴν σὴν ψυχήν."

friends. Yet, of course, the new philosopher is looking for new teachings. He is attracted especially to ideas he has not heard before from his family and his community. Indeed, the search for truth, as Plato espoused it, requires the philosopher to seek new sources of knowledge, to go beyond what he has studied before. Indeed, as Socrates explained, this leads to an inevitable dilemma:

> On one hand, if you are a knowledgeable consumer, you can buy teachings safely from Protagoras or anyone else. But on the other hand, if you are not, my blessed one, please do not risk what is most dear on a roll of the dice, for there is a far greater risk in buying teachings than in buying goods. . . . You cannot carry teachings away in another container. You put down the money and take the teaching away in your own soul by having learned it, and you leave, either helped or injured.[12]

As a compromise, Hippocrates agreed that Socrates should come to hear Protagoras with him so that together they could evaluate the sophist's promises. For future philosophers, Plato created a set of written dialogues in which Socrates was portrayed as a model of vigorous questioning that might help anyone going to listen to new teachings.

But Augustine had not yet come upon the books of the Platonists when the *Hortensius* of Cicero awakened his desire for truth. He recognized himself as a creature who hungered, thirsted, and lusted for wisdom and he set off to find truth on his own. He tried to consult the books that his mother had claimed held wisdom. But he did not know how to read them, and more importantly he wanted to prove himself as a mature thinker who had grown beyond his childish dependence on his mother's advice. As a newly converted philosopher, he was in a precarious position.

The Manicheans were poised for just such a seeker. They flattered him for recognizing that he needed the truth. They mocked and ridiculed the common beliefs held by Augustine's mother. As Augustine explained it, his was a familiar story, one that the author of *Proverbs* warned the wisdom seeker about:

> I stumbled on that bold woman [Folly] who was empty of prudence, from Solomon's allegory, sitting on a stool by the door,

---

12. Plato, *Protagoras*, 313e–314b: "εἰ μὲν οὖν σὺ τυγχάνεις ἐπιστήμων τούτων τί χρηστὸν καὶ πονηρόν, ἀσφαλές σοι ὠνεῖσθαι μαθήματα καὶ παρὰ Πρωταγόρου καὶ παρ᾽ ἄλλου ὁτουοῦν. εἰ δὲ μή, ὅρα, ὦ μακάριε, μὴ περὶ τοῖς φιλτάτοις κυβεύῃς τε καὶ κινδυνεύῃς. . . . μαθήματα δὲ οὐκ ἔστιν ἐν ἄλλῳ ἀγγείῳ ἀπενεγκεῖν, ἀλλ᾽ ἀνάγκη, καταθέντα τὴν τιμήν, τὸ μάθημα ἐν αὐτῇ τῇ ψυχῇ λαβόντα καὶ μαθόντα ἀπιέναι ἢ βεβλαμμένον ἢ ὠφελημένον."

"Eat freely of the secret bread and drink of the sweet furtive water." She seduced me, she who came and found me by the door,
living in the eye of my flesh and ruminating by myself while I ate
voraciously what I could see through my own eyes.[13]

The Manicheans promised to teach Augustine a new and secret truth, and
their promises enflamed his desire. So he followed them.

Both Plato's and Solomon's descriptions of the vulnerability of the passionate seeker of wisdom continue to be apt in the contemporary world.
Contrary to some common opinions about those people who join cults or
supremacist groups and even about those who simply believe conspiracy
theories, it is not apathy towards truth that is the cause of false belief. Rather,
excitement about the possibility of learning something that no one else
knows is what attracts the seeker to a secret error. A contemporary description of this vulnerability is given in the account of Frank Meeink in his
Autobiography of a Recovering Skinhead, a confessional work dedicated to
exposing the techniques used to recruit and sustain white supremacist cults
in the twenty-first century. Frank Meeink recounted his first encounter with
white supremacist skinheads: "They knew what to do and say to a half Irish,
half Italian kid who was abused."[14] While as a teenager from the streets of
Philadelphia he was a skeptic and a "hard sell," the supremacists used this
to their advantage. By the middle of the first conversation with members
of the group, the teenage Meeink asked, "Why didn't I learn this at Mass?"
He received the gnostic answer, "God chose for you to learn now"[15] They
followed up his "millions of questions" with what appeared to Meeink at the
time to be evidence and logic.[16] He became excited to know the real truth
about what was going on in the United States.

Some psychologists say this excitement is easily aroused because it is
an evolutionary benefit for humans to seek out knowledge that goes beyond
the community's ascribed beliefs.[17] An evolutionary benefit or not, there is

---

13. Conf. III.vi.11: "offendi illam mulierem audacem, inopem prudentiae, aenigma
Salomonis, sedentem super sellam in foribus et dicentem 'panes occultos libenter edite,
et aquam dulcem furtivam bibite' quae me seduxit, quia invenit foris habitantem in
oculo carnis meae et talia ruminantem apud me qualia per illum vorassem." See Prov 9.

14. Meeink, *Autobiography of a Recovering Skinhead*, 52.

15. Meeink, *Autobiography of a Recovering Skinhead*, 54.

16. Meeink, *Autobiography of a Recovering Skinhead*, 55

17. See psychologist Karen Douglas's comments as reported in Hogenboom, "Enduring Appeal of Conspiracy Theories": "'On some level, we are all predisposed to be
suspicious or mistrustful of government,' says Douglas. That we are wary of groups or
people we do not understand makes sense from an evolutionary perspective. 'In some
ways, it is quite adaptive to be suspicious of other groups for your own personal safety.'"

clearly a human psychological drive to uncover a secret. The web designers for white supremacist groups, the creators of sites that sport conspiracy theories, and the makers of political clickbait all understand this well. Using the same process as the recruiters for the Manicheans, they seek out those who are unsatisfied with the current level of their knowledge and want to know more. The first access point is created especially for the person who is looking to know the real truth behind some specific phenomena. At the second access point, a commonly held belief is deconstructed and the authority that issued the information is belittled. The goal is to inflame the reader's desire to know the real truth. Ironically, the more passionate seeker of truth is more vulnerable as she is more likely to keep clicking forward at this point. At the third access point, the beliefs of the group begin to be made manifest. Set before the ravenous mind of the truth seeker, conspiracies, fallacies, and dogma are swallowed with little examination as sweet, secret truths.

The Danger of Simplicity

These secret teachings are initially presented as straightforward teachings and simple to understand. The recruiters laugh that it is amazing that somehow these simple truths have been ignored by the majority of mainstream thinkers. The paradoxical promise offered is that the cult has simple and obvious truths that are easily grasped by the initiate but hidden from most people who cannot see or understand them. Ironically, the desire for simple but hidden truths often leads to the acceptance of doctrines that appear wildly fantastic compared with common knowledge. Part of the problem is that the seeker of truth, by definition, does not yet have the truth and therefore cannot discern it from error. As Augustine explained,

> Here again arises a most difficult question. Indeed, in what manner can fools find a wise person? . . . The fool is ignorant of wisdom, therefore, the fool does not know wisdom. . . . Therefore, he does not know this, and since he does not know, he cannot recognize this in any place. Therefore, he cannot, so long as he remains a fool, recognize with absolute certainty a wise person who, if he followed, might liberate him from the evil of his folly.[18]

18. UC xiii.28: "Hic rursus oritur difficilissima quaestio. Quonam enim modo stulti sapientem invenire poterimus, . . . Caret autem stultus sapientia: non igitur novit sapientiam. . . . Nescit hanc igitur, et dum nescit, in alio loco cognoscere non potest. Non ergo potest, quamdiu stultus est, quisquam certissima cognitione invenire sapientem, cui obtemperando tanto stultitiae malo liberetur."

Famished, the passionate truth seeker prefers simple, easily digestible teachings. While many scientific studies, religious doctrines, and philosophical accounts are complex and require abstract thinking, the doctrines of gnostic teachings are almost always simplistically materialist and easy to understand. But this does not mean that the people attracted to false teachings are typically uneducated. When Augustine joined the Manichean sect as a hearer he was already one of the top scholars in his class at Carthage. Furthermore, he remained as a hearer even after finishing his studies and becoming a professor of rhetoric himself. Not only was he educated in the liberal arts generally, he had specific training in how to use words to make an appealing argument. This education did not inoculate him against the false teachings of the Manicheans. Nor has education inoculated many citizens in the contemporary world from believing a barrage of internet conspiracy theories, fake news, and simply bad information. Reports have shown that the school districts with some of the highest rates of "anti-vaxxers" (people who believe that, contrary to the evidence provided by the American Medical Association, vaccines cause significant health risks that outweigh their benefits) and, correspondingly, some of the highest rates of measles outbreaks are in school districts that educate the children of highly educated parents with degrees from elite universities.[19] In fact, the believer in false teachings is usually a person who is proud of her intellectual ability and education level and thus less likely to question her own beliefs. That said, the false knowledge that is dogmatically believed is almost always in an area in which the believer is not an expert.

At age nineteen, and even later, at age twenty-eight, Augustine was not an expert in theology or metaphysics. Of course, by his own account, he was remarkably gifted intellectually. He noted that he learned quickly in classes where others struggled. But while his studies were well-rounded in the liberal arts, he spent most of his time as a young man studying rhetoric, not metaphysics. He said that he was at that stage of development in which he

> could not think about any substance other than the kind of substance that can be seen by the eye. . . . I did not think of you [God] to be in the form of a human body, but nevertheless I could only think of you as some kind of corporeal substance extended in space, either infused throughout the world or diffused in infinity beyond it.[20]

19. See Keneally, "Parents Who Don't Vaccinate Kids."

20. Conf. VII.i.1: "qui cogitare aliquid substantiae nisi tale non poteram, quale per hos oculos videri solet. . . . ut quamvis non forma humani corporis, corporeum tamen aliquid cogitare cogerer per spatia locorum, sive infusum mundo sive etiam extra mundum per infinita diffusum."

Moreover, the philosophical texts he did encounter in his academic studies in his teens and early twenties were mainly those written by materialists and skeptics, neither of whom required him to think abstractly. He asserted that this inability to imagine anything other than visible substance led him to accept Manichean dualism easily. The Manichean god was a material god who was present in the souls of the elect and in a distant realm beyond the world.

Augustine insisted that the doctrines of the Manicheans did not have much to offer on their own. They appealed only to those with a lack of philosophical and theological training and who did not understand their own religious traditions, which the Manicheans deliberately made sound absurd. Manichean materialism was attractive to him only because at the time he simply could not think spiritually of an incorporeal realm. Untrained in theology and metaphysics, Augustine had no concept of a noetic reality that included a God who creates substance but is not substance and a soul that informs matter but is not material. Yet Augustine easily grasped the materialist teachings of Manichean dualism with their ethereal depiction of God and the soul as sharing a substance that differed from the substance of earthly things but still could be easily imagined.

Especially appealing was the simple Manichean explanation of the problem of evil, a quandary that had long troubled Augustine. He wondered at the existence of evil in a world supposedly created and controlled by a good God. Moreover, he wondered why it was that he did evil things even though he wanted so badly to be good. The Manichean dualism gave a full and simple account of the nature of evil:

> Here indeed I believed evil to be a type of substance—as if it had a shapeless hideous mass that was deformed and crass as they say about earth or else thin and subtle like the way air has a body, in these ways did they imagine the malignant mind on this earth. And my piety thought that I ought to believe a good God could create nothing bad in nature. Thus I constructed a theory that there were two shapeless masses, and both were infinite, but the bad was narrow and the good was grand, and from that pestilent foundation other sacrilegious ideas followed.[21]

21. Conf. V.x.20: "Hinc enim et mali substantiam quandam credebam esse talem et habere suam molem taetram et deformem et crassam, quam terram dicebant, sive tenuem atque subtilem, sicuti est aeris corpus, quam malignam mentem per illam terram repentem imaginantur. Et quia deum bonum nullam malam naturam crease qualiscumque me pietas credere cogebat, constituebam ex adverso sibi duas moles, utramque infinitam, sed malam angustius, bonam grandius, et ex hoc initio pestilentioso me cetera sacrilegia sequebantur."

Furthermore, Manichean psychology explained sin as the result of the uncontrollable force of evil in material bodies that acted contrary to the goodness of the will of the elect. This psychology asserted that the soul of the elect is divine and good. Human error never results from a weakness of the will of the elect but only from the overwhelming influence of the evil force of material flesh. This ability to accuse something outside of himself appealed to Augustine. Such teachings flattered his pride and did not demand that he inquire further into the nature of himself and his urge to do evil. He wrote,

> Before this, indeed, it seemed to me that it is not we who sin but some other, I know not what, in our nature that sinned, and it delighted my pride to be without blame. When I might do something evil, I did not confess that I did it, so that you could heal my soul when it sinned before you, but I loved to excuse myself and to accuse I know not what other that was with me but was not me.[22]

A common view in cults and even conspiracy theories is that some evil force or evil power is the source of a specific problem. Such a position protects the members and teachings of the group in two ways. First, it removes the blame and the guilt for a difficult problem from the members of the group and creates an alternate explanation. The Manicheans, like most gnostic religious groups, blamed a powerful evil force for creating and sustaining all the suffering in the world. Manicheans themselves were urged to follow a strict code of conduct in order to separate themselves as much as possible from this evil influence, but any failures to act properly served only to confirm the power and danger of the evil force. Manicheans were told they, in themselves, were completely blameless for all sin and suffering. This freedom from the pain of guilt was especially attractive to many members.

Similarly, white supremacists in the twenty-first century also proclaim their own blamelessness in a world of suffering. They blame people of color and Jews for creating a system that they believe has undermined the success of white people, causing them to be unemployed, impoverished, and victims of drug addiction and violence. For many white supremacists, this view is religious in nature. They see themselves as children of a different God than that of people of color. Interestingly, many secular conspiracy theories also encourage believers to blame something other than

---

22. Conf. V.x.18: "adhuc enim mihi videbatur non esse nos qui peccamus, sed nescio quam aliam in nobis peccare naturam, et delectabat superbiam meam extra culpam esse et, cum aliquid mali fecissem, non confiteri me fecisse, ut sanares animam meam, quoniam peccabat tibi, sed excusare me amabam et accusare nescio quid aliud quod mecum esseet et ego non essem."

themselves for the current problems that might plague them. For example, climate-change deniers suggest that government officials and professional scientists created a fictional crisis in order to line their own pockets with government funding for new projects while small businesses and private individuals face unemployment and poverty because of new regulations. Central to the recruiting of believers is the perspective that the members of this group are blameless victims of a dangerous power.

Second, this recruiting tool also inoculates the believers against any counter arguments. Because conspiracy theorists and cult members are told they are victims of a dangerous power, they must be constantly wary of how this dangerous power might try to deceive them. For example, an "anti-vaxxer" must discount a pamphlet on vaccine safety from his doctor if he believes that scientists and doctors are in the pockets of pharmaceutical companies. They assert that doctors deliberately falsify evidence in order to profit from both the use of vaccines and the medical problems they cause. Similarly, climate-change deniers ignore scientific evidence because they believe that the government and green energy corporations coerce scientists to give false evidence. Ultimately, all conspiracy theories, supremacist cults, and gnostic teachings protect themselves with a fundamentally anti-philosophical claim: reason and empirical evidence cannot be trusted because some malevolently deceptive force is holding the reigns of power.

Ironically, this view is at odds with their initial claims to recruits that their theories are obvious, observable, and straightforward. Interestingly, the theory of the powerful deceiver is not needed at first; once a view is adopted, many believers will filter evidence in order to confirm their initial beliefs. "At its core is the need for the brain to receive confirming information that harmonizes with an individual's existing views and beliefs,"[23] said Mark Whitmore in a piece published by the American Psychological Association concerning the popularity of "fake news." Whitmore explained, "In fact, one could say the brain is hardwired to accept, reject, misremember or distort information based on whether it is viewed as accepting of or threatening to existing beliefs."[24] For this reason, the doctrine of the powerful deceiver is only discussed when members who have joined the group begin to consider outside arguments for leaving it. Dangerously, this doctrine ensures that the more counter evidence that is presented, the stronger is their claim that an evil power has tampered with it. This may be the reason why many "birthers" believed that Barack Obama was not a US citizen even after his birth certificate was published in 2008 and his original certificate

23. "Why We're Susceptible to Fake News."
24. "Why We're Susceptible to Fake News."

of live birth was made public in 2011.[25] All evidence presented against a conspiracy theory serves as evidence that that the malevolent power is more engaged in manipulating data than previously thought.

While many twenty-first-century conspiracy theorists claim governmental or corporate powers are the source of false evidence, the Manicheans grounded their extreme epistemological claim in their religious belief that most of the visible world is the product of a dark and evil force. They, like most gnostic religious groups, believed that the creator of the earthly material world was a deceiver who hoped to plunge the noble minds of the elect into deeper relationship with darkness. Not only could members of the cult not trust scientists or others outside of their community, they could not even trust their own lived experience. Bodily eyes, ears, fingers, noses, and tongues could not be trusted to give the truth. As such, Manicheism, like most gnostic cults, was profoundly opposed to Jewish theology.

The Danger of Anti-Semitism and Anti-Judaism

Augustine reports that the Manichean recruiters who approached believers in catholic Christianity always began with an attack on Judaism. "Therefore the Manicheans are accustomed to attack the Scriptures of the Old Testament which they do not recognize in order to mock and deceive by that attack our weak and little ones who find no way to respond to them."[26] This was critical because the African church understood itself as a descendent of Judaism and took the Old Testament seriously. According to Peter Brown, "Many of its institutions and practices may have stemmed directly from the Jewish synagogue."[27] Augustine admitted that as a young man he knew little about Christian scriptures and, as explained above, was unable to think abstractly. He could not counter the attacks on Judaism. Despite his academic prowess, Augustine had been a little one in his theological knowledge:

> I did not know that there was another, which truly is, and I was moved by this condition to suffer from the deception of fools, when they asked me: Where does evil come from? Is God contained in the form of a body, and does he have hair and nails? Can it be said that they are just who have many wives at once and who kill people, and who sacrifice animals? I was troubled

25. Clinton and Roush, "Persistent Partisan Divide."

26. DGM I.i.2: "Solent ergo Manichaei Scripturas Veteris Testamenti, quas non noverunt, vituperare, et ea vituperatione infirmos et parvulos nostros, non invenientes quomodo sibi respondeant, irridere atque decipere."

27. See Brown, *Augustine of Hippo*, 42.

by my ignorance of these things, and departing from the truth I
saw myself as running towards the truth.[28]

Chief among the elements of Judaic teaching opposed by Manicheanism is the Jewish understanding of creation as an act of God in accordance
with God's wisdom. The Manicheans mocked the view that a supremely good
God created the world. They listed as counter examples: vipers, vermin, vi-
cious beasts, and poisonous plants. In addition, they reminded their listeners
of the pain and suffering caused by fire, hail, snow, ice, wind, and storms.[29]
Most of all, they ridiculed the Genesis account of God lovingly creating human beings out of mud, for this account demoted the human person to a
bit of warmed earth and denied the divine nature of the soul of the elect
human being. Emphasizing the lowness, the baseness, and the ugliness of the
earthly sphere, the Manicheans painted a contrasting picture of a bright, pure
ethereal realm that lay beyond the terrestrial one. The earth was not the true
home of the elect, they insisted, a celestial heaven was.

The anti-Judaism of the Manicheans, like the anti-Semitism that remains a central aspect of many twenty-first-century white supremacist
cults and a common element in many contemporary conspiracy theories, is
built on an epistemological foundation that serves as an impenetrable wall
against empirical or scientific evidence. The Manicheans did not trust any
physical evidence because they believed that the physical terrestrial world
was created by a deceptive and evil force. Contemporary anti-Semitic conspiracy theorists are similarly "immune to fact, logic, and reason," according
to Talia Lavin in her 2019 article on the subject in the *Nation*, because anti-
Semitism is at its core "a postulation of nefarious, transnational control by
Jews of institutions, inspired by malevolence and cunning unique to us as a
people."[30] Many anti-Semites insist that Jews control government agencies,
scientific organizations, and the media. As a result, the more evidence an
interlocutor provides about a given issue, the more evidence the conspiracy
theorist has that Jews have used their wealth, influence, and cleverness to
pollute the mainstream sources of information.

The accusation concerning Jewish cleverness is an especially protec-
tive defense used by anti-Semites. To explain, Talia Levin cites the 1920
publication *The International Jew*, which proclaimed that the Jew does not

28. Conf. III.vii.12: "Nescibam enim aliud vere quod est, et quasi acutule movebar
ut suffragarer stultis deceptoribus, cum a me quaerent unde malum, et utrum forma
coporea deus finiretur et haberet capillos et ungues, et utrum iusti existimandi essent
qui haberent uxores multas simul et occiderent homines et sacrificarent de animalibus.
quibus rerum ignarus perturbabar, et recedens a veritate ire in eam mihi videbar."

29. See Conf. VII.xvi.22; VII.xiii.19; DGM 1.xiii.19; 1.xvi.26; 1.xviii.18; 1.xx.31.

30. Lavin, "Maddening, Baffling, Exhausting."

simply rule by wealth and influence but rather by the "masterful genius of his race."[31] Jewish "genius" comes from a religious worldview espoused in Genesis. Historically, many Jewish theologians have considered human beings to be creatures of this world, created from earth to dwell on the earth. From this worldview comes a faith in a personal God who regularly met humans in the earthly realm: in burning bushes, in clouds and whirlwinds, and in the promise of an embodied messiah. There is, throughout the Hebrew Torah, a theological hope in a God who is a friendly hearted non-deceiver. Moreover, an epistemology arises from the creation narrative, an epistemology that expects humans can find God's wisdom in examining creation. Therefore, much Jewish theology, like much Christian and Muslim theology that is grounded in Genesis, encourages the study of science and the examination of lived experience. In contrast, in attacking Jewish thought, the Manichean gnostics and twenty-first-century anti-Semites both contend that arguments based on empiricism and reason are dependent on a Jewish type of intellectualism, which they reject. The anti-Semitic attack on Jewish philosophical method makes itself immune to all arguments from empiricism, reason, and authority figures outside their own group.

And, of course, anti-Semitism also protects itself with a wall of elitism. Manichean doctrine proclaimed that Jews were children of the dark and evil creator of the natural world, thus inferior to the Manichean elect in every way. Contemporary anti-Semites are equally vitriolic in their rhetoric and often more violent in their actions as they maintain that Jews are racially inferior, their bodies substantially different from "white" bodies. This elitism simultaneously gives anti-Semites a reason to ignore Jewish voices and promotes a dangerous pride in themselves and their own views. Importantly, many white supremacist groups go far beyond disdain for Jews and actively encourage hatred and violence. Meeink, in his confessional autobiography, admits to feeling pleasure when he committed mandated acts of violence. For some personalities, guilt-free opportunities to commit sadistic acts of torture and murder are relished. Psychological experiments, like the Stanford experiments, as well as historical events, like the Holocaust and the Rawandan genocide, suggest that a majority of human beings may be easily lured into participating in sadistic acts if the activity is considered blameless and praiseworthy by leaders. Furthermore, those who have participated in such violence may be unwilling to question their groups' core beliefs later, as doing so would require admitting painful guilt for their actions. Ironically, the very desire to be good, to be blameless, can

---

31. Lavin, "Maddening, Baffling, Exhausting."

lead a believer to do violent acts and to refuse to examine her own motive or the motive of the group that led her to these acts.

The Danger of Pride

Indeed, pride in one's self, one's own merits, and one's own knowledge is one of the greatest dangers in any human's quest for true knowledge, according to Augustine. The desire to seek the truth is often tempered by the desire to already know the truth and to be seen as knowing the truth. The Manicheans carefully made their arguments to Augustine in order to appeal to his pride. Claiming to offer a Christianity for intellectuals, they prepared their missionaries to be "exceedingly well spoken and fashionable" in contrast to many catholic Christian preachers who were unskilled in rhetoric.[32] They promised that everything they taught could be explained clearly and rationally. They ridiculed other religious sects who demanded believers follow with faith, saying that members of their sect walked with full knowledge and understanding of all Manichean teachings. This was particularly appealing to Augustine, who had been disappointed by what he saw as anti-intellectualism in the catholic Christian church. Augustine explained:

> I fell among these people for no other reason except that they said that they would put aside all terrible threats of authority, and by plain and simple reason would introduce those who were willing to listen to them to God, and to liberate them from all error. What, indeed, other than that compelled me for nearly nine years to spurn the religion implanted in me as a boy by my parents, to follow these people and listen diligently to them. Only that they said we were awed by superstition and they said we were commanded to faith rather than reason. They, however, said no one was pressured to believe unless the truth had been discussed and elucidated? Who would not be enticed by these promises, especially if one had the soul of an adolescent with a lust for truth, but made proud and garrulous by the dispute of learned men in school?[33]

32. Brown, *Augustine of Hippo*, 42.

33. UC I.i.2: "non aliam ob causam nos in tales homines incidisse, nisi quod se dicebant, terribili auctoritate separata, mera et simplici ratione eos qui se audire vellent introducturos ad Deum, et errore omni liberaturos. Quid enim me aliud cogebat, annos fere novem, spreta religione quae mihi puerulo a parentibus insita erat, homines illos sequi ac diligenter audire; nisi quod nos superstitione terreri, et fidem nobis ante rationem imperari dicerent, se autem nullum premere ad fidem, nisi prius discussa et enodata veritate? Quis non his pollicitationibus illiceretur, praesertim adolescentis animus cupidus veri, etiam nonnullorum in schola doctorum hominum disputationibus superbus et garrulus."

In particular, the Manicheans raised questions about the morality of other groups in order to highlight their own elite status. They derided the idea that catholic Christians shared the same God as Jews, a God who created in his own image. Throughout their speeches, they laughed at polytheists too. They claimed that Manicheans alone were the true church, the true children of the good God. In contrast, they preached that polytheists, Jews, and catholic Christians were substantially, intellectually, and ethically inferior to them. Indeed, one of the keys arguments of the Manicheans concerning their own superiority was in regard to their morals. By the late fourth century, beliefs about polytheist immorality were commonly held by many philosophers and monotheists. The very term "pagan" is a derisive term for polytheists, deriving from the Latin for hill (*pagus*). To Latin speakers, a pagan was a "hillbilly." The Manicheans played on this anti-pagan attitude and proclaimed that the heroes honored by Jews and catholic Christians were no better than the lecherous gods and goddesses of polytheists in Greece, Egypt, and Rome. The Manicheans jeered at the stories of the Hebrew patriarchs who were often, according to Scripture, lustful, jealous, and idolatrous. Moreover, the Manicheans claimed that Jews followed strict rules, which were irrational, while catholic Christians were easily swayed to do whatever the dominant culture dictated as moral. The Manicheans claimed that Jews and catholic Christians acted just like pagans: killing animals for feasts, drinking wine, having sex with their wives and concubines. In contrast, Manicheans were proud of their own moral code. They believed their abstinence from meat, wine, and sex demonstrated their superiority to all other groups.

Similarly, many contemporary cults have specific moral rules that they uphold in order to demonstrate their superiority. Meeink writes that he was proud to be part of a group that did not allow any type of drug use. The irony that he himself was a drug addict was not enough for him to see the hypocrisy in the group. Of course, in a similar way, Augustine's unwillingness to give up sex made him only more proud to be part of a group where the most elite members bragged of their abstinence. Flattery is a guaranteed method to recruit members to cults; proclaiming the inferiority of others is a guaranteed method to keep members from leaving. Even if this group is not perfect, explain the leaders, the people in this group are at least better than those other people. Often the distrust of those outside a cult is so deep that no matter what occurs within the cult, members will not want to leave.

This danger of pride is therefore significant because it blocks the seeker of truth from talking to people outside of the group. Cult members often refuse to be in the presence of others, and conspiracy theorists can become unwilling to talk and debate with those who do not hold their views.

Importantly, pride can prevent self examination and serious dialogue in all people, whether or not they are part of a gnostic type of cult. Augustine encountered this proud elitism when he confronted the Donatists later in his life when he was bishop.

The Donatists were a Christian group.[34] They were not gnostics. They did not espouse a conspiracy theory, and they did not distrust empirical evidence or rational discourse. Based on historical events, they saw themselves as the most pure Christians because they had refused to renounce their faith even when threatened with persecution. These African Christians claimed that Christians who had hidden and even recanted their Christianity out of fear of persecution were false Christians who needed to be re-baptized if they wanted to return to the church. The Donatists further claimed that baptisms were not efficacious if they were done by priests who had been apostates during times of persecution. The Donatists' belief in their own superiority made them resist debate with non-Donatists. Further, many Donatist leaders encouraged violence against non-Donatists.[35] Augustine understood that much of the Donatists' popularity came from its resistance to Roman rule. He was sympathetic but believed that their pride was problematic. They did not accept those baptized by Roman priests as brothers and sisters in Christ. Their pride made them unwilling to examine their own faith in order to seek understanding. Their pride gave them an excuse to be violent. Later in his life, as a bishop in North Africa, Augustine found the Donatists' refusal to accept equality with other Christians to be almost as dangerous as gnosticism. And yet, Augustine was surprised to find that even as he was working to quell the pride of the Donatists about their superiority to the Roman church, the Roman See was starting to claim itself as the authority and source of knowledge from which all other churches might draw.[36]

In general, Augustine came to see pride as a constant obstruction in the path of true wisdom seeking. Augustine continued to dialogue with both Roman Catholics and African Donatists throughout his life. Later, those who carried his legacy continued the dialogue between Carthaginian and Roman Christians as the African church challenged the secular authority of Rome. The commitment to dialogue in the church rather than the use of secular force stems from his hope in Wisdom's friendly heart to seek out those who love wisdom. Giving the credit to Wisdom rather than

---

34. For a scholarly account of the Donatist church, see Frend, *Donatist Church*.

35. See Possidius, *Vita* 10; 12.

36. See Markus, *Saeculum*, 128–32.

the wisdom seeker was essential to quelling the dangerous pride that kept believers clinging to ignorance.

Escape from False Teachings

As dangerous as false teachings can be, Augustine claimed that the grip of gnosticism is ultimately weak. Indeed, if Manicheanism, other gnostic cults, elitist sects, or conspiracy theorists were serious competitors with scientists and truth tellers, Augustine's argument for hope in philosophy would be refuted. Fake news and real facts are not simply different opinions. Every system of belief is not an equally valid choice with any other. Augustine asserted that gnosticism, which inoculates itself against critique with a metaphysics that forbids the use of empiricism, logic, and debate, is ultimately unstable as a system. It will not satisfy the seeker of truth. Indeed, the same impulse that drives a truth seeker to secret teachings will, if given freedom, lead the truth seeker away from false teachings. Importantly, this means that no one needs seriously fear the teachings of any group as long as one continues to investigate those teachings.

Augustine was driven to the Manicheans by his proud desire for a simple truth, and this same proud desire for a simple truth led him away from the Manicheans. Augustine's first indication that the teachings of the Manicheans were incomplete, if not entirely false, was a general feeling of dissatisfaction, a sense that something was not right. This is often noted by cult members who write about their decisions to leave. Augustine realized that the Manicheans were better at refuting others than actually proving their own doctrines. Generally, gnostic cults and conspiracy theory websites rarely initially reveal their own teachings. The first contact is usually a set of questions that aim to ridicule the teachings of the mainstream. The reason for this, according to Augustine, is that their teachings are not that impressive. Only by destabilizing the hearer's sense of her own knowledge can they expect that the hearer will be charitable to their own theories. Only out of despair towards mainstream sources of knowledge will a seeker of truth turn towards the secret knowledge offered by cults and conspiracy theorists.

On one hand, the epistemology of gnosticism forbids a member of the sect to learn from those outside the sect. On the other hand, the teachings of gnosticism are logically incoherent, and the same type of investigative personality who is attracted to gnosticism will often eventually unravel its errors. Indeed, when Augustine's mother begged a catholic Christian bishop to persuade Augustine to leave the Manicheans, the bishop said such an attempt would be ineffective and unnecessary. "But, just leave him alone and pray to God for him. By himself, reading, he will discover what the error is and how great the impiety."[37] The bishop said this from his own experience. As a young man he "had not only read almost all their books but had also made written copies of them, and even though no one disputed with him or convinced him, it appeared to him that he ought to flee the sect; and therefore he had fled it."[38] The bishop insisted that while gnosticism may bewitch a student for a time, even for a long time, the truth seeker will see eventually that the teachings are false if she continually seeks understanding of the truth.

Seeking understanding of the teachings that he believed is exactly what led Augustine to deny these teachings. He asserted that as he grew older, he began to be less charmed by the elegant speech of the Manicheans. No longer impressed by their rhetoric, still on fire for truth, he began to investigate the teachings of the Manicheans with vigor. He raised questions to the most highly educated members of the group. When Augustine spoke with the teacher Faustus, whom all the Manicheans had promised would be able to answer any concern, he was unimpressed by the man's understanding. The man was a charismatic public speaker but not liberally educated; he was not up to the task of debating someone like Augustine.[39] Augustine began to see that this sect which had flattered his pride, promising to be a sect for the most intellectual people, was actually a cult led by a teacher who was less educated and less clever than Augustine himself. As Augustine had become more advanced in his own rhetorical skills, he was able to ask questions that made the Manichean system seem as absurd as they had once made other systems seem to him.

Particularly, the Manicheans had ridiculed the Genesis account of creation, asking why God would make such a world. But Augustine found their own creation story was worse than laughable; it was metaphysically incoherent. The Manicheans held that there was a battle between the forces of Light and Dark. But if these were equal forces, if the battle was real, there was no basis for naming one force superior and the other inferior. To declare that there is a creative force that is evil and the opposite of the good is to declare that there is a second god.[40] If there are two gods, one of the light and one of the dark, the Manichean allegiance to the force of light would

37. Conf. III.xii.21: "'sed,' inquit, 'sine illum ibi. tantum roga pro eo dominum. ipse legendo reperiet quis ille sit error et quanta impietas.'"

38. Conf. III.xii.21: "omnes paene non legisse tantum verum etiam scriptitasse libros eorum, sibique apparuisse nullo contra disputante et convincente quam esset illa secta fugienda; itaque fugisse."

39. See Conf. V.vi.11

40. See NB xviii.

simply be tribalism rather than true goodness. This was blasphemous to the cult whose foundation was built on the claim of the ultimate goodness of the force of light. But if one force was truly incorruptibly good, and the light and the dark were not equal forces, then the battle was unnecessary. If the force of light was good and the souls of the elect that were part of this force of light were superior to their material bodies and to other beings who were the products of the force of dark, they had nothing to fear from darkness. There was no possibility of a real battle in which the light could be harmed by the force of evil. The elect did not need to avoid eating meat, drinking wine, or having sex because their souls could not be corrupted. Divine sparks in fruits and vegetables did not need to be freed by the consuming of ritual feasts. And certainly the elect did not need to fear engagement with others outside of the sect or with the material world. In short, "Therefore, if they said that you [God] were a substance that is incorruptible, all their theories were proved to be false and repugnant. If however they said you [God] were a corruptible substance, if would be an obvious falsehood, an abomination as soon as it was said."[41] The Manichean story simply did not make sense. Augustine insisted that this logical refutation "was therefore enough against these and I ought to have vomited all this to relieve the pressure in my chest."[42]

Augustine was also disheartened by their physics. They had recruited believers by finding small inconsistencies in widely held scientific theories. They used, as many conspiracy theorists do, anecdotal evidence to contradict a scientific theory. For example, climate-change deniers point to single snow storms and "anti-vaxxers" point to a single vaccinated child that has autism. Yet, in general, Augustine discovered later, their own theories were far less congruent with the empirical evidence than the scientific theories. They had taught him to use his eyes and mind to examine his own experiences instead of trusting authorities in mainstream science. But when Augustine began to seriously examine the stars and when he watched a scientifically predicted eclipse, the phenomena he experienced seemed to fit the predictions of the natural scientists and not those of the Manicheans:

> These [secular] teachings seemed rational to me, through calculation, orders of time, and the visible testimony of the stars. I compared them with the teachings of the Manicheans, which say quite a lot about these things as he, being delirious, wrote

41. Conf. VII.ii.3: "itaque si te, quidquid es, id est substantiam tuam qua es, incorruptibilem dicerent, falsa esse illa omnia et exsecrabilia; si autem corruptibilem, idipsum iam falsum et prima voce abominandum."

42. Conf. VII.ii.3: "sat erat ergo istuc adversus eos omni modo evomendos a pressura pectoris."

a copious amount. These Manichean teachings did not seem rational to me—not the teachings about the solstices or those about the equinox or those about the eclipses of light or those about other things I had studied in the books of secular wisdom. The rules of math and my own eyes told me something quite contrary to the the the teachings of the Manicheans.[43]

At first, the Manicheans told their hearers to pay attention to clear and certain facts. But later, Augustine recognized that the Manicheans themselves had failed to pay attention to clear and certain facts. They ignored overwhelming evidence. Their claims about the natural world were wrong. This would not in itself necessarily have been their undoing. Augustine said that in general, "When indeed I hear some brother of the Christians not knowing this or that thing and feeling one way or another, I look patiently at that person's opinions and I do not see him as dangerously biased."[44] But, Augustine insisted, "However, this is a fault if he dares to affirm that these things he holds ignorantly are pertinent to the doctrines of piety."[45] People make mistakes in science all the time, and these mistakes are not dangerous unless the people in error cling to the error as a tenet of religious faith and refuse to examine it in the light of empirical evidence. "Is it not just to detest these teachings and object to them?"[46] Ironically, the Manicheans claimed to be superior to other religions, especially catholic Christianity, because they offered scientific truths as well as religious truths. Mani had "believed himself to be a doctor, an authority, a leader, the first of those who followed him. He was so bold that those who followed him did not consider him to be like a human being but to be a holy spirit, although he was demented and teaching falsely."[47] This, indeed, is the mark of gnostic teachings. They are teachings given by a leader who is believed to be divine or believed to

43. Conf. V.iii.6: "et occurrebat mihi ratio per numeros et ordinem temporum et visibiles attestationes siderum, et conferebam cum dictis Manichaei, quae de his rebus multa scripsit copiossime delirans, et non mihi occurrebat ratio nec solistitiorum et aequinoctiorum nec defectuum luminarium nec quidquid tale in libris saecularis sapientiae didiceram. ibi autem credere iubebar, et ad illas rationes numeris et oculis meis exploratas non occurrebat, et longe diversum erat."

44. Conf. V.v.9: "Cum enim audio christianum aliquem fratrem illum aut illum ista nescientem et aliud pro alio sentientem, patienter intueor opinantem hominem nec illi obesse video,"

45. Conf. V.v.9: "obest autem, si hoc ad ipsam doctrinae pietatis formam pertinere arbitretur et pertinacius affirmare audeat quod ignorat."

46. Conf. V.v.9: "non detestandam longeque abiciendam esse iudicaret?"

47. Conf. V.v.9: "in illo autem qui doctor, qui auctor, qui dux et princeps eorum quibus illa suaderet, ita fieri ausus est, ut qui eum sequerentur non quemlibet hominem sed spiritum tuum sanctum se sequi arbitrarentur, quis tantam dementiam,"

have direct access to the divine so as to know secrets that others cannot see or understand but must only believe. And yet this is in direct opposition to the initial message of the cult recruiter who first promised a clear and simple teaching that is obviously superior to mainstream knowledge. Once the hearer realizes that the promise of full understanding has been replaced with a demand for blind faith, Augustine promised, the hearer, who is driven by a desire for truth, will begin to reject the teachings.

As Augustine himself began to be skeptical of the doctrines of Manichean physics, he also began to become skeptical of their promise of perfect moral standards. First, Augustine began to question why there were two sets of rules: one for catechumens and another for the elite.[48] He questioned why, if certain actions were wrong, anyone should be allowed to do them. Moreover, he found the elite's practice of gorging on food in order to free the divine particles trapped inside to be obviously harmful to their own health. Their practices resulted at least once in the death of children who choked while engaged in forced gluttony.[49] Moreover, Augustine was bothered by the edict that beggars were never to be given food and thus left to die of hunger.[50] The Manicheans, who wept for fig trees and the angels trapped in melons, "feel more compassion for a cucumber than for a human person."[51] Finally, despite his strong desire to avoid blame for any of his own actions, he felt guilt in his heart. When Augustine examined himself, he did not perceive that he was compelled by his body to do evil acts. He did not seem to himself to be a soul driven against its own will by demonic forces. Rather, he saw himself as doing actions that arose from his own conflicted will. He was the origin of his actions; he was to blame for his crimes.[52] Manichean doctrine could not protect him from this feeling of guilt.

In general, proud Augustine began to find the elitism of the Manicheans more and more suspect. He found they were less intellectual and less kind than his friends and family members who were not Manicheans. He discovered that he simply could not pretend otherwise in order to appear blameless for his own lack of knowledge and his own lack of morality. Like many truth seekers who have left cults and supremacist groups, Augustine was too proud to remain with a group that did not give him the wisdom it had promised. After nine years, he officially left.[53] "Thereafter, I felt secure in

48. See DME I.xxxv.71; II.xvii.57.

49. See DME II.xvi.52.

50. See DME II.xvi.53.

51. DME II.xvi.52: "benignus magis cucumerem quam hominem miseraris\."

52. See Conf. VIII.x.22.

53. Of course, Augustine was lucky. Some cults do not allow escape, and those who try to leave do so at risk of suffering violence at the hands of the cult leaders.

continuing to search, as I was certain that they were not speaking the truth, and I fled with my whole soul from those who were seeking the source of evil and were themselves full of evil."[54]

But like many others who have escaped cults, while Augustine was certain the group he left was wrong, he was quite uncertain about what group was correct. While later he would say that the whole experience demonstrated that the Truth has a friendly heart and works to free all those caught in error, he would acknowledge that at first he was left with only skepticism, which quickly became nihilism.

54. Conf. VII.iii.4: "itaque secures eam quaerebam, et certus non esse verum quod illi dicerent quos toto animo fugiebam, quia videbam quarendo unde malum repletos militia,"

Chapter 4

"Never Mind, It's Only My Opinion"

The Despair and Apathy of Skepticism

The Fall into Skepticism

And, indeed, I began to think that those philosophers called the academics were more prudent than the rest, because they considered everything to be dubitable. They discredited any possibility that humans could understand the truth. Therefore, indeed, they were seen by me to be most sensible. I held this just like a vulgar, common person, as I did not yet understand their intention.[1]

WHEN AUGUSTINE FINALLY LEFT the Manicheans, he decided that the position of academic skepticism was the most pragmatic stance to adopt. In the fourth-century Roman empire, the term "academic" was synonymous with the school of thought that proclaimed that the wisest person was the person who understood how little she knew. They taught that no human being could hope to have true understanding but must be content to acknowledge the limits of the human mind. In order to abstain from error and deception, the best philosopher, the academics claimed, withheld her assent to any opinion. The wisest person never pretended to know anything at all but claimed that she simply acted upon what seemed most plausible.

When Augustine left the Manicheans, angry at having been deceived for so long, he was attracted to academic skepticism. He was ashamed that he had adhered to the false teachings of a gnostic group whose doctrines now seemed absurd to him. He was eager to avoid further deception, so he found an academic refusal to assent to any specific teachings to be the safest

---

1. Conf. V.x.19: "Etenim suborta est etiam mihi cogitatio, prudentiores illos ceteris fuisse philosophos quos academicos appellant, quod de omnibus dubitandum esse censuerant nec aliquid veri ab homine comprehendi posse decreverant. ita enim et mihi liquido sensisse videbantur, ut vulgo habentur, etiam illorum intentionem nondum intellegenti."

path. Moreover, academics were considered wise in the popular culture, had prestigious positions as teachers, and claimed to live happy human lives. Even Augustine's mother was happier when Augustine became an academic skeptic. Augustine claimed in his *Confessions* that when she arrived in Italy, he was "in danger and gravely desperate of tracking down the truth."[2] Yet she leapt with joy that he had left the Manicheans. She believed it was better that he had no faith than that he be trapped in bad faith, and she was confident that he was on the path to health.[3]

However, Augustine was unable to remain "academic" in his skepticism. He wrote, "I came to the depths of the sea, and I lost faith, and I despaired of finding the truth."[4] Augustine tossed and turned in the sea of doubt. At times, he considered turning back towards Manicheanism in order to find some stability. At other times, he tried to live a life based on the secular culture's values. Generally, throughout this period, he was miserable.

Interestingly, the European and American academy in the late twentieth century bore a strong resemblance to the New Academy of the fourth century. Philosophers began to advocate their discipline as a means to keep oneself from error, bias, and superstition. In order to do so, twentieth-century philosophical skeptics dedicated much effort to explaining the limits of human reason. In many academic circles, the vocation of the learned thinker was considered to be the deconstruction of hegemonic thought. Academics held dialogues and debates in order to demonstrate the shortcomings in the knowledge of authority figures and their audiences. They believed that the wisest people were those who recognized how little was known and how much was simply believed. They hoped that educating students in critical thinking would prevent them from falling into needless error. But in many ways, twentieth-century academic skepticism contributed to the "post-truth" society of the twenty-first century, where skepticism and conspiracy theory work together to undermine the hope that any truth can be really known. Indeed, Augustine asserted that academic skepticism, carefully considered, is a gateway to radical skepticism and the nihilism that can accompany it.

2. Conf. VI.i.1: "periclitantem quidem graviter desperatione indagandae veritatis."

3. See Conf. VI.i.1.

4. Conf. VI.i.1: "et veneram in profundum maris, et diffidebam et desperabam de inventione veri."

The Position of Ancient Academic Skepticism

In the Greek world, skepticism seems to have reigned in Plato's Academy soon after Plato died and perhaps even during his lifetime. Indeed, many twentieth-century scholars of Plato claimed that the Academy was never a place of doctrinal instruction but always one of vigorous debate and discussion.[5] Twentieth-century interpretations of Plato's dialogues often suggested that Plato learned academic skepticism from Socrates. In these readings, Plato's dialogues are explained as invitations to encourage the reader into deeper thought about the questions Socrates posed rather than treatises containing a systematic metaphysics or a theory of forms.[6] Of course, Aristotle, Plato's most famous student, considered Plato's dialogues to articulate specific theories, and many philosophers who called themselves Platonists adopted the theories of the soul and metaphysics that they believed Plato had espoused. But, interestingly, these philosophers taught outside the Academy that had been established by Plato. In the Academy, at least by 264 BC, when Arcesilaus became the sixth leader of the Academy, Academics stressed that the vocation of philosophy was to lead the philosopher out of false belief rather than to lead the philosopher towards any truths. A little more than a century later, in 155 BC, Carneades, who was then head of the Academy, came to Rome, bringing this Academic understanding of philosophy with him. Soon thereafter, Cicero became the main advocate for the skeptic's understanding of the vocation of philosophy in Rome.

The ancient academic skeptics all made the same basic claims. First and foremost, they asserted, humans could not be certain of any truths. Authority figures could err or lie. Even propositions that relied on one's own sense perception were not reliable for the senses were often deceived by optical illusions, dreams, and madness. Second, they believed that to be wise meant to hold nothing false as true. Since nothing can be known to be certainly true, the wise person is the one who holds nothing as true. Augustine explained in the *The Handbook on Faith, Hope, and Love*, "Among them, all error is thought to be sin, and they contend that it is not possible to avoid this unless assent is suspended. They say one errs who gives assent to anything uncertain."[7] Thus, the academic philosopher's goal was not to find truth but simply to avoid error. Cicero explained in *Academica*, "Both your

5. See, for example, Dancy, *Two Studies in the Early Academy.*

6. See, for example, Strauss, *On Plato's Symposium; Studies in Plato's Political Philosophy.* See also Rosen, *Plato's Symposium; Plato's Sophist; Plato's Statesman.*

7. Ench. vii.20: "Apud illos ergo error omnis putatur esse peccatum, quod vitari non posse contendunt nisi omnis suspendatur assensio. Errare quippe dicunt eum quisquis assentitur incertis."

wise person and ours, then, inquires about these things, but your person assents, believes, and affirms; our person fears to hold an opinion and thinks it is excellent if in this manner he can act on something which he finds is similar to truth."[8] The wise academic will never assent to any opinion as if it is true but will act in accordance with the proposition that seems most likely to be true. By admitting that he does not know that this proposition is true, he avoids error while still being able to live in a practical manner.

The academics set up a dichotomy that suggested human beings have only two choices: to race headlong into error or to refrain from holding any opinions. The academics did not see this as a cause for despair. They believed that human beings could be happy with the search for wisdom once they humbly and piously acknowledged that true wisdom was out of their reach. As the academic character Licentius explained in *Against the Academics*, "I think that truth is known by God alone, or maybe by the soul of a human being when it abandons the body which is a dark prison."[9] But this does not mean that happiness is beyond human reach. Licentius continued, "This is the goal for human beings: to search for truth perfectly. Indeed, we seek perfectly, but nevertheless as human beings. . . . And this is happiness for human beings . . . to search for truth perfectly. This indeed is to arrive at the goal, we can't progress beyond that."[10] The academics were still in the erotic paradigm of philosophy that suggests the desire of the human being is to seek wisdom. But they insisted that human beings will delight in the quest for truth, although they cannot hope for satisfaction of having truth.

Skepticism in the Twentieth-Century Philosophical Academy

A similar view was especially prominent in philosophy departments in the last half of the twentieth century, particularly in Europe and the United States. Perhaps paradigmatic of this understanding of philosophy was the view of German-American philosopher Leo Strauss. Strauss, who spent most of his career at the University of Chicago, was extremely influential

8. Cicero, *Academica* 2.31.128: "Quaret igitur haec et vester sapiens et hic noster, sed vester adsentiatur credat adfirmet, noster ut vereatur temere opinari praeclarique agi secum putet si in eius modi rebus veri simili quod sit invenerit."

9. CA I.iii.9: "Veritatem autem illam solum Deum nosse arbitror, aut forte hominis animam, cum hoc corpus, hoc est tenebrosum carcerem, dereliquerit."

10. CA I.iii.9: "Hominis autem finis est, perfecte quaerere veritatem: perfectum enim quaerimus, sed tamen hominem. . . . At hoc ipsum est beatum hominis, . . . , perfecte quaerere veritatem: hoc est enim pervenire ad finem, ultra quem non potest progredi."

as a philosopher and as a classicist who read Plato's dialogues through the lens of academic skepticism. Many of his students became prominent philosophers in their own right. His view, thus, in many ways, re-formed the vocation of philosophy in the United States in the latter half of the twentieth century. Strauss said:

> Philosophy as such is nothing but genuine awareness of the problems, i.e., of the fundamental and comprehensive problems. It is impossible to think about these problems without becoming inclined toward a solution, toward one or the other of the very few typical solutions. Yet as long as there is no wisdom but only quest for wisdom, the evidence of all solutions is necessarily smaller than the evidence of the problems. Therefore, the philosopher ceases to be a philosopher at the moment at which the 'subjective certainty' of a solution becomes stronger than his awareness of the problematic character of that solution. At that moment the sectarian is born. The danger of succumbing to the attraction of solutions is essential to philosophy which, without incurring this danger, would degenerate into playing with the problems. But the philosopher does not necessarily succumb to this danger, as is shown by Socrates, who never belonged to a sect and never founded one.[11]

Strauss, like Cicero, urged his students to avoid assenting to any particular opinion. Strauss, like Carneades, insisted that this was the best lesson taught in the Academy founded by Plato, Socrates's student.

In addition to the prominent thinking of Leo Strauss, there were other types of skepticism at play in late twentieth-century philosophy. An especially important influence came out of the natural sciences, specifically in the anti-realist philosophy of science espoused in Thomas Kuhn's 1962 paper *The Structure of Scientific Revolutions*. Kuhn, an American physicist, suggested to the scientific community that in the history of science there are radical revolutions of thought, total paradigm shifts, in which previously held theories were not adjusted but destroyed. One such example is the Copernican Revolution, which demolished not only the astronomical map of the Ptolemaic system but also the foundational theories of physics that had dominated since Aristotle. The Copernican revolution changed the way Galileo looked at the night sky, giving him a new lens through which he observed new phenomena. The Copernican revolution allowed Newton to come up with a new understanding of forces on Earth—including his theory of gravity. Further, the Copernican revolution led to a new system

---

11. Strauss, *What Is Political Philosophy?*, 116.

of mathematics called calculus, new interpretations of Scripture, and new axiological paradigms. Kuhn's point was that when Copernicus drew his new model of the stars, he created a paradigm shift that did not expand fifteenth-century European scientific theory, it demolished it. Kuhn argued this is to be expected in scientific revolutions, for a scientific theory is not a transcendent truth but a human construct that organizes the empirical data available. Scientists and the public should expect to revise and even overthrow scientific theories continually in response to new evidence. Kuhn suggested that scientists be trained to think critically about current scientific theories and to think creatively about new ways to organize the data. Kuhn's paper was a significant part of a philosophical revolution in its own right. After Kuhn, scientific constructivism, a type of anti-realism, became a seriously held position in both philosophy and science departments.

Other prominent philosophers in the late twentieth century went so far as to assert that the reason that human beings cannot find truth is because there is no transcendent truth, only culturally agreed upon values and propositions. The French philosopher Michel Foucault famously considered the relationship between truth and power:

> The important thing here, I believe, is that truth isn't outside power, or lacking in power: contrary to a myth whose history and functions would repay further study, truth isn't the reward of free spirits, the child of protracted solitude, nor the privilege of those who have succeeded in liberating themselves. Truth is a thing of this world: it is produced only by virtue of multiple forms of constraint. And it induces regular effects of power. Each society has its regime of truth, its "general politics" of truth: that is, the types of discourse which it accepts and makes function as true; the mechanisms and instances which enable one to distinguish true and false statements, the means by which each is sanctioned; the techniques and procedures accorded value in the acquisition of truth; the status of those who are charged with saying what counts as true.[12]

Foucault's understanding of truth and power went beyond the call of social critics to deconstruct dominant cultural truths in order that thinkers might create a more equal and truly liberal society. Rather, Foucault insisted that all truth is culturally defined through the use of power and restraint. His view became prominent throughout the French and American philosophical academy.

---

12. Foucault, "Truth and Power," 131.

Strauss, Kuhn, and Foucault are just three examples of types of philosophical skeptics prominent in the twentieth century. Their works, along
with the writings of many other philosophers in the twentieth century, led
to a flourishing of contemporary academic skepticism. Importantly, these
thinkers, like Cicero, did not find anything desperate or despairing in their
point of view. Their understanding of their own vocation as philosophers
was to continually challenge the dominant points of view in order that
readers might think more critically and more deeply about the questions at
hand. Indeed, American philosopher Richard Rorty claimed that this view
led to the most honest and helpful kind of pragmatism. In his 1989 book,
Contingency, Irony and Solidarity, Rorty wrote,

> It is central to the idea of a liberal society that, in respect to
> words as opposed to deeds, persuasion as opposed to force,
> anything goes. This openmindedness should not be fostered
> because, as Scripture teaches, Truth is great and will prevail, nor
> because, as Milton suggests, Truth will always win in a free and
> open encounter. It should be fostered for its own sake. A liberal
> society is one which is content to call "true" whatever the upshot
> of such encounters turns out to be.[13]

Rorty, like Kuhn, was not concerned that apathy, nihilism, or culture wars
might erupt in a post-truth society. He strongly advocated for acting pragmatically on the advice of any theories that appeared to account for the
phenomena while being useful to human life.

However, there were other philosophers in the twentieth century who
saw this type of skepticism as the harbinger of the end of philosophy. Famously, Ludwig Wittgenstein, who early in the twentieth century argued
that philosophers should forego the search for truth, said in his 1922 *Tractatus Logico-Philosophicus*:

> The correct method in philosophy would actually be this: not to
> say anything other than what is allowed to be said, except what
> can be said, such as propositions of natural science—something
> that does not have to do with philosophy—and then always,
> when some other person wanted to say something metaphysical,
> to demonstrate to him that he had given no meaning to certain
> signs in his propositions. This method would be unsatisfying to
> the other person—he would not have the feeling that we were
> teaching him philosophy—but this method would be the only
> strictly correct one.[14]

13. Rorty, *Contingency, Irony, and Solidarity*, 51–52.

14. Wittgenstein, *Tractatus Logico-Philosophicus* 6.53: "Die richtige Methode der

Wittgenstein himself took this advice seriously. In order to not say what cannot be said, he attempted several times to leave the profession of philosophy and refused to publish most of his later writings. However, he did, in the end, maintain a long career as professor of philosophy at the University of Cambridge and many volumes of his works were published posthumously.

Nearing the end of the twentieth century, many philosophers were beginning to wonder if they, too, should attempt to escape philosophy. Cornel West's *The American Evasion of Philosophy*, published in 1989, is generally an optimistic book about the future of American pragmatism. Nonetheless, the book opens with a diagnosis of the crisis in philosophy. West wrote,

> First, there is a widespread disenchantment with the traditional image of philosophy as a transcendental mode of inquiry, a tribunal of reason which grounds claims about Truth, Goodness, and Beauty. The professional discipline of philosophy is presently caught in an interregnum.... The situation has left the discipline with an excess of academic rigor yet bereft of substantive intellectual vigor and uncertain of a legitimate subject matter.[15]

West, always a philosopher for the people, acknowledged how this situation in academic philosophy was mirrored in the public: "In this worldweary period of pervasive cynicisms, nihilisms, terrorisms, and possible extermination, there is a longing for norms and values that can make a difference, a yearning for principled resistance and struggle that can change our desperate plight."[16] While West concluded his book with a hope in "prophetic pragmatism" that calls for a "reinvigoration of a sane, sober, and sophisticated intellectual life in America,"[17] which owes no small debt to the Augustinian hope in the hearts of earlier pragmatists, such as Charles Sanders Pierce and William James, other philosophers were more discouraged. As an example, Lawrence Cahoone wrote in *The Ends of Philosophy* in 1995, "No belief can receive ultimate validation as true. Thus philosophy cannot ultimately validate its judgments. But philosophy by its very nature demands such validation."[18] Cahoone articulated this as a crisis:

Philosophie wäre eigentlich die: Nichts zu sagen, als was sich sagen läßt, also Sätze der Naturwissenschaft—also etwas, was mit Philosophie nichts zu tun hat—und dann immer, wenn nein anderer etwas Metaphysisches sagen wollte, ihm nachzuweisen, daß er gewissen Zeichen in seinen Sätzen keine Bedeutung gegeban hat. Diese Methode wäre für den anderen unbefriedigend—er hätte nicht des Gefühl, daß wir ihn Philosophie lehrten—aber sie wäre die einzig streng richtige."

15. West, *American Evasion of Philosophy*, 3.

16. West, *American Evasion of Philosophy*, 4.

17. West, *American Evasion of Philosophy*, 239.

18. Cahoone, *Ends of Philosophy*, 325.

The question of the validity of philosophy ought to be the most radical and interesting, the deepest and most vital discussion philosophers could have. It is, after all, a continuation of Socrates's defense of his philosophic (and non-philosophic) life at his trial, immortalized in Plato's *Apology*. For those philosophers who believe we have but one life on earth, the stakes remain only slightly less high than for Socrates. For if philosophy cannot do or be what it claims, if it cannot serve the ends for which we choose to practice it, then our lives are threatened too, not with death, which must befall everyone, but with *waste*, a fate Socrates would have thought considerably worse than hemlock.[19]

Skepticism as Despair

Augustine, too, back in the fourth-century Roman Empire, considered academic skepticism as a crisis. While he, like the academics of the fourth and twentieth century, was initially drawn to academic skepticism for its pragmatism, he came to find skepticism to be a cause for despair. He was unable to find happiness in searching for a truth he knew he could not find. He was unable to find rest in deconstructing opinions held by the dominant culture. Therefore, he felt that he could not continue the philosophical journey at all. But the end of philosophy for Augustine was the end of his hope for human happiness.

Augustine had come to philosophy as a teenager who believed that truth would satisfy his restless soul. "I, in my nineteenth year, having received in the school of rhetoric that book of Cicero which is called *Hortensius*, was burning with love of philosophy, so that immediately I meditated on bringing myself to her."[20] But "a childish superstition"[21] drove him off course as he followed the Manicheans. When he left the Manicheans, he was horrified and embarrassed by how long he had believed false teachings: "This sharp care irritated my insides, because I was ashamed that I had held as certain what was most uncertain, babbling the nonsense that was untrue, deceived as I was with childish error."[22] Augustine wanted desperately to

---

19. Cahoone, *Ends of Philosophy*, 4–5.

20. BV i.4: "Ego ab usque undevigesimo anno aetatis meae, postquam in schola rhetoris librum illum Ciceronis, qui 'Hortensius' vocatur, accepi, tanto amore philosophiae succensus sum, ut statim ad eam me ferre meditarer."

21. BV i.4: "superstitio quaedam puerilis."

22. Conf. VI.iv.5: "tanto igitur acrior cura rodebat intima mea, quid certi retinerem, quanto me magis pudebat tam diu inlusum et deceptum promissione certorum puerili errore et animositate tam multa incerta quasi certa garrisse."

avoid adhering to error ever again; he hoped that simply avoiding error would be enough to satisfy his soul.

Similarly, many people in the late twentieth century, horrified by the societal errors of recent times, were also desperate. Wanting to get beyond the bad faith of sexism, racism, colonialism, and other harmfully false constructs, many people were drawn to the deconstructive arguments of skeptical philosophers. Perhaps for this reason, the skepticism of academic philosophers flowed easily into late twentieth- and early twenty-first-century European and American culture. It was considered educated and pragmatic to condemn hegemonic opinions. Like Augustine, many people believed skepticism was the only honest route. Augustine had come to think, as Cicero insisted, that the wise person was the one who "never holds an opinion, never assents to a thing that is either false or unknown."[23] Fear of error led Augustine to the skeptics, and a similar fear directed many of the educated elite in the late twentieth century toward a view of philosophy as a way of critical thinking rather than a search for truth itself.

While academic skepticism was not as satisfying as Augustine had hoped philosophy would be, it did foster a kind of intellectual pride. Augustine not only feared error, he especially feared childishness. The Manicheans had played into this fear when they first recruited him, suggesting that catholic Christianity was a religion for children and childish people. When he came to see Manichean materialist dualism as untenable, he became disturbed that he had for so long believed such a "childish error."[24] He was immediately attracted to academic skepticism in part because it promised to be a way of philosophy for the most intelligent adults. He was especially enamored by the point made by Cicero, that

> the Academics are seen to be the wisest by all the other sects, who seem to themselves to be wise. They give second place to the Academics, since it is necessary that they vindicate themselves as first. From this if can be confirmed, probably, that he is judged rightly to be first whom all the others judge to be second.[25]

Pride caused both his adherence to Manicheanism and later to skepticism. This is typical. Wishing to appear wise and wishing not to appear

23. Cicero, *Academica* 2.18.59–60: "nihil opinari, id est numquam adsentiri rei vel falsae vel incognitae."

24. Conf. VI.iv.5: "puerili errore."

25. CA III.vii.15: "Nam est in libris Ciceronis . . . Academico sapienti ab omnibus caeterarum sectarum qui sibi sapientes videntur, secundas partes dari, cum primas sibi quemque vindicare necesse sit. Ex quo posse probabiliter confici, eum recte primum esse iudicio suo, qui omnium caeterorum iudicio sit secundus."

foolish, a would-be philosopher too quickly agrees with false teachings or too quickly refuses to assent to any teachings. Indeed, Augustine insisted that pride is "one most immense mountain"[26] which blocks the path of philosophers who would pursue the happy life were they not deterred with the promise of vainglory.

Siding with the academics, Augustine felt proud that he was no longer a child who believed in childish tales. But this pride did not protect him from a dark despair. He had come to philosophy wanting to understand the truth, not simply to be free of error. He could not settle for a view of philosophy that was only critical, not redemptive. Furthermore, he did not believe that many people could settle for such a view. "Which, indeed, is harder to bear: that a person cannot be wise or that the wise person cannot know wisdom?"[27] For Augustine, academic skepticism meant that philosophy was incompatible with the happy life. He could not accept the argument that seeking—but not finding—wisdom was the happy life. Augustine argued that such a view in the end drives people away from the attempt to find wisdom. He explained, thus, that skeptics present a view that is a massive obstruction "put before those who are entering into philosophy. Casting darkness from I know not what hiding places, it threatens that the whole of philosophy is such as this, and nothing permits one to hope that any light is going to be found in it."[28] Augustine insisted that the student of philosophy needs to have confidence that truth can be found or she will abruptly abandon the pursuit, crying out, "What, indeed, then do we desire to investigate with such great effort? What do we wish to attain? Where do we desire to arrive? To that which we do not believe exists or can be reached by us? Nothing is more perverse that this mentality."[29]

Worse, Augustine came to find that skepticism did not protect him from false teachings. In fact, because he felt that he could find no truth, he stayed in contact with the Manicheans. He no longer assented to their doctrines, but he believed that since there were not better answers to be found, he might as well enjoy the company of the group. He did not look elsewhere for better

---

26. BV i.3: "unus immanissimus mons."

27. CA III.ix.19: "Quid enim est durius, hominem non posse esse sapientem, an sapientem nescire sapientiam?"

28. CA III.xiv.30: "quae intrantibus ad philosophiam sese opponit, et nescio quibus receptaculis tenebras tegens, talem esse philosophiam totam minatur, nihilque in ea lucis inventum iri sperare permittit."

29. UC xiii.29: "Quid enim tandem tanto molimine investigare cupimus? Quid optamus attingere? Quo pervenire desideramus? Eone quod esse aut ad nos pertinere non credimus? Nihil est tali mente perversius."

answers and did not encourage others to leave the group. He explains that while he felt that the academic skeptics were more prudent,

> I did not try to dissuade my host from holding too much trust, as I sensed he held, in the fabulous things which filled the books of the Manicheans. I was used to the more familiar friendship of these people than to that of other people who were not follow- ers of this heresy. I did not defend it with pristine boldness, but nevertheless the familiarity of them (indeed Rome secretly hid many of these) made me slower to seek another way.[30]

While academic skepticism promises to protect the skeptic from error, it removes the motive for avoiding error. If truth cannot be found, most people would rather enjoy their friendships without argument. The Manicheans found they had a new protection in their line of defense. An academic skeptic like Augustine might not think the Manicheans had the truth, but because he believed that no other sect had the truth he was un- likely to debate with them.

Indeed, Augustine discontinued his philosophical inquiry entirely for a time and concentrated on his career in rhetoric and his secular life. When he listened to the speeches of others, he listened only for style not content; "this empty cure remained—despairing as I was to find a path for a human being to you [who are Truth]."[31] Augustine figured he had reached the end of philosophy and did not need to engage in any further search for truth. He wrote in *Against the Academics,*

> Accordingly, I had become totally lazy and inactive, nor did I dare to seek what the sharpest and most learned men were not allowed to find. Unless, therefore, I first am persuaded that truth can be found, since they have persuaded me that it cannot, I will not dare to seek, nor do I have anything to defend.[32]

---

30. Conf. V.x.19: "nec dissimulavi eundem hospitem meum reprimere a nimia fiducia quam sensi eum habere de rebus fabulosis quibus Manichaei libri pleni sunt. amicitia tamen eorum familiarius utebar quam ceterorom hominum qui in illa haeresi non fuissent. nec eam defendebam pristina animositate, sed tamen familiaritas eorum (plures enim eos Roma occultat) pigrius me faciebat aliud quaerere."

31. Conf. V.xiv.24: "(ea mihi quippe iam desperanti ad te viam patere homini inanis cura remanserat)."

32. CA II.ix.23: "unde piger et prorsus segnis effectus eram, nec quaerere aude- bam, quod acutissimis ac doctissimis viris invenire non licuit. Nisi ergo prius tam mihi persuasero verum posse inveniri, quam sibi illi non posse persuaserunt; non audebo quaerere, nec habeo aliquid quod defendam."

For Augustine, ceasing his search for wisdom had ramifications for his life, morality, and spirit. On one hand, many ancient and twentieth-century skeptics boasted that they had a superior, yet less judgmental, morality. On the other hand, Augustine recognized that his own integrity faltered during his skeptical period. As a skeptic, Augustine consented to nothing; he became apathetic. He had no motivation to do anything that might be his duty since it might not be his duty. "Someone who gives approval to nothing does nothing."[33] Augustine thus tried to continue the habits that pleased him, but he realized that he could not even determine what would please him. As such, he compared himself to a drunk beggar and decided he, as a skeptic chasing culturally sanctioned joys, was actually worse off at finding joy than the committed hedonist:

> I chased honors, profit, marriage. . . . I suffered in this the most bitter difficulties in these desires. . . . Then, therefore, I was miserable as I acted in such a way. I felt my misery on the day when I was prepared to recite praise to the emperor, as I was to lie about many things and I was to be favored by those who knew I was lying. My heart inhaled these cares and it burned with fever about these all consuming cogitations. As I was crossing through a certain street of Milan I came across a poor man begging. Yet, I believe, he was satiated for he was joking and happy. And I groaned and told my friends who were with me that we were insane with our many troubles. We had labored so hard as we chased after our unhappy desires, dragging our flesh around and securing nothing at all. We wanted nothing other than to reach joyfulness, that is why we worked so hard, and yet this beggar was more joyful than we. Indeed, he was adept with just the little bit he had acquired by begging, whereas I had walked in circles, taking troublesome turns. In terms of temporal felicity, indeed he had more true joy which was what I was seeking with my false ambitions. And certainly he was made joyful, and I was only anxious. He was secure, and I was trepid. And if anyone asked me whether I would rather be exultant or be afraid, I would respond I would want to be exultant. But if he asked me what type of suffering I would want—my own or this one's I would elect the cares and fears of my own situation. But this is perverse, is it truly not?[34]

33. CA III.xv.33: "qui nihil approbat, nihil agit." Augustine was quoting Sextus Empiricus, *Against the Logicians* 7.158.

34. Conf. VI.vi.9: "Inhiabam honoribus, lucris, coniugio, . . . patiebar in eis cupiditatibus amarissimas difficultates, . . . quam ergo miser eram, et quomodo egisti ut sentirem miseriam meam die illo quo, cum pararem recitare imperatori laudes, quibus

Augustine had found that skeptics, in trying to live pragmatically and happily, failed to be pragmatic or happy.

Indeed, Augustine insisted, skepticism, thoughtfully followed, would tear apart the skeptics' understanding of herself, her identity, and her place in her community, making her totally unable to act pragmatically, not to mention joyfully, in her community:

> Indeed, I ask, if that which is not known is not to be believed, how will children serve their parents and delight them with mutual devotion, if they do not believe that they are their parents. Indeed, not by any rational means can this pact be known: the paternity of the father is believed by the authority of the mother, and truly as to the maternity, not by the authority of the mother but by the authority of midwives, nurses, and maids. For the child can be stolen and another put in its place, and can she who is deceived not thus deceive? We believe, nevertheless, and without any doubt, we believe what we confess we cannot know.[35]

---

plura mentirer et mentienti faveretur ab scientibus, easque curas anhelerat cor meum et cogitationum tabificarum febribus aestuaret, transiens per quendam vicum Mediolanensem animadverti pauperem mendicum, iam, credo, saturum, iocantem atque laetantem. et ingemui et locutus sum cum amicis qui mecum erant multos dolores insaniarum nostrarum, quia omnibus talibus conatibus nostris, qualibus tunc laborabam, sub stimulis cupidatatum trahens infelicitatis meae sarcinam et trahendo exaggerens, nihil vellemus aliud nisi ad securam laetitiam pervenire, quo nos mendicus ille iam praecessisset numquam illuc fortasse venturos. quod enim iam ille pauculis et emendicatis nummulis adeptus erat, ad hoc ego tam aerumnosis anfractibus et circuitibus ambiebam, ad laetitiam scilicet temporalis felicitatis. non enim verum gaudium habebat, sed et ego illis ambitionibus multo falsius quaerebam. et certe ille laetabatur, ego anxius eram, secures ille, ego trepidus. et si quisquam percontaretur me utrum mallem exultare an metuere, responderem, 'exultare'; rursus si interrogaret utrum me talem mallem qualis ille, an qualis ego tunc essem, me ipsum curis timoribusque confectum eligerem, sed perversitate—numquid veritate?"

35. UC xii.26: "Quaero enim, si quod nescitur, credendum non est, quomodo serviant parentibus liberi, eosque mutua pietate diligant, quos parentes suos esse non credant. Non enim ratione ullo pacto sciri potest: sed interposita matris auctoritate de patre creditur; de ipsa vero matre plerumque nec matri, sed obstetricibus, nutricibus, famulis. Nam cui furari filius potest, aliusque supponi, nonne potest decepta decipere? Credimus tamen, et sine ulla dubitatione credimus, quod scire non posse confitemur. Quis enim non videat pietatem, nisi ita sit, sanctissimum generis humani vinculum, superbissimo scelere violari? Nam quis vel insanus eum culpandum putet, qui eis officia debita impenderit quos parentes esse crediderit, etiamsi non essent? Quis contra non exterminandum iudicaverit, qui veros fortasse parentes minime dilexerit, dum ne falsos diligat metuit? Multa possunt afferri, quibus ostendatur nihil omnino humanae societatis incolume remanere, si nihil credere statuerimus, quod non possumus tenere perceptum."

One's identity as the child of one's parents is believed on the authority of one's parents, nurses, and servants. But, a person must trust those authorities about her identity and assent to the bonds of necessary relationships:

> If it is not so, who indeed does not see that devotion, the most sacred knot of humankind, might be violated by the most overbearing wickedness? . . . Many cases could be brought forth by which it is shown that nothing would remain stable in all human society if we determined to believe nothing that we could not hold by perception.[36]

An academic skeptic who truly refuses to assent to any opinion would be unable to participate in healthy human relationships as she would be unable to trust that those who say they are her family are her family and that those who say they love her really love her.

Augustine knew that the academic skeptics claimed that this was not a real problem because, while they refused assent to any opinion, they acted in accordance with what they could "induce" to be "probable" or "truthlike."[37] The wise person, according to the academic skeptics, honored his parents because it was probable that they were who they said they were. But Augustine could not understand this argument for probability. If a skeptic could not recognize truth, how could she recognize what is truth-like. Augustine asks rhetorically, "If anyone affirmed that your brother had a similar face to your father, and he did not know your father; would not he seem to you to be insane or inept?"[38] Lest there be any temptation to disagree, Augustine continued to explain,

> Behold, suppose, I don't know, this person whom we were describing were present. And your brother arrives from somewhere. Then this one says, "Whose son is this child?" It is responded: "This is Romanius's." And then: "How similar to his father he is! The rumor reported to me is accurate!" Here you, or someone else, says: "Indeed, do you know of Romanius, good fellow?" "No, I don't know him," he says, "nevertheless

36. UC xii.26: "Quis enim non videat pietatem, nisi ita sit, sanctissimum generis humani vinculum, superbissimo scelere violari? . . . Multa possunt afferri, quibus ostendatur nihil omnino humanae societatis incolume remanere, si nihil credere statuerimus, quod non possumus tenere perceptum."

37. CA II.v.12: "Hic illi inducto quodam probabili, quod etiam verisimile nominabant" (Here, I induce what is probable, that which they name as truthlike).

38. CA II.vii.16: "Si quisquam fratrem tuum visum patris tui similem esse affirmet, ipsumque tuum patrem non noveri; nonne tibi insanus, aut ineptus videbitur?"

this one seems similar to him to me." Could anyone be able to hold in the laughter?[39]

Just as a person cannot judge that a child is similar to a parent whom she has never met, so neither can a person who cannot see truth claim to recognize what is similar to truth.

In general, Augustine figured that the average skeptic used her own cultural criteria for what is probable, truth-like, and useful. These criteria are as biased as any other. Indeed, the skeptic might end up following paths more ridiculous than that chosen by a more gullible believer. Augustine told the following story to explain:

> Let's suppose there are two travelers intending to go to one place. One of these has decided to believe nothing, the other is very credulous. They come to a fork in the road. The credulous one addresses a shepherd or other country person, "Hello, honest person. Please tell me by which way should we continue to that place." The response: "If you go here, you will err in no way." He says to the companion, "He says the truth, let's go." The most cautious man laughs that the other would give his assent so quickly. While this other one departs, he stands thinking at the fork in the road. And he begins to see that he is stopped when, behold, from around the corner of the other path appears a clean city-dweller on a horse who is coming closer. Then he congratulates himself. Then he approaches and indicates a salutation and asks him about the path. He says that he remained here because he prefers this one's advice to that of a shepherd. This one, however, is full of tricks, he is what the common people call a trickster. This bad man held to his morals freely. "Here, take this way," he says. "Now, I just came from there." He deceives him and goes away. But how can he be deceived? "No, indeed, I do not approve that this information is true; but it is truth-like. And to be idle is not appropriate, nor is it useful, so here I go." Meanwhile the traveler who erred by giving assent to the words of the shepherd, is already refreshing himself in the place. However, the one not erring, who followed what is probable, is wandering about in some woods, I know not where, and has not found anyone who knows how to come to his destination.[40]

39. CA II.vii.19: "Ecce fac illum nescio quem hominem quem describimus, esse praesentem: advenit alicunde frater tuus; ibi iste: Cuius hic puer filius? Respondetur: Cuiusdam Romaniani. At hic: Quam patri similis est! quam ad me hoc non temere fama detulerat! Hic tu, vel quis alius: Nosti enim Romanianum, bone homo? Non novi, inquit: tamen similis eius mihi videtur. Poteritne quisquam risum tenere?"

40. CA III.xv.34: "Faciamus enim duos viatores ad unum locum tendentes, quorum

With this allegory, Augustine asserted that the proud skeptic may be in the most danger of becoming lost. If he takes his assertion seriously that nothing can be known, he is bound to inactivity. If this apathy seems incompatible with the good life and the skeptic acts on the probable, he finds himself in no better place than the naïve believer. In fact, he may be in a worse place if his arrogance leads him to trust his own biases as more reliable than common sense. Indeed, he may be more vulnerable to follow the lie of a wealthy trickster or the esoteric position of a gnostic. In this way, skepticism and conspiracy theories are two sides of the same coin. In common, they do not trust that truth can be known through empiricism, reason, dialogue, and human interactions. They leave the discernment completely to the individual human being.

Skepticism and Radical Individualism

The despair of skepticism is related to the radical individualism that is proposed by the academics. As Augustine asserted, the academic skeptic cannot assent to the opinions of others and thus cannot consent to human relationships and duties within human communities. The skeptic stands alone. Moreover, the happiness of the academic skeptic depends on the individual person's ability to accept that her erotic need for something outside of herself to satisfy her will not be met. For Augustine, whose vision of Truth includes maternal, paternal, and romantic characteristics, the academic skeptics were asking him to forego his hope in a transcendent Truth that would guide him, rule him, and satisfy him. According to the skeptics, the philosopher must create his own guide, create his own rules, and satisfy himself. Augustine compared the academic skeptic to a sick person who

---

alter instituerit nulli credere, alter nimis credulus sit. Ventum est ad aliquod bivium: hic ille credulus pastori qui aderat, vel cuipiam rusticano: Salve, frugi homo; dic quaeso, qua bene in illum locum pergatur. Respondetur: Si hac ibis, nihil errabis. Et ille ad comitem: Verum dicit, hac eamus. Ridet vir cautissimus, et tam cito assensum facetissime illudit, atque interea illo discedente in bivio figitur: et iam incipit videri turpe cessare, cum ecce ex alio viae cornu lautus quidam et urbanus equo insidens eminet, et propinquare occipit: gratulatur iste. Tum advenienti, et salutato indicat propositum, quaerit viam; dicit etiam remansionis suae causam, quo benevolentiorem reddat, pastori eum praeferens. Ille autem casu planus erat de iis quos Samardocos iam vulgus vocat. Tenuit suum morem homo pessimus etiam gratis. Hac perge, ait: nam ego inde venio. Decepit, atque abiit. Sed quando iste deciperetur? Non enim monstrationem istam tamquam veram, inquit, approbo; sed quia est veri similis. Et hic otiosum esse nec honestum, nec utile est; hac eam. Interea ille qui assentiendo erravit, tam cito existimans vera esse verba pastoris, in loco illo quo tendebant, iam se reficiebat: iste autem non errans, siquidem probabile sequitur, circumit silvas nescio quas, nec iam cui locus ille notus sit, ad quem venire proposuerat, invenit."

refuses to listen to a doctor or take any medical advice. Ill as he is, he believes he must try to heal his sickness on his own. In this attempt, he is in an all the more precarious situation.[41]

Augustine asserted that as they are social animals, human beings learn in community. A human being simply cannot live pragmatically without trusting other people:

> I considered that I believed countless things which I had not seen or had taken place when I was not present; so many events in the history of people, so many facts about places and cities which I had not seen, and so much that I believed of friends, of medics, of many other people that unless they are believed, we could accomplish nothing in this life. Afterwards, I retained how fixed and unshakable was the faith about who my parents were, because I could not know this unless I listened with the most credulity.[42]

Augustine explained that academic progress is rendered impossible by skepticism, which prohibits taking any information on authority. And Augustine repeated again that human relationships require trust in other people.

In twentieth-century American and European philosophical thought, skeptical philosophers urged students to question authority, think critically, and withhold assent. Many of these held that plausible and pragmatic theories should be accepted, leaving the individual thinker to puzzle out which theories were most plausible and pragmatic. By the beginning of the twenty-first century, this skeptical view had become a mainstream marker of an educated person. At the same time, conspiracy theories began to flourish on the internet and there was a marked rise in cult-like activity and supremacist groups. This would not have surprised Augustine. He had asserted that a society that does not foster confidence in its citizens that truth can be found through science, philosophy, debate, and dialogue will be a society with citizens incapable of carrying out their duties to and with their community.

41. See Conf. VI.iv.6: "tenebam enim cor meum ab omni adsensione timens praecipitium, et suspendio magis necabar. . . . sed sicut evenire adsolet, ut malum medicum expertus etiam bono timeat se commmitare, ita erat valetudo animae meae," (Indeed, I refused to assent to anything in my heart because I was afraid of a fall, but in my refusal to assent, I was I was hanging suspended in a way which was more likely to be fatal than a fall. . . . Just as one who has had an experience of a bad expert in medicine will be timid to commit to a good, so it was with my soul.)

42. Conf. VI.v.7: "consideranti quam innumerabilia crederem quae non viderem neque cum gererentur adfuissem, sicut tam multa in historia gentium, tam multa de locis atque urbibus quae non videram, tam multa amicis, tam multa medicis, tam multa hominibus aliis atque aliis, quae nisi crederentur, omnino in hac vita nihil ageremus, postremo quam inconcusse fixum fide retinerem de quibus parentibus ortus essem, quod scire non possem nisi audiendo credidissem."

Escape from Skepticism

As dangerous as skepticism can be, Augustine realized that skeptical arguments are a necessary part of the search for truth. Properly applied, skepticism can lead a person out of error and even out of skepticism. Augustine remembered that his mother, who had been frantic while he was Manichean, was at peace while he floundered in skepticism. "She leapt with joy, since she was secure for her part that my misery was not going to flow towards death but to resuscitation in you [who are Truth]. . . . I was not yet won by truth, but I was torn from falsehood."[43] One who is certain that she already knows cannot learn. Often the first step to learning is unlearning what is falsely believed.[44] As a skeptic, Augustine believed that his philosophical desire would never be satisfied, but at least he knew he was not already satisfied. He was aware of his need and hunger for truth.

Importantly, academic skepticism, if held honestly, must be applied to skepticism itself. In doing just this, Augustine noticed that as a system, academic skepticism is unstable. First, the skeptics admonish seekers of truth to be wary of trusting the opinions of authority figures. But as Augustine became more proficient at identifying appeals to authority, he recognized how often the Academics appealed to authorities themselves. They were careful to appeal to those authorities that carried the most weight in the culture of their audience. Augustine demonstrated this in *Against the Academics,* as the character of Licentius argued for skepticism through a series of appeals to authority, suggesting if his friends want to be wise, they should follow the advice of past wise people. "'Carneades,' he said, 'does not he seem wise to you?'"[45] But he was surprised when one of his friends scoffed at Carneades, saying that he had no reason to trust a Greek. Quickly changing course, Licentius asked if they would not be pleased to follow Cicero. Licentius believed he could win the argument simply by mentioning the name of Cicero. But, incongruously, the argument that he wished to win was the argument that authorities should not be trusted. Ironically, Cicero himself appealed to authority to make this same argument. Augustine noted that Cicero said Marcus Varro was "without any doubt the most learned."[46] Augustine wrote, "Of course, he was so certain about this thing, that he laid aside that doubt which he required to keep in all matters, as if, when

43. Conf. VI.i.i: "exilivit laetitia, cum iam secura fieret ex ea parte miseriae meae in qua me tamquam mortuum sed resuscitandum tibi flebat, . . . veritatem me nondum adeptum sed falsitati iam ereptum."

44. See UC xi.25.

45. CA I.iii.7: "Carneades, inquit, tibi sapiens non videtur?"

46. CD VI.2: "sine ulla dubitatione doctissimo"

about to dispute in favor of the doubt of the Academics he forgot that he was an Academic."[47] Augustine noted that the skeptics, who often tried to give weight to their skepticism of authority by referring to authority, should have been aware that their own skepticism refuted their own authority. "But an Academic, who contends that all is uncertain, is unworthy to be one who has authority about these things."[48]

Indeed, as Augustine continued to investigate academic skepticism using its tools and techniques, he found that its most fundamental tenets are self-refuting. First, those who do not know anything do not know that they cannot know anything. Their foundation is contradictory. Second, the pragmatic claim of the academic skeptic is that by living a life of academic questioning, one can live the best human life. This claim must also fall to the knife of skepticism. This means that the skeptic cannot claim that the life of philosophy is the best life but only assert that it is plausible. A gnostic or a conspiracy theorist might argue that her position is also plausible and that the standards of plausibility are manipulated by those in power. Thus, all theories are, according to the honest academic skepticism, equal. If the academic skeptic refutes the gnostic or conspiracy theorist by insisting on her own academic standards of plausibility, she asserts that human beings do have some standards that are better than others. Insofar as academic skeptics live their lives by these standards and deny other standards, they make an assent to standards agreed upon by many academic skeptics. But in so doing, they have undone the very first tenet of academic skepticism, which is to give no assent. Thus, the whole system is both foundationally and pragmatically untenable according to Augustine.

Academic Skepticism Is Demonstrably False

Augustine asserted that a deeper problem with academic skepticism is that their core tenet is not only untenable, it is demonstrably false. The foundational tenet of academic skepticism is that human beings cannot know anything perfectly. Yet the skeptics did claim that human beings are capable of seeing some things are more truthlike or more probable than others. Yet they were unable to account for how this is possible, and when pressed, they asserted that this was not possible. Indeed, when the defender of the skeptics in *Against the Academics* was asked this very question, he was stumped.

47. CD VI.2: "Profecto de hac re sic erat certus ut auferet dubitationem quam solet in omnibus adhibere, tamquam de hoc uno etiam pro Acaemicorum dubitatione disputaturs se Academicum fuisset oblitus."

48. CD IV.30: "Sed iste Academicus, qui omnia esse contendit incerta, indignus est qui habeat ullam in his rebus auctoritatem."

His argument with the others did not go beyond a sparring match about the meaning of the words "truthlike" (*verisimile*) and "probable" (*probabile*). And yet, it seems that the skeptic is not foolish to suggest that people follow the most probable advice rather than do nothing at all. Indeed, some opinions do seem more truth-like than others. Thus, the question remains, how is it that one can recognize which statements are truth-like?

The question is sharpened in *Against the Academics,* when Augustine introduced a number of statements that are not only plausible but most certainly true. To his friends, Augustine said,

> Nevertheless, I, who am a long way from being anywhere close to having wisdom, do not know nothing in physics. I have certainty that the world is either one or not one. And if it is not one, the number of worlds is either finite or infinite. Let Carneades teach that this sentence is similar to the false. Also, I know that our world has been arranged by the nature of bodies or by some other providence, that it always was and will be, or began to be and lacks a destiny, or it did begin in time and has an end to its being, or began to remain and will remain forever. I know innumerable ideas in physics or this manner. These disjunctions are true, and nobody can confound them with any likeness to what is false.[49]

Augustine continued in the same vein, "If there are four elements in the world, there are not five. If there is one sun, then there are not two."[50] He insisted, whether a person is asleep or awake, insane or sane, these statements are true and cannot be doubted.[51]

In the *Soliloquies,* the character of Reason calmed the anxiously skeptical Augustine with similar arguments, "Although, indeed, you do not believe by the senses and you can respond that you do not know whether what is before you is a tree, nevertheless you will not deny, I suppose, that truly

---

49. CA III.x.23: "Tamen ego qui longe adhuc absum vel a vicinitate sapientis, in istis physicis nonnihil scio. Certum enim habeo, aut unum esse mundum, aut non unum; et si non unum, aut finiti numeri, aut infiniti. Istam sententiam Carneades falsae esse similem doceat. Item scio mundum istum nostrum, aut natura corporum, aut aliqua providentia sic esse dispositum; eumque aut semper fuisse et fore, aut coepisse esse minime desiturum; aut ortum ex tempore non habere, sed habiturum esse finem; aut et manere coepisse, et non perpetuo esse mansurum: et innumerabilia physica hoc modo novi. Vera enim ista sunt disiuncta, nec similitudine aliqua falsi ea potest quisquam confundere."

50. CA III.xiii.29: "Si quatuor in mundo elementa sunt, non sunt quinque. Si sol unus est, non sunt duo."

51. See CA III.xi.25.

it is a tree if it is a tree?"[52] And in the *Confessions*, Augustine sighed, "Oh would that I knew anything that I desire to know that is useful in such a way as I know that no creature was before any creature was."[53] While some later philosophers might argue that the laws of logic and mathematics are themselves human constructs, these were rules that the academic skeptics accepted. Thus, Augustine asked how it was possible that they were able to discover these rules. Even if anachronistically, Augustine had to answer contemporary physicists who assert that an electron can be both a wave and not a wave, the fact that human scientists can recognize in the empirical data this apparent contradiction to the law of excluded middle only makes his question more urgent. How is it that human beings discover such things? How is it that human beings have found equations that make sense of the world in a way that is more mathematically probable given the empirical data than the previous model of physics? The academic skeptics say that knowledge is not possible, and yet it seems knowledge is quite possible.

Beyond logical disjuncts, Augustine asserted that, at the very least, he knows true things through his senses. He knew that the leaves of wild olive trees tasted bitter to him. While he could not be sure that they taste bitter to everyone or would always taste bitter to him, he knew at the moment he was tasting them they tasted bitter.[54] He explained,

> I say this: a person can when he eats, judge in good faith and know that it is sweet to his palate or the contrary, and no Greek trickery can lead him away from this knowledge. Who indeed is impudent and says to me while I am relishing the flavor of something; "Perhaps you're not eating, since what if it is a dream?" Do I resist this in anyway? But nevertheless, it would delight me even in the dream.[55]

Thus, even if a person is dreaming that she is enjoying her dessert or even if she is awake while enjoying her dessert but has been conditioned to enjoy it by advertisements or because of some fluke of evolution, the true fact

52. Sol. I.xv.28: "Quamvis enim non credas sensibus, possisque respondere, ignorare te prorsus utrum arbor sit; tamen illud non negabis, ut opinor, veram esse arborem, si arbor est:"

53. Conf. XI.xii.14: "et utinam sic sciam quidquid utiliter scire cupio, quemadmodum scio quod nulla fiebat creatura antequam fieret ulla creatura."

54. See CA III.xi.26.

55. CA III.xi.26: "Illud dico, posse hominem cum aliquid gustat, bona fide iurare, se scire palato suo illud suave esse, vel contra, nec ulla calumnia graeca ab ista scientia posse deduci. Quis enim tam impudens sit, qui mihi cum delectatione aliquid ligurienti dicat: Fortasse non gustas, sed hoc somnium est? Numquidnam resisto? Sed me tamen illud in somnis etiam delectaret."

remains that she is enjoying this. Her recognition of her enjoyment is therefore real knowledge. And central to all of these claims is the recognition that she is a being that can recognize her enjoyment.

But the final death blow to academic skepticism, said Augustine, is the recognition by any doubter that no matter how far she doubts, she cannot doubt her own existence.

> I am most certain that I am and that I know and delight in this. And I am not, in respect of these truths, concerned by the arguments of the Academics, who say, "What if you are deceived?" For if I am deceived, I am. For one who is not cannot be deceived and used, and thus I am, if I am deceived. Therefore, if I am deceived, in what manner am I deceived about being me, since it is certain that I am, if I am deceived? Since therefore, I am, who is deceived, even as I am deceived, I cannot doubt in this—that I know that I am. In this I am not deceived. Consequently, I know that I know that I am not deceived. Just as I know indeed that I am, I know that I know that I am.[56]

Augustine made this argument over and over, in his early, middle, and late writings.[57] Each time he repeated it, Augustine showed the skeptic that in the heart of skepticism one finds a very clear and distinct truth. Even the skeptic cannot deny the fact that she is doubting, and therefore that there is some she who is doubting.

Now a committed skeptic might sigh and say that this knowledge simply extends to the individual doubter. The proof does not work to give certainty to the existence of anything else or any other being. It only declares that one cannot doubt one's own existence. But Augustine demonstrated that this lone fact shows the skeptic the way out of her solipsistic world, empty of other truths. Indeed, this lone fact requires an explanation of how this truth is known. The skeptic who denies that truth can be found must account for that fact that she can know her own existence so clearly. If this knowledge is possible, a new question surfaces, "How is this knowledge possible?" Augustine's answer requires that the philosopher accept the existence of a Truth outside of herself that is in friendly relationship to her.

---

56. CD XI.26: "mihi esse me idque nosse et amare certissimum est. Nulla in his veris Academicorum argumenta formido dicentium: Quid si falleris? Si enim fallor, sum. Nam qui non est, utique nec falli potest; ac per hoc sum, si fallor. Quia ergo sum si fallor, quo modo esse me fallor, quando certum est me esse, si fallor? Quia igitur essem qui fallerer, etiamsi fallerer, procul dubio in eo, quod me novi esse, non fallor. Consequens est autem, ut etiam in eo, quod me novi nosse, non fallar. Sicut enim novi esse me, ita novi etiam hoc ipsum, nosse me."

57. See, for example, Trin. X.x.14; XV.xii.21; Sol. II.i.1; VR I.xxxix.73.

Chapter 5

Wisdom's Friendship

*A Relational View of Truth as the
Ground for Philosophical Hope*

Recognizing the Love of Wisdom

"When I first knew you, you raised me up, so that I could see."[1]

WHEN AUGUSTINE REALIZED THAT there are truths he could recognize
(mathematical facts, logical tautologies, his own existence), he turned to the
epistemological question, "How is it that I know what I know?" Augustine
discovered that his knowledge came through relationships. He began to
see that he was foundationally a relational creature. No individual human
mind discovers or creates knowledge by itself; all human knowledge grows
from relationships. For Augustine, the most fundamental relationship for
the philosopher is with Wisdom herself. While other philosophers, including Aristotle, Plato, and their followers, recognized the need for students to
engage in learning with others, Augustine found that they failed to explain
how knowledge was gained through these relationships. Without this explanation, they lacked a certain amount of hopeful trust in the enterprise that
made them liable to skeptical doubt. Augustine insisted that philosophers
must recognize that the foundation for all optimistic investigation is Truth's
friendly hearted compassion for people, especially for those caught in the
shadows of error. It is Truth's friendship with philosophers that allows them
to be literally philosophers (friends of wisdom), boldly investigating wisdom in their communities with optimism.[2]

---

1. Conf. VII.x.16: "et tu cum te primum cognovi, tu adsumpsisti me ut viderem."

2. See CA III.xix.42: "nunquam ista ratio subtilissima revocaret, nisi summus Deus
populari quadam clementia divini intellectus auctoritatem usque ad ipsum corpus
humanum declinaret, atque submitteret; cuius non solum praeceptis, sed etiam factis
excitatae animae redire in semetipsas, et resipiscere patriam, etiam sine disputationum
concertatione potuissent." (Never would the most subtle reason have called us back,
unless the highest God, moved by a certain compassion for the people, submitted the

Augustine's trust in Truth's compassion (*clementia*) and friendly heart-edness (*misericordia*) was the ground of his argument against radical skepticism. For Augustine, this compassion is personal in nature. Throughout the corpus of his Christian writings, Augustine never used the pronoun "it" to denote Truth or Wisdom, terms he used interchangeably. For Augustine, Truth, like Wisdom is a "she." In part, this is because of the structure of Latin's gendered language. Truth (*veritas*) and wisdom (*sapientia*) are both feminine words in Latin that grammatically take feminine rather than neuter pronouns. But more importantly, Augustine's use of the word "she" for Truth engaged the personal nature of that pronoun.[3] The language Augustine used to describe Truth is often maternal, sometimes romantic, and always friendly. In fact, the most common pronouns Augustine used for Truth and Wisdom were actually not third-person pronouns at all. In the corpus of his works, the most common pronoun Augustine used for Truth is "you" in its friendliest and most familiar Latin form—*tu*. Augustine's description of his relationship with this friendly Truth became the foundation that grounded him as a philosopher for the rest of his life.

Augustine's Experience of Wisdom's Friendship

Importantly, Augustine's refutation of skepticism did not come from faithfully accepting Christian doctrines but from his analysis of his own lived experience. In examining his own intellectual activities, Augustine recognized that he had experienced learning new knowledge by the help of an interior teacher. This recognition unfolded as he strove to understand how he knew what he knew. "What torments labored in my heart, which sighs, my God! And your ears were open, although I did not know it. And when in silence I sought you, the wordless sorrows of my soul were calling loudly to your friendly heart."[4] Augustine could not see that the Truth was holding him as he sought Wisdom. "I was separated from you by a tumor of my pride, which was such that my inflated cheeks clouded my eyes."[5] His pride, a product of sin, made him think that he was alone, a mind with no guaranteed access

---

authority of divine intellect even to the human body itself; so that not only by precepts but indeed by acts could souls be aroused to reflect and consider their true country without dissolving into quarreling disputation.)

3. See Hockenbery Dragseth, "He, She, and It of God."

4. *Conf.* VII.vii.11: "quae illa tormenta parturientis cordis mei, qui gemitus, deus meus! et ibi errant aures tuae nesciente me. et cum in silentio fortiter quaererem, magnae voces erunt ad misericordiam tuam tacitae contritiones animi mei."

5. *Conf.* VII.vii.11: "et tumore meo separabar abs te et nimis inflata facies claudebat oculos meos."

to the world outside of itself, a mind without relationship.[6] But he was not alone. Moreover, Truth refused to let him wallow in his false loneliness for long. Augustine claimed in the *Confessions* that the Truth came to find him underneath his puffed up cheeks:

> You are empathetic to earth and ashes. And it pleased you, as you looked at me, to reform my deformity. You agitated me by prodding me internally so that I became impatient until I could see with my interior sight that you certainly exist. My tumor of pride receded by the secret hand of your medicine. And my salty tears of grief were a saline solution for my disturbed and troubled mind so that I could see more clearly day by day.[7]

Augustine's relationship with Truth was intimate, personal, and loving. As such, it was not a Platonic relationship in which a disinterested light of Truth shone upon his individual mind. Yet Augustine acknowledged that he came to recognize this friendly relationship only after an acquaintance introduced some books of the Platonists to him. This acquaintance was, according to Augustine, a gift of the divine Truth. He explained, "You procured for me though a certain person who was puffed by immense and wild pride, some of the books of the Platonists which were translated into Latin words from the Greek language."[8] In Augustine's view, Truth shows her friendly heart by bringing people together to share ideas. Even people puffed by immense and wild pride, as Augustine's friend and Augustine himself were, are loved and sought by Truth. Moreover, Truth allows such people to be occasions for their own and other people's learning. Augustine read the books provided. He was not persuaded to become a Platonist, but he found the Platonic description of Truth as an incorporeal being helpful.

While reading the books of the Platonists, he found that they proclaimed the existence of a transcendent Truth that is the source of all true things and the source of light that allows all true things to be recognized as true. This description of Truth made sense to Augustine, who suddenly found that he could think about beings that were not physical or material

6. For more discussion on Augustine's understanding of sin and the feeling of the individual being alone inside of her mind, see Cary, *Augustine and the Invention of the Inner Self*, 122–23.

7. Conf. VII.viii.12: "miseratus es terram et cinerem. Et placuit in conspectu tuo reformare deformia mea, et stumulis internis agitabas me ut impatiens essem donec mihi per interiorem aspectum certus esses. et residebat tumor meus ex occulta manu medicinae tuae aciesque conturbata et contenebrata mentis meae acri collyrio salubrium dolorum de die in diem sanabatur."

8. Conf. VII.ix.13: "procurasti mihi per quendam hominem immanissimo typho turgidum, quosdam platoniciorum libros ex graeca lingua in latinam versos."

but intellectual in substance. This idea was important to him, but more important to him was the insight that in order for Truth to be known, she had to come in love to dwell amongst her people. Yet he did not find that insight written in the works of the Platonists but in his experience of being able to understand the teachings of the Platonists. Augustine said that when reading the books of the Platonists he suddenly found that he could conceive of God, who is Goodness and Truth, as completely incorporeal rather than as the thin, ethereal substance that he had imagined God to be as a Manichean. More importantly, he had a recognition that he did not come to this idea of incorporeal substance on his own. He learned to think in this new way through reading the writings of others and through the intimate teaching of Truth herself. He learned this idea only by being in relationship with others and with God. "You hide this indeed from the wise and reveal it to little ones,"[9] he explained. A little one, a child who understands his dependence on his mother, on his community, and on his creator, understands something more true than the older person who foolishly thinks himself wise and self-reliant because he understands a difficult philosophical text.[10]

Indeed, reading and understanding difficult philosophical texts is an experience that does not point to the reader's individual potency as an intellectual. It points to the reader's need for relationship with external sources. On one hand, Augustine was clear that anyone who reads the books of Platonism and considers himself capable of ascending to the Truth on his own is a fool. On the other hand, Augustine insisted that the ideas of the Platonists are remarkable; they are the gold that God told the Hebrew slaves to take when they were escaping Pharaoh;[11] they are the gifts the Athenians used to understand Paul.[12] In Augustine's view, Truth brings people of dif-

---

9. Conf. VII.ix.14: "Abscondisti enim haec a sapientibus et revelasti ea parvulis."

10. See Conf. VII.ix.14: "discentes se esse sapientes stulti facti sunt." (Those who say they are wise by themselves, are made fools.) See also Rom 1:22.

11. See Conf. VII.ix.15: "et ego ad te veneram ex gentibus et intendi in aurum quod ab Aegypto voluisti ut auferret populus tuus, quoniam tuum erat, ubicumque erat." (And I came to you from the Gentiles and I aimed for the gold which you wanted your people to take, as it was yours, wherever it was.) See Exod 3:22 NIV: "Every woman is to ask her neighbor and any woman living in her house for articles of silver and gold and for clothing, which you will put on your sons and daughters. And so you will plunder the Egyptians." See Exod 12:35–36 NIV: "The Israelites did as Moses instructed and asked the Egyptians for articles of silver and gold and for clothing. The Lord had made the Egyptians favorably disposed toward the people, and they gave them what they asked for; so they plundered the Egyptians." See ODonnell, Commentary, 432–34. "The Egyptian gold is Platonism." O'Donnell also noted that Plotinus was born in Egypt and studied at Alexandria with Ammonius Saccas. Egypt is frequently cited as the place where Platonism is born.

12. See Conf. VII.ix.15: "et dixisti Atheniensibus per apostolum tuum quod in te

ferent places and cultures together to share philosophical ideas so that they can grow in wisdom. He had been told by Ambrose that Plato had studied with the Jewish prophets in Egypt.[13] He believed this showed that Christians can learn much from the Platonists and Platonists can learn much from Christians as they had from Jews. But essential to this learning is a recognition that the students are not ascending to these truths by their own individual aptitude but rather by their relationship with each other and with the Truth that they all seek. Otherwise, one foolishly takes Egyptian gold and turns it into an idol. In worshipping one's own mind, one worships the creature rather than the Creator.[14]

Platonic theory is valuable according to Augustine. It provides the golden idea that there is a metaphysical (not material) light that allows one to understand what one understands. Just as the eye sees only with the aid of physical light, the mind knows only by the aid of a non-corporeal light. There is a transcendent light that is the ground of all truth and enlightens all who know truths. However, Augustine believed this light of Truth is not like the light of the sun; this light is not indifferent to the creatures that depend on her. Because the books of the Platonists admonished him to meditate on his own interior experiences of knowing, Augustine decided to do so. And in so doing, he was graced with a remarkable experience of a graceful interaction with Truth. It is that gracefulness—and not the immateriality—of Truth which he emphasized in his moment of conversion from skepticism.

This is clear in the central passage of the *Confessions* that has often been quoted and used to explain Augustine's epistemology. In chapter 10 of the seventh book of the *Confessions*, Augustine recounted:

> And having been admonished to return to myself, I entered
> into myself with you leading me. I could do this because you

---

vivimus et movemur et sumus, sicut et quidam secundum eos dixerunt, et utique inde erant illi libri." (And you said to the Athenians through your Apostle that we live and we move and we are in you, just as their own scholars said, and certainly these were their books.)

13. See O'Donnell, *Commentary on Books 1–7*, 433: "Augustine believed, following Ambrose, that Plato himself had derived his teaching from contact with Jewish scripture during a sojourn in Egypt. Augustine thought he recalled—as late as 397 and so perhaps even while writing the *Confessions*—that Ambrose had said that Plato met Jeremiah personally and was instructed by him. The notion of influence goes back to Hellenistic Judaism and was sometimes admitted by non-Christians."

14. See Conf. VII.ix.15: "et non attendi in idola Aegyptiorum, quibus de auro tuo ministrabant qui transmutaverunt veritatem dei in mendacium, et coluerunt et servierunt creaturae potius quam creatori." (I did not aim for the idols of Egypt, which are made of your gold, which transmuted the truth of God into lies, for they worshiped and served the creatures rather than the creator.)

are my helper. I entered, and I saw as it were with the eye of my
soul that above the eye of my soul and above my intellect was
an unchangeable light, not the common light seen by all flesh.
Nor was this light similar but just greater as if shining more
brightly and occupying more space. No, this light was another,
much greater than any other light. Nor was this light above my
intellect as oil is above water nor as the heavens are above the
Earth, but this light was superior because she made me and
and I was inferior because I was made by her. One who knows
the truth knows her, and one who knows her knows eternity.
And one who knows love knows her. O Eternal Truth, O True
Love, O Loving Eternity, you are my God. To you I sigh day and
night. And when I first knew you, you lifted me so that I might
see that which I could see and that I was not one who could
see it myself. And you reverberated through my infirmity, ra-
diating passionately around me, and I trembled with love and
dread. And I found I was a long way from you in a place so
dissimilar to you. And I heard a voice from on high, "I am the
food of great people: Grow and you will feed on me. You will
not change me into you as you do food of the flesh, but you
will be changed into me." And I knew that you teach people in
proportion to their vices. And you made my soul collapse like
a spider web. I said, "Is the Truth nothing? For truth is not dif-
fused through finite or infinite space?" And you shouted from a
long way off, "Truly, I am who I am."[15] And I heard as one hears
in the heart. And there was no room for doubt. It is easier to
doubt that there is life in me than to doubt the Truth which is
seen intellectually through what she has made.[16]

15. See Exod 3:14 NIV: "God said to Moses, 'I am who I am. This is what you are to
say to the Israelites: "I Am has sent me to you."'"

16. Conf. VII.x.16: "Et inde admonitus redire ad memet ipsum, intravi in intima
mea duce te, et potui, quoniam factus es adiutor meus. intravi et vidi qualicumque
oculo animae meae supra eundem oculum animae meae, supra mentem meam, lucem
incommutabilem, non hanc vulgarem et conspicuam omni carni, nec quasi ex eodem
genere grandior erat, tamquam si ista multo multoque clarius claresceret totumque
occuparet magnitudine. non hoc illa erat sed aliud, aliud valde ab istis omnibus. nec
ita erat supra mentem meam, sicut oleum super aquam nec sicut caelum super terram,
sed superior, quia ipsa fecit me, et ego inferior, quia factus ab ea. qui novit veritatem,
novit eam, et qui novit eam, novit aeternitatem; caritas novit eam. o aeterna veritas et
vera caritas et cara aeternitas, tu es deus meus, tibi suspiro die ac nocte! et cum te primum cognovi, tu adsumpsisti me ut viderem esse quod viderem, et nondum me esse
qui viderem. et reverberasti infirmitatem aspectus mei, radians in me vehementer, et
contremui amore et horrore. et inveni longe me esse a te in regione dissimilitudinis,
tamquam audirem vocem tuam de excelso: 'cibus sum grandium: cresce et mandu-
cabis me. nec tu me in te mutabis sicut cibum carnis tuae, sed tu mutaberis in me.' et

Augustine beheld the Truth that is because the Truth lifted him up to see her.

Over the centuries since Augustine wrote his *Confessions*, philosophers have analyzed this passage and compared it with other passages in his early philosophical dialogues and his later works, especially *On the Trinity*. With careful analysis of the texts, many have tried to get clear on the mechanics of his epistemology. Ironically, the goal of clarifying Augustine's epistemology has led to complicated and divisive arguments between various schools of thought. There is the Platonic interpretation that insists Augustine accepted that the divine light completely informs the human mind of all truths *prior* to sensation. There is a Thomistic interpretation that claims Augustine spoke of a divine light that allows the human mind to derive truth *from* (*a posteriori*) sense perceptions. There is a proto-Kantian interpretation that argues Augustine claimed that the divine light structured the mind in such a way that the mind is able to make sense out of sense data. Beyond these three, there are other interpretations. All these published interpretations can be demonstrated to be viable readings of various passages in Augustine's works, for indeed Augustine's writings certainly influenced the work of later Christian Platonists as well as Thomas and Kant. However, too often these analyses, in their zeal to lend Augustinian authority to their own epistemological ideas, miss the main point that Augustine wished to emphasize. His point was to testify to his own experience of a loving Truth who is in relationship with him and who exposed this relationship to him. It is the immanent and loving relationship with Truth that is most essential to Augustine's epistemology for that is the foundation for his hope in philosophy. This is clear in his tender description of how he came to understand more deeply the abstract, or noetic, understanding of God rather than the materialist concept with which he still struggled—even after the experience recounted above. He wrote that his soul

> had imagined for itself a god extended through all space to infinity and it thought that this was you and enshrined this in its heart. And once again, it was made into a temple of idols which were abominable to you. But afterward, unknown to me, you soothed my head and closed my eyes so that they should not look upon vanities and I stopped for a little while and slept away

---

cognovi quoniam pro iniquitate erudisti hominem, et tabescere fecisti sicut araneam animam meam, et dixi, 'numquid nihil est veritas, quoniam neque per finita neque per infinita locorum spatia diffusa est?' et clamasti de longinquo, 'immo vero ego sum qui sum.' et audivi, sicut auditur in corde, et non erat prorsus unde dubitarem, faciliusque dubitarem vivere me quam non esse veritatem, quae per ea quae facta sunt intellecta conspicitur."

my madness. I awoke in you and saw that you were infinite in
another way. This came to me but not as a vision of the flesh.[17]

For Augustine, his testimony concerning his relationship with Truth is the
most essential part of his teaching on epistemology. Every time he explained
a new insight, he gave credit to God who is the Truth. And he insisted that
the reader consider how her own insights bear testimony to Wisdom's relationship with her:

> Indeed, wherever you turn, she speaks to you through the
> vestiges of her operations. When you are retreating towards
> external things she recalls you back inside by the very forms of
> external things so that anything that delights you bodily and en-
> tices you through the senses of the body, you can see is governed
> by number, and when you ask how that is so, you will return
> into yourself, and you will understand that by touching with the
> senses of the body, you could not prove or disprove anything,
> unless you had in relationship with you as it were laws of beauty
> by which you judge all beautiful things which you see externally
> by your senses.[18]

By Augustine's account, each human experience of making a useful
judgment, of creating a helpful classification, and of postulating a scientific
theory is evidence of an intimate and immanent relationship with Truth,
herself. The academic skeptics had shown Augustine that his mind was
mutable, easily altered by moods, disease, sleep, and madness. He knew
that the human mind is easily fooled by dreams, optical illusions, and
grand hallucinations. Yet the human being who is honest must admit that
she does make correct judgments sometimes and that she knows certain
things that cannot be doubted despite the fluctuating conditions of the human brain, heart, and psyche. The best explanation Augustine found for his
ability to see order, to recognize beauty, and to make claims about justice
from the buzz of sense data that bombarded his changeable psyche is that

---

17. Conf. VII.xiv.20: "fecerat sibi deum per infinita spatia locorum omnium et eum
putaverat esse te et eum conlocaverat in corde suo, et facta erat rursus templum idoli sui
abominandum tibi, sed posteaquam fovisti caput nescientis et clausisti oculos meos, ne
viderent vanitatem. cessavi de me paululum, et consopita est insania mea, et evigilavi in
te et vidi te infinitum aliter, et visus iste non a carne trahebatur."

18. LA II.xvi.41: "Quoquo enim te verteris, vestigiis quibusdam, quae operibus
suis impressit, loquitur tibi, et te in exteriora relabentem, ipsis exteriorum formis intro
revocat; ut quidquid te delectat in corpore, et per corporeos illicit sensus, videas esse
numerosum, et quaeras unde sit, et in te ipsum redeas, atque intellegas te id quod at-
tingis sensibus corporis, probare aut improbare non posse, nisi apud te habeas quasdam
pulchritudinis leges, ad quas referas quaeque pulchra sentis exterius."

there is some eternal light that helped him process it. This is the light of Truth that lovingly shone within his mind and helped it to make sense of the sense data. While the skeptics are correct that many times human beings make errors in their judgments and postulates, human experience shows that human beings sometimes judge correctly. These moments bear witness to a friendly hearted Truth who illuminates the mind and teaches it through an intimate relationship.

But of course individual human beings more often err. Human beings make false judgments, create dangerously impractical categories, and postulate empirically false scientific theories. Augustine had been plagued by his knowledge of this fallibility of the human mind. At times, he blamed "the serpent";[19] more often, he blamed the broken nature of the human being and creation after the original sin in Eden. While Augustine never found a systematic answer to the problem of evil and error, he did come to a methodological solution for philosophers. Philosophers must not work alone, they must question, dialogue, and debate with other thinkers in order to uproot errors and grow in their understanding. Philosophers are not individuals in relationship only with Wisdom. Human beings are created to be in relationship with each other.

That this is possible, that human beings can learn from each other in community, is itself an empirical sign of the graciousness of Truth. Augustine noted this in *On the Teacher,* when he and his son Adeodatus discussed how it is that teaching from father to son and from teacher to student is possible through the use of words. Spoken words are simply sounds that pass away before the words are even completed. And yet, thoughts, laws, plans, desires, fears, and loves are made manifest from from one person to another through spoken language. To a human listener who understands the same language as the speaker, the sounds communicate the ideas inside the speaker's mind. This testifies to the relationship of Wisdom with each and every human mind.

> Concerning universals of which we understand, we do not listen to a person speaking outside ourselves, but inside of our minds we hear truth which presides in our minds so that we are admonished by the words most strongly. Thus, this is the one who is heard, the one who teaches, who dwells in the interior person

---

19. Conf. VI.xii.21: "insuper etiam per me ipsi quoque Alypio loquebatur serpens, et innectebat atque spargebat per linguam meam dulces laqueos in via eius, quibus illi honesti et expediti pedes implicarentur." (Moreover, the serpent spoke through me to Alypius, and it wove words and sprinkled from my tongue the sweet liquor in his way, so that his honest and expedient feet might be tripped.)

and is named Christ—the one who is the unchangeable Virtue
and eternal Wisdom of God.[20]

Augustine insisted that this Wisdom speaks through all who speak truly—
even through Cicero, the skeptic. Whenever Cicero spoke truly, Wisdom
spoke through his lips.[21]

Thus, while experiences of error led Augustine to skeptical despair,
experiences of insight gave him renewed optimism for the possibility of
philosophy, not as an individual's search for wisdom but as a communal
friendship with Wisdom. His conversion to this understanding of philosophy required that he reconsider not only the nature of Truth but also the
nature of himself.

Relationship as the Ground of the Self

Throughout the *Confessions*, it is clear that Augustine understood himself
as a creature dependent upon God, who is Truth: "What indeed am I in
myself without you except a leader in a headlong fall. Or what am I when
all is well with me, except a nursling suckling your milk, the food that never
perishes? And what is a human, any human, if he is human."[22] There can be
no creature without the Creator and no being without Being itself.[23] Thus,
Augustine's existence required the ongoing sustenance of the Sustainer who
gave him life and the friendship of his Savior who gave him the will to live.
Augustine cried out, "If we could not sob into your ear, there would be nothing of hope that remains for us."[24]

---

20. DM xi.38: "De universis autem quae intellegimus non loquentem qui personat
foris, sed intus ipsi menti praesidentem consulimus veritatem, verbis fortasse ut con-
sulamus admoniti. Ille autem qui consulitur, docet, qui in interiore homine habitare
dictus est Christus, id est incommutabilis Dei Virtus atque sempiterna Sapientia."

21. Epis. 130.5.10, "To Proba" (411): "haec verba nonne ab ipsa veritate per quemlibet hominem dicta sunt?" (Were these words not said by Truth herself through the
speech of a human being?)

22. Conf. IV.i.1: "quid enim sum ego mihi sine te nisi dux in praeceps? aut quid
sum, cum mihi bene est, nisi sugens lac tuum aut fruens te, cibo qui non corrumpitur?
et quis homo est quilibet homo, cum sit homo?"

23. See Conf. I.xx.31: "ita enim servabis me, et augebuntur et perficientur quae dedisti mihi, et ero ipse tecum, quia et ut sim tu dedisti mihi." (Therefore, indeed, you will
serve me, and what you've given me will be increased and perfected, and I will be with
you, for you have made it so that I can be.)

24. Conf. IV.v.10: "et tamen nisi ad aures tuas plorarermus, nihil residui de spe
nostra fieret."

Nevertheless, throughout Augustine's work, it is clear that he understood himself not only to be dependent on God but dependent on all of creation. His existence depended on his relationship to nature and especially to the human community. The Creator made Augustine from "earth and ashes,"[25] forming him in the flesh of his mother and out of the flesh of his parents.[26] Augustine was sustained by the milk of the breasts of his mother and his nurses. His very body's particles were made from their milk. By taking their milk and growing strong, he gave them joy even as they gave him life.[27] Augustine understood the secular world to be interconnected. Each part relies on every other part, and the whole is sustained by God. While Augustine claimed he had wanted independence as an adolescent, as the adult writer of the *Confessions* he recognized that independence was an illusion. As much as any child, he was a dependent. He depended upon the water and the dirt and the air, upon his family and his friends and his community, upon his God. His very existence depended on his relationships, and so did his ability to know.

Christian Philosophy and the Significance of the Doctrine of Incarnation

Augustine believed that Truth, the teacher, understands that her students are creatures she formed from earth and ashes to be social animals who depend on the help of their community.[28] Thus, to teach human beings, the Truth had to dwell amongst them on earth and in their society. Such was the lesson Augustine derived from the Gospels' account of the Incarnation. Augustine believed that the Incarnation was wholly in line with Jewish theology, whose Scriptures began with an account of God creating human beings in the midst of nature and declaring all of creation as good. The Hebrew Scriptures describe the God of Wisdom speaking to these human beings even after they sinned against God. God spoke to people through burning bushes, whirlwinds, and a myriad of prophets in order to lead them

25. Conf. I.vi.7: "terram et cinerem."

26. See Conf. I.vi.7: "sicut audivi a parentibus carnis meae, ex quo et in qua me formasti in tempore." (Just as I have heard from the the the flesh of my parents, out of whom and in whom you did form me in time.)

27. See Conf. I. vi.7: "dare enim mihi per ordinatum affectum volebant quo abundabant ex te. nam bonum erat eis bonum meum ex eis." (Indeed, they wanted to give to me through their ordinary affection which they had abundantly from you. Now it was good for them that what was good for me came from them.)

28. See Gen 2:7–18.

out of the wilderness and rescue them from repeated errors.[29] Augustine found that the Gospel accounts did not contradict the writings of the Old Testament but, in his view, fulfilled them. In the Incarnation, God fulfilled the promises made to the prophets, making Truth fully manifest to human beings as human beings, creatures who come to knowledge through rational processing of sense data and through discussions held in community. Of course, Augustine recognized that there were tensions between Christians and Jews on this very point; he acknowledged that Jews do not see the Incarnation as the fulfillment of the Old Testament nor accept Christian teachings as legitimate. While he criticized their theology on this point, he also preached tolerance for Jewish people and their teachings as they witnessed to Gentiles fundamental truths concerning the relationship of God to creation.[30] This understanding of the relationship of God to creation, Augustine found to be unique to Jewish and Christian teachings.

In contrast, the idea of the Incarnation was scandalously impossible to many other schools of thought. Certainly, gnostics could not accept that flesh, being dark matter, could hold the divine. The anti-Semitic Manicheans had repudiated the entire Old Testament account that God was the one who created the earth and the flesh of bodies. The Manicheans could not accept that the divine was born from a woman's body, laid in a manger stall, and suffered death and humiliation. Nor could the Platonists accept the possibility of the Incarnation, for while they refuted the gnostic view of the

---

29. See Epis. 147, "To Paulina" (413), Augustine's long letter to Paulina, a woman who had asked a difficult question of whether God can be seen by bodily eyes. Augustine mentioned the many Old Testament people who were able to see God through their bodily senses—not just Adam but even Cain. He mentioned that Jacob wrestled with God and Moses was able to to talk to God face to face as a friend. Even the Devil was given a meeting with God according to the Book of Job. Augustine indicated to Paulina that, in his opinion, God can show an aspect of the divine to the bodily senses of whomever he desires to show. But in the end, he noted the full essence of God is beyond our sight and Paulina would be profited in cleansing her mind of too many corporeal images of God and striving to think of God spiritually, a being that is not seen corporeally but known intellectually, as are the concepts of love, goodness, and faith.

30. See, for example, CD xviii.46. For a general description of Augustine's position on Jews and Jewish theology, see Goodwin, "Jews and Judaism," 1214–18. See also Fredriksen, *Augustine and the Jews*. While most of Augustine's arguments in support of Jewish theology can be found in his polemics against the Manicheans or the polytheists, he did write a less sympathetic treatise on the subject later in his life. See Augustine's *Tractatus adversus Iudeos* [Tractate against the Jews] (428–29), in which he argued against the Jews that Christianity has a legitimate interpretation of the Hebrew Scriptures and that Christians are not obligated to follow the Law literally while also arguing to Christians that they must recognize that the Jews had an important and continuing role in bringing the books and teachings of the Hebrew Scriptures to Gentile communities.

material world as evil, they saw the material world as merely a reflection of the divine, incapable of actually containing the divine.

Indeed, Augustine noted that belief in the Incarnation is a radical separation point between Christians and Platonists. As he read the Platonic books he found that their insights coincided with some Christian teachings. "I read there . . . that in the beginning was the Word and the Word was with God and God was the Word that was in the beginning with God. All things were made through it and without it nothing was made."[31] But while Christians teach that the Incarnation of the Word is a supreme act of the care of Truth, Platonists could not conceive such care in their metaphysical One. "But that the Word was made flesh and dwelled among us, that I did not read there,"[32] explained Augustine. Truth was considered intelligible and not physical; it could not become physical according to a Platonist.[33] Moreover, as an intelligible reality, the highest Good simply did not have the property of thinking or caring.[34] Indeed, the concept of a caring Truth was an ethical impossibility for Platonists. Plotinus explained,

> But, on one hand, it says that those who have become good will have a good life and later go to a good life, and for the wicked it will be the opposite. But, on the other hand, it is not right that for those who have become wicked to ask others to be their saviors and to sacrifice themselves in answer to their wishes. Nor then is it right to ask the gods to rule their affairs in detail, sacrificing their own lives or those of good men.[35]

Plotinus held that not even good people should be expected to sacrifice for the wicked, much less should divine beings be expected to do so.

31. Conf. VII.ix.13: "et ibi legi, . . . quod in principio erat verbum et verbum erat apud deum et deus erat verbum. Hoc erat in principio apud deum. Omnia per impsum acta sunt, et sine ipso facum est nihil." See John 1:1–3.

32. Conf. VII.ix.14: "sed quia verbum caro factum est et habitavit in nobis, non ibi legi." See John 1:14.

33. For example, see Plotinus, *Enneads* V.5.12–13, for a long explanation of the metaphysical difference between the Good and any particular good thing. Of course, this was a paradox with which Augustine also struggled; however, unlike the Platonists, he insisted that somehow the eternal and the intelligible was present in the temporal and physical person of Jesus.

34. See Plotinus, *Enneads* V.6.5–6, where he discusses that the nature of the Good is a being beyond thinking.

35. Plotinus, *Enneads* III.2.9: "Λέγει δὲ τοῖς μὲν ἀγαθοῖς γενομένοις ἀγαθὸν βίον ἔσεσθαι καὶ κεῖσθαι καὶ εἰς ὕστερον, τοῖς δὲ κακοῖς τὰ ἐναντία. Κακοὺς δὲ γενομένους ἀξιοῦν ἄλλους αὐτῶν σωτῆρας εἶναι ἑαυτοὺς προεμένους οὐ θεμιτὸν εὐχὴν ποιουμένων. οὐ τοίνυν οὐδὲ θεοὺς αὐτῶν ἄρχειν τὰ καθέκαστα ἀφέντας τὸν ἑαυτῶν βίον οὐδέ γε τοὺς ἄνδρας τοὺς ἀγαθούς."

Moreover, all human suffering is inconsequential in the grand scheme of the cosmos according to the Platonists. A person only suffers if he is self-centered, refusing to look at what is good and providential for the whole. A truly wise person, and certainly a god, would not fall into such an error as to concern himself with the crying of human beings any more than a spectator seriously concerns herself for an actor playing a part on stage or a parent concerns himself with his child's tears over a game of ball.[36]

When combatting the Platonists, the gnostics, and the skeptics, Augustine admitted that relying on Scriptural authority is necessary to know of the Incarnation. Importantly, Augustine came to embrace the authority of Scripture not out of forced reverence but because of his own experiences. As he considered why Scriptural authority might be necessary, he remarked, "As I thought about this, you were present to me, and I sighed and you heard me, I fluctuated and you governed me, I ran through secular paths and you did not not desert me."[37] As such, his experience was simply contrary to the doctrinal position of the Platonists. He experienced a God who is the Truth and who is concerned with the troubles of creatures who are in error. He found in the Gospels an account that helped him understand his experiences and gave him hope of continuing to grow in understanding:

> And I sought a way of gaining the strength that is necessary to enjoy you, but I did not find such a way until I comprehended the mediator between God and human beings, the human Christ Jesus, who is God over all, praised forever, who was calling and saying "I am the way and the truth and the life," and the food, which I was too weak to take, mixed with flesh so that the Word was made flesh, so that your wisdom might be made milk for our infancy. Through her, you created all things. Indeed, I, a humble one, did not hold my God Jesus, who is the humble

36. Plotinus, *Enneads* III.2.15: "Ὥσπερ δ᾽ ἐπὶ τῶν θεάτρων ταῖς σκηναῖς, οὕτω χρὴ καὶ τοὺς φόνους θεᾶσθαι καὶ πάντας θανάτους καὶ πόλεων ἁλώσεις καὶ ἁρπαγάς, μεταθέσεις πάντα καὶ μετασχηματίσεις καὶ θρήνων καὶ οἰμωγῶν ὑποκρίσεις. . . . Σπουδάζεται δὲ καὶ τὰ παίγνια τοῖς σπουδάζειν ο᾽θκ εἰδόσι καὶ τοῖσ αὐτοῖς οὖσι παιγνίοις. Εἰ δὲ τις συμπαίζων αὐτοῖσ τὰ τοιαῦτα πάθοι, ἴστω παραπεσὼν παίδων παιδιᾳ τὸ περι αὐτὸν ἀποθέμενος παίγνιον. . . . ὅτι δὴ καὶ παῖδες ἐπὶ οὐ κακοῖσ καὶ δακρύοθσι καὶ ὀδύπονται." (Therefore, it is necessary that we observe murders and all deaths and the corruption and taking of cities, as if they were on the stages of theaters, all changes of scenery and costume and acted struggles. . . . But games also are seriously studied by those who do not know how to study seriously and are players themselves. But if anyone plays with them and suffers in this same way, of course, he has tumbled amongst children in a game for children. . . . For children, too, weep and wail about things that are not evils.)

37. Conf. VI.v.8: "cogitabam haec et aderas mihi, suspirabam et audiebas me, fluctuabam et gubernabas me, ibam per viam saeculi latam nec deserebas."

one, nor did I know the things this schoolmistress would teach us with weakness. Indeed, your Word, the eternal Truth, superior to your creatures picks these lower ones up to herself. In this inferior realm, she built herself a humble home out of our clay through which she presses down those who needed to be subdued and brings them over to her, healing their swollen pride and nourishing their love. Thus, they might not progress far in their faith in themselves, but rather they are made weak, seeing before their feet the humble divine sharing the tunic of our skin. Thus they might prostrate themselves before her, that she might, as she rises, lift them.[38]

According to Augustine, the Incarnation was a physical manifestation of Truth's effort to teach human beings; Christ was a divine school mistress teaching in a humble house of clay. Peter Brown noted in his biography of Augustine that the most popular icon of the fourth century was Christ portrayed as a teacher before a crowd of students.[39] The Gospels were seen as an account of the teachings of this divine professor. In the Gospels, a student could read the words of Truth, who spoke using a human tongue and lips so as to be heard by human ears. As Augustine explained,

> This is your word, that is the beginning, that is spoken to us. It speaks through the flesh, as in the Gospel, where it sounds to human ears, so that it can be believed and sought and found as the eternal truth internally, where the one good Teacher teaches all disciples. There I hear your voice, Sir, saying to me that as it is spoken to us, he teaches us, for he cannot teach if it is not spoken and if it is not spoken to us. Who can teach us except the firm Truth?[40]

38. Conf. VII.xviii.24: "Et quaerebam viam comparandi roboris quod esset idoneum ad fruendum te, nec inveniebam donec amplecterer mediatorem dei et hominum, hominem Christum Iesum, qui est super omnia deus benedictus in saecula, vocantem et dicentem, 'ego sum via et veritas et vita,' et cibum, cui capiendo invalidus eram, miscentem carni, quoniam verbum caro factum est ut infantiae nostrae lactesceret sapientia tua, per quam creasti omni. non enim tenebam deum meum Iesum, humilis humilem, nec cuius rei magistra esset eius infirmitas noveram. verbum enim tuum, aeterna veritas, superioribus creaturae tuae partibus supereminens subditos erigit ad se ipsam, in inferioribus autem aedificavit sibi humilem domum de limo nostro, per quam subdendos deprimeret a seipsis et ad se traiceret, sanans tumorem et nutriens amorem, ne fiducia sui progrederentur longius, sed potius infirmarentur, videntes ante pedes suos infirmam divinitatem ex participatione tunicae pelliciae nostrae, et lassi prosternerentur in eam, illa autem surgens leveret eos."

39. Brown, *Augustine of Hippo*, 42.

40. Conf. XI.viii.10: "ipsum est verbum tuum, quod et principium est, quia et loquitur nobis. sic in evangelio per carnem ait, et hoc insonuit foris auribus hominum, ut

For Augustine, the words recorded in the Gospels are the words of the Word. And the words of the Word hold a promise. He explained,

> My heart, Sir, in the neediness of my life, is busy knocking at the doors of the words of your Holy Scriptures. . . . "Ask and you shall receive, seek and you shall find, knock and it is opened to you. All indeed who ask receive and the seeking one finds and the for the one knocking, the door is opened." These are our promises and who fears falsehood when the Truth promises?[41]

Moreover, because human beings learn by actions as well as words, the deeds of the Teacher are also recorded in the gospel. These acts demonstrate that Truth goes to great lengths to make sure that the promise of enlightenment is fulfilled. Augustine preached,

> Look, O human person, what God did for you. . . . You once in paradise were so fluent that you gave names to every living animal; yet for you, your Creator became an infant, who did not even call the name of his mother. You lost yourself in the broad orchard of fruit trees by neglecting obedience; he obediently came as a mortal to a narrow lodging house, in order by dying to seek those who were dead. You when you were a human being wished to be God, and so you were lost; He when he was God wished to be human so to find what had been lost. Human pride pressed you down so much it was not possible for you to rise, except with the aid of divine humility.[42]

While many African Christians in the fourth century were concerned that Christmas was simply a created holiday, modeled after the pagan festivities of Saturnalia, Augustine believed that it was good to celebrate the birth

---

crederetur et intus quaereretur et inveniretur in aeterna veritate, ubi omnes discipulos bonus et solus magister docet. ibi audio vocem tuam, domine, dicentis mihi, quoniam ille loquitur nobis qui docet nos, qui autem non docet nos etiam si loquitur, non nobis loquitur. quid porro nos docet nisi stabilis veritas?"

41. Conf. XII.i.1: "Multa satagit cor meum domine in hac inopia vitae meae, pulsatum verbis sanctae scripturae tuae, . . . 'petite et accipietis, quaerite et invenietis, pulsate et aperietur vobis. Omnis enim qui petit accipit, et quaerens inveniet, et pulsanti aperietur.' promissa tua sunt, et quis falli timeat cum promittit veritas?" See Matt 7:7–8.

42. Sermon 188.3: "Vide, o homo, quid pro te factus est Deus: . . . Tu quondam in paradiso tam facundus fuisti, ut omni animae vivae nomina imponeres: propter te autem Creator tuus infans iacebat, et nomine suo nec matrem vocabat. Tu in latissimo fructuosorum nemorum praedio te perdidisti, obedientiam neglegendo: ille obediens in angustissimum diversorium mortalis venit, ut mortuum quaereret moriendo. Tu cum esses homo, Deus esse voluisti, ut perires; ille cum esset Deus, homo esse voluit, ut quod perierat inveniret. Tantum te pressit humana superbia, ut te non posset nisi humilitas sublevare divina."

of Christ at the winter solstice as a reminder of the light that shines in the darkness, the Truth that makes herself incarnate in order to be known. His Christmas sermons celebrated the nativity as the ground of philosophy:

> It is the day of the birth of the Master of the house, when the Wisdom of God is shown as an infant and the Word of God is sent as a voice in the flesh without words. . . . Truth, by which holds the world, has sprung from the earth, in order to be carried in a woman's arms. Truth, on which the bliss of the angels is incorruptibly nourished, has sprung from the earth, in order to be suckled at breasts of flesh. Truth, which heaven is not sufficient to hold, has sprung from the earth, in order to be placed in a manger.[43]

The message of Christmas radically changed Augustine's hope for philosophy because it proclaimed that Truth seeks human beings. Moreover, the Incarnation reinforced that human beings learn through their bodily senses in a world in which and for which they were created, thus encouraging secular science.

Importantly, for Augustine the rhetorician, the Incarnation also redeemed the possibility of truth-telling through language. Augustine explained in his *Narrations on the Psalms,*

> All other things can be said in some way; this one alone is ineffable, this one who spoke and made everything. He spoke and we were made, but we could not speak of him. His word, by whom we were spoken into existence, is his Son. For us, he was made weak so that he might be spoken by us, despite our weakness.[44]

For Augustine, God's presence in the historical person of Jesus was evidence that speech about God is possible in all of human history. God's Word is effable through the Incarnation; this allowed words to hold the fullness of truth. God holds human words in such esteem that God used them to preach to his creatures in both the Old and New Testament. Words therefore are not only symbolic but also iconic or even sacramental for Augustine. Words can

43. Sermon 185.1: "Natalis Domini dicitur, quando Dei Sapientia se demonstravit infantem, et Dei Verbum sine verbis vocem carnis emisit. . . . Veritas quae est in sinu Patris, de terra orta est, ut esset etiam in sinu matris. Veritas qua mundus continetur, de terra orta est, ut femineis manibus portaretur. Veritas qua beatitudo Angelorum incorruptibiliter alitur, de terra orta est, ut carnalibus uberibus lactaretur. Veritas cui coelum non sufficit, de terra orta est, ut in praesepio poneretur."

44. See Enn. Ps. xcix.6: "Postremo caetera dici possunt utcumque. ille solus est ineffabilis, qui dixit, et facta sunt omnia. Dixit, et facti sumus: sed nos eum dicere non possumus. Verbum eius quo dicti sumus, Filius eius est: ut a nobis utcumque infirmis diceretur, factus est infirmus."

convey the fullness of Truth. As Marcia Colish explained in the *Mirror of Language*: "The doctrine of the Incarnation and the manner in which Augustine understands his conversion to it are thus essential to his conception of the redemption of language, which he holds, makes theology possible."[45] Colish asserted this Christian philosophy of language was redemptive for theology and philosophy for Augustine because it explained that human beings can hear and read words and understand their true meaning.

For Augustine, accepting the Incarnation changed his understanding of the vocation of the philosopher. The philosopher is not on a solo journey towards self-discovery but has Truth herself as his philosophy teacher. Truth is revealed on the pages of John's Gospel. Truth rings internally in the ears of the heart. Truth is the philosophy teacher, the Socratic gad-fly that stirs the philosopher towards further investigation and understanding. In Augustine's words:

> You called and you cried out, and you broke my barrier of deafness. You shone with splendor and you made my blindness flee. You shed your fragrance and I drew breath and I inhaled you. I tasted and I hunger and thirst. You touched me and I am burning for your peace.[46]

After Augustine's conversion to Christianity, philosophy for Augustine was no longer a quest for truth but a friendship with Truth. The Truth was not an ideal yardstick by which he measured propositions. The Truth was the friendly teacher, guiding Augustine in his wanderings, laying a gentle finger on his heart and setting his thoughts in order.[47] This is not to say that Augustine expected the seeker of Truth simply to wait for the divine Teacher to appear. The Truth can be beseeched. Augustine, like his mother before him, begged the Teacher for help often. Augustine saw the movement of Truth bound inextricably with the movements of creation in a way that he could not explain fully. While in some places he seemed to suggest pre-destination, in other places he seemed to insist on the full and active participation of all members of the relationship. Augustine's difficulty in explaining where agency lies is due to the entangled nature of relationship as such. And it is relationship that Augustine wished to stress. Truth is not a principle to be discovered but a loving being in relationship with every truth seeker. All in all, his experience of this relationship and his belief in the Incarnation made

---

45. Colish, *Mirror of Language*, 22.

46. Conf. X.xxvii.38: "vocasti et clamasti et rupisti surditatem meam; coruscasti, splenduisti et fugasti caecitatem meam; fragrasti, et duxi spiritum et anhelo tibi; gustavi et esurio et sitio; tetigisti me, et exarsi in pacem tuam."

47. See Conf. VI.v.8.

it possible for him to continue as a philosopher with optimism. He advocated for this redeemed philosophy for the rest of his life.

Credo ut Intelligam: The Proper
Method for Philosophy

While Augustine grounded his apologetics for Christian philosophy in his lived experience, he understood that Christians grounded their philosophical foundations in Scripture, believing in doctrines—such as the Incarnation—that could only be known by being read. He explained, "At the same time we are too weak to discover truth by clear reason, and here for us there is the authority of sacred scriptures."[48] While he had rejected assenting to any propositions on faith as an academic skeptic, as a Christian, he advocated the method of believing in order to understand. Importantly, Augustine's use of the nouns faith (*fides*) and belief (*opinio*) and the verb to believe (*credo*) did not change much between secular and Christian contexts. This means his use of these words is somewhat different than that of later medieval thinkers who often considered faith as a religious kind of knowledge in itself. Augustine's commendation of faith was a result of his assessment that a philosopher must believe principles that seem plausible and then investigate and explore these in order to understand them. Indeed, according to Augustine, this is not a uniquely Christian method but the usual human method of investigation. Children, scientists, citizens, and even philosophers commonly seek knowledge by believing first in order to understand later.

Augustine recounted that in his own childhood he was taught, as most children are, to trust authorities.[49] Parents and teachers assume that such faith is the only possible starting place for a child's future development. If a small child were left to her own rational faculties to accept only those tenets which she could fully understand, the child would never acquire the skills of reading, writing, and critical thinking that she needs in order to understand the need for education. She probably would not even survive. So, children are told to believe that they must go to school, that they must eat their vegetables, and that they must trust their parents' goodwill in order that they might mature and later be able to understand. While a good teacher will try to give a child rational reasons for what the child must accept, if the child

48. See Conf. VI.v.8: "ideoque cum essemus infirmi ad inveniendam liquida ratione veritatem et ob hoc nobis opus esset auctoritate sanctarum litterarum."

49. For an account of all the things Augustine was told to trust as a child, especially in regards to attending school, see Conf. I.viii.13—I.ix.14.

cannot understand these, it is a rare educator who allows the child to return to the playground to conduct his life according to his own self-discovered maxims. Humans are nourished and educated under a paradigm of education that requires trust and belief before understanding.

Furthermore, Augustine claimed that this paradigm is also the usual path of inquiry for adults. Any human being who wants to learn about the world needs to believe much on the authority of teachers, scientists, and historians. There simply is no other way to learn about events that happened before one is born or in places where one is not. In fact, anyone who simply wants to learn about her own self needs to rely on the authority of others. Augustine noted that he believed the accounts of his mother and nurses in order to understand who he was as a baby. He explained, "This was indicated to me about myself and I believed it, for we see the same in other infants: I could not remember this myself."[50] Anyone who wants to know oneself must learn from others; much must be believed "on the authority of women."[51] Indeed, the method of faith seeking understanding is the human method of inquiry, a necessary method for a wisdom-seeking, social animal who is finite. Human finitude requires that humans believe other human beings. Humans' social nature allows them to do just that.

Despite the claims of the skeptics and the gnostics that no one ought to take assertions on authority, every sect requires followers to do just that. Therefore, Augustine asserted that the mark of a legitimate teaching is the admission that certain premises are taken on faith. In the end, this is what brings him to consider seriously catholic Christian teachings—the honesty of those Christians who admitted that their foundational statements were beliefs that were open to all:

> After this, I started to be a proponent of the catholic doctrine. I judged it to be more modest and I felt it to be less false in claiming that it believed that which was not demonstrated (either because there was no one who was able to understand, or because it could not be demonstrated). This was more honest than those who laughed at belief and promised to be scientific and then taught fabulous and absurd things which, when they could not be demonstrated, were commanded to be believed.[52]

50. Conf. I.vi.8: "hoc enim de me mihi indicatum est et credidi, quoniam sic videmus alios infantes: nam ista mea non memini."

51. Conf. I.vi.10: "auctoritatibus etiam muliercularum multa de se credere." (On the authority of women, indeed, much must be believed.)

52. Conf. VI.v.7: "Ex hoc tamen quoque iam praeponens doctrinam catholicam, modestius ibi minimeque fallaciter sentiebam iuberi ut crederetur quod non demonstrabatur (sive esset quid, sed cui forte non esset, sive nec quid esset), quam illic

He found the catholic Christians were more honest than the gnostics and even the skeptics, who followed the authority of Cicero even as they asserted that one ought never to adhere to the positions of authorities.

The reason that this honest humility is so important is because such humility encourages students and followers to investigate their premises. The finite nature of the human being means that the search for truth requires faith. But human corporeal nature allows thinkers to investigate their beliefs through empiricism, and human social nature allows them to investigate that faith through questioning and dialogue in community. The inherent passion in human hearts for wisdom drives human beings to investigate statements that are believed in order that these examined premises be understood or denied.

Augustine claimed that all who want wisdom—and he believed that all people desire wisdom—must follow this usual path of wisdom seeking. They must believe and trust authorities, and they must investigate what they believe using empiricism and reason. They must even give themselves the opportunity to doubt. Elie Weisel, the famous theologian, philosopher, and novelist, once said, "It is easy to fool ourselves, to think we have more faith than we actually do. Doubt is a kind of inoculation against this."[53] Such was Augustine's point. Augustine even asserted that heretical claims were important because they helped people understand true beliefs better. Moreover, he preached to members of his congregation that they needed to investigate all they believed, if not for their own sake, for their neighbor's sake. "For you simple faith was sufficient; it will not suffice for him."[54] Augustine insisted that each congregant must knock on the door of Truth and seek answers and discuss these answers with their friends intellectually. The happiness of their community depended on this. Augustine insisted in *On Order*:

> As to those who are content only to follow authority and constantly devote themselves to good morals and right choices but condemn or do not value the liberal disciplines and highest studies—I do not know in what way I would call them happy when they live among human people.[55]

temeraria pollicitatione scientiae credulitatem inrideri et postea tam multa fabulosissima et absurdissima, quia demonstrari non poterant, credenda imperari."

53. Elie Weisel quoted in Burger, *Witness*, 78.

54. Sermon 105.2: "Tibi forte sufficiebat simplex fides, illi non sufficit."

55. Ord. II.ix.26: "Qui autem sola auctoritate contenti bonis tantum moribus rectisque votis constanter operam dederint, aut contemnentes, aut non valentes disciplinis liberalibus atque optimis erudiri, beatos eos quidem, cum inter homines vivant, nescio quomodo appellem."

Augustine's method, taken as a whole, respects the human person as human, as a social corporeal animal that learns through its senses and in community. His method encourages human philosophers to tread boldly in the quest for wisdom, following the natural path of human discovery: trusting authorities in their community, using their senses, asking questions, and having dialogues in and beyond their communities. Importantly, dialogue and debate are essential aspects of his method.

The Importance of Public Dialogue and Debate

Dialogue and debate must always accompany faith, for Augustine's Christian philosophy does not discount the well-reasoned arguments of the academic skeptics in regard to the possibility of error. As a convert to Christianity, Augustine did not become a naïve realist who believed that his senses gave unfettered access to literal truth. He believed that because of the brokenness of the world post-Eden there is error. The most common error is due to the sin of pride as it is the most common obstacle to the kind of cooperation that human beings as social animals require. Human beings, finite as they are, need to learn from those that lived before them, those that have different experiences than they do, and those that live in other places. Humans are constructed to seek knowledge in relationship with each other; pride makes individuals forget this. However, Augustine also insisted that while human beings need to rely on the authority of others, they also need to continue to investigate this information in ever widening circles of community. Augustine's experiences with the gnostics made him concerned about insular communities. As a bishop, Augustine constantly advocated for broadening community. He even condemned the marriage of first cousins because he believed that such marriages encouraged parochialism. In his view, marriage should be used to bring people from diverse communities together in the deepest friendship.[56] Human happiness profits from friendly dialogues between diverse peoples.

    Importantly, a commitment to dialogue and debate requires a trust that dialogue can lead to real learning and not just persuasion. When Augustine was first trained as a rhetorician, he had no confidence in words as vehicles for anything more than pleasure and persuasion. After his conversion to Christianity, he developed a new understanding of language that

---

56. See Corbier, "Family and Kinship in Roman Africa," 277. Coribier explained that Augustine's condemnation of cousins marrying cousins is "not based on divine law, which he himself points out imposes no ban, but rather on his desire to multiply alliances . . . and to enlarge the circle of kinship."

allowed him to use his skill with rhetoric to do more than "to recite praise of the emperor which was full of lies, to those who, knowing I was lying, would give favors."[57] Instead, he began to use rhetoric to admonish friends to philosophy, to debate about the nature of the happy life, and to apologize for Christian teachings. As a pastor and a bishop, he believed that preaching was a vehicle for congregants to arrive at truth since he himself had only recognized Wisdom "through the ministry of your preacher."[58]

Other Christians sometimes claimed that rhetoric was a worthless study. But Augustine advocated for the teaching and use of rhetoric to all who would preach and teach Christianity. He explained in *On Doctrine,*

> Now because both true and false things seem persuasive through the art of rhetoric, who would dare to say that one ought to defend truth against liars while unarmed, so that those who know how to persuade about false things should know how to induce their listeners to be willing, attentive and docile, while the defenders of truth do not know how to do this? Should they proclaim their falsehoods briefly and openly, as if they are like the truth, while they who tell the truth tell it so that it is tedious to hear, hard to understand, and not likely to be believed?[59]

While Augustine had been ambivalent about his profession before his conversion, as a Christian, he was a bold advocate for the study of rhetoric. Humans learn in community through communication with language. Learning to communicate well with language is necessary for all who pursue and teach truth.

Good rhetoric skills are especially necessary in public dialogue and debate. And Augustine insisted that dialogue and debate are necessary for those involved in philosophical, theological, and ecclesiological conflicts. Augustine explained in the *Confessions* that it was a discussion with Faustus that helped lead him away from the Manicheans. Public debate was not encouraged by the gnostics, and he had to meet privately with their bishop to ask the questions he had. So Augustine, as a catholic Christian bishop, insisted upon public debates with Manichean leaders as well as with

57. Conf. Vi.vi.9: "recitare imperatori laudes, quibus plura mentirer et mentienti faveretur ab scientibus."

58. Conf. I.i.1: "per ministerium praedicatoris tui."

59. Doct. IV.ii.3: "Nam cum per artem rhetoricam et vera suadeantur et falsa, quis audeat dicere, adversus mendacium in defensoribus suis inermem debere consistere veritatem, ut videlicet illi qui res falsas persuadere conantur, noverint auditorem vel bene volum vel intentum vel docilem proemio facere; isti autem non noverint? Illi falsa breviter, aperte, verisimiliter et isti vera sic narrent ut audire taedeat, intellegere non pateat, credere postremo non libeat?"

Pelagians and Aryans. In a position of ecclesial power, he held fast to his claim that theological matters should not be decided by force but should be questioned, discussed, and debated. His confidence in the friendly heart of Truth grounded his desire for public debate.

Importantly, Augustine held the same belief about the necessity of public debate for political and ecclesial matters. The Donatists were not so much theological as ecclesial and political rivals to the catholic church in Africa. They insisted that their church was purer because they held apostates accountable. The Donatists believed their church had more authority because it was more pure. Augustine, a proponent of the catholic church because it was a universal church, found the Donatists to be narrowly and dangerously provincial and, like "frogs," they "clamored from the swamp, 'We alone are Christians.'"[60] At first, the Donatists refused to debate Augustine in public, claiming that he was a seducer of souls who could not be vanquished in debate but must be silenced with violence.[61] Augustine called their leaders cowardly for this position. He announced publicly that a call to violence demonstrated a lack of confidence in the accessibility of true propositions. Trust in Truth led to confidence to struggle with words rather than in violent acts.[62] Thus, Augustine spoke, preached, and wrote treatises against those whose doctrines he believed were incorrect.[63] According to Possidius, this increased the attendance at catholic Christian churches and made the Donatists more violent in protest. Possidius claimed that Augustine finally found a way to get the Donatists to debate. He condemned Crispinus, the Donatist bishop, for inciting violence through the teaching of heresy. He demanded that Crispinus be arrested and brought to court to pay a fine in gold. Brought to court, the Donatist had to prove that he was not a heretic, and Augustine was brought to debate him. The procounsel judge, after hearing the debate, declared Crispinus a heretic. The debate being the crucial matter, Augustine begged that the court not penalize Crispinus and asked for a pardon. According to Possidius, this public debate and Augustine's appeal to truth-telling rather than punishment led to a further

---

60. Enn. Ps. xcv.11: "clamant ranae de palude: Nos soli sumus christiani." See also Wilhite, *Ancient African Christianity*, 252.

61. See Possidius, *Vita* 9.

62. See Possidius, *Vita* 10.

63. See Bourke, *Augustine's Quest of Wisdom*, 162–66. Bourke noted that Augustine believed in disputation and public preaching; secular force was to be used only against the Donatists when they were upsetting the unity and peace of the region. Similarly, Augustine only advocated for the use of secular force against Polytheists when they became violent to Christians. See Epis. 93, "To Vincent" (407–408), for Augustine's own long discussion about the topic, which troubled him greatly.

diminished following for the Donatists and an increase in participation by those who called themselves catholic Christians who did not try to enforce a purity code on their congregants.[64] Augustine was then called to Caesarea to debate Emeritus, the Donatist bishop in that region. Their debate was also public. Augustine had the last word as Emeritus found that he could not answer Augustine's charges.[65]

According to Possidius, Augustine, throughout his time as Bishop of Hippo, only called for the use of secular force in order to stop violence and force public debate. His epistle to Vincentius, written in 408, explains how complicated his position could be, as he found ample examples in the Scriptures of prophets and teachers who did not fight back in any way against persecution. On one hand, he trusted that public debate, disputation, and discussion would lead to cooperation on all matters of diverse beliefs. On the other hand, he did not want people dissuaded from true principles by fear or ignorance. And he knew that tolerance and love on the part of catholic Christians could not mean that intolerance, hatred, and censorship of true ideas should be tolerated. While Augustine was conflicted on how to use secular power to best allow public debate and community dialogue, he was clear that public debate and community dialogue were the best human paths for truth.

Wisdom's Redemption of Philosophy

At the end of his life, Augustine was concerned about the collapse of trust in the public in the liberal arts, in public debate, and in the enterprise of philosophy generally. He spent his years as a priest and as a bishop advocating for all of these by evangelizing the Christian trust that Wisdom has a friendly heart. He held that Truth is immanently in relationship with all human truth seekers, not as an impassive light that can be ignored but a personally-involved, loving friend who grabs and pokes both those who earnestly wish to know and those who do not seem to care to know.

This Truth uses human community and discussion to teach in particular and immanent ways. For example, Possidius claimed that Augustine would change course mid-sermon saying that he felt that God was telling him to say something that perhaps some straying member of the congregation might need to hear. In one incident recounted by Possidius, Augustine found that he had suddenly found himself talking about the Manicheans in a sermon on a different matter. He learned later that a

64. See Possidius, *Vita* 12.
65. See Possidius, *Vita* 14.

businessman had been in the church and was struck particularly by this tangential comment. This man came to Augustine in tears days after hearing the sermon saying he was a Manichean who had given significant funds to the Manichean elite. He claimed that the words of Augustine's sermon had converted him away from the sect. Then he quoted the exact tangential phrase in the sermon as the phrase that rescued him. Possidius wrote that when Augustine told his friends about this incident, they were filled with wonder at God's working on behalf of human healing through their relationships with other human beings.[66]

Augustine's faith in a graceful God who is the Truth was not tangential but foundational to his way of talking and acting as a friend, teacher, pastor, and bishop. He believed that the love of Wisdom that burns in every human heart is not unrequited love; philosophy is a friendship with Wisdom. Augustine's philosophical prayers were not prayers that he might simply see the Truth but that he might deepen his relationship with Wisdom. He asked, "What are you, my God?"[67] and he understood the answer. "The highest, the best, the most powerful, the omnipotent, the friendliest and the most just, the most secret and the most present, the most beautiful and the most strong, the most firm and the most incomprehensible."[68] And then he begged,

> Speak to me through your mercy, tell me who you are to me,
> Sir, My God. Tell my soul, "I am your salvation." Tell me so that
> I may hear. Behold the ears of my heart before you, Sir. Open
> them and tell my soul, "I am your salvation." I will run after your
> voice and I will grab you. Don't hide your face from me.[69]

He believed that Wisdom could remake him into the kind of person who could know wisdom.[70] He believed Wisdom to be his omnipotent friend. Because Augustine was in relationship with Wisdom, a caring personal relationship, he could boldly ask questions and debate others.

66. See Possidius, *Vita* 15.

67. Conf. I.iv.4: "Quid es ergo, deus meus?"

68. Conf. I.iv.4: "summe, optime, potentissime, omnipotentissime, misericordissime et iustissime, secretissime et praesentissime, pulcherrime et fortissimo, stabilis et incomprehensibilis."

69. Conf. I.v.5: "dic mihi per miserationes tuas, domine deus meus, quid sis mihi. dic animae meae, 'salus tua ego sum': sic dic, ut audiam. ecce aures cordis mei ante te, domine. aperi eas et dic animae meae. 'salus tua ego sum.' Curram post vocem hanc et apprehendam te. Noli abscondere a me faciem tuam."

70. Conf. I.v.6: "Angusta est domus animae meae, quo venias ad eam: dilatetur abs te. ruinosa est: refice eam." (The house of my soul is too narrow, you will come to her, she will be broadened by you. She is in ruins, you will remake her.)

Augustine's method and admonition for philosophy is foundationally Christian. However, it is not parochial. Rather than clinging to his foundational premises about the friendly nature of Truth without further investigation, Augustine demanded that he, his friends, his readers, and his congregants constantly question, discuss, and debate. Because of his Christian foundations, he did not claim that there was a Christian method to finding truth but rather encouraged everyone to continue to pursue knowledge by examining faithfully held hypotheses with empiricism, reason, and dialogue. This admonition and the optimism that fueled it influenced the next 1,500 years of philosophical thought after his death.

Chapter 6

The Influence of Hope

Augustine's Epistemology and Later Philosophy,
Part I

And what human being can give understanding to another
human being? What angel can give understanding to another
angel? What angel can give understanding to a human? It must
be asked of you, sought in you, knocked at your door: then it
will be received, then it will be found, then it will be opened.[1]

AUGUSTINE ENDED HIS *CONFESSIONS* with the admonition that the reader
keep seeking Truth by knocking on Truth's door with the hope that this
door will be opened. While Augustine believed that human beings learn
in community with each other, he also insisted that the true ground of
their hope for wisdom was in Wisdom's friendly heart, not in accepting
his doctrinal stance. That said, his writings as the Doctor of Grace were
tremendously influential for the next 1,500 years of philosophy and theology. The recently released three-volume collection of *The Oxford Guide to
the Historical Reception of Augustine* bears witness to his enormous influence. Thus, no two chapters in a monograph could justly account for this.
Instead, this section of the book provides a few central examples of how
Augustinian hope in Truth's relationship with philosophers aided specific
thinkers and traditions. These examples will lead the reader to the final
chapter's analysis of how this hope might help twenty-first-century thinkers re-establish hope in the philosophical process so that, despite an up-
surge in conspiracy theories and nihilistic skepticism, readers today might
ask and seek, receive and find.

1. Conf. XIII.xxxviii.53: "et hoc intellegere quis hominum dabit homini? quis angelus angelo? quis angelus homini? a te petatur, in te quaeratur, ad te pulsetur: sic, sic
accipietur, sic invenietur, sic aperietur."

Late Antique North African and African-American Thought

While Augustine was an African who saw himself as an African preaching to Africans in Africa, his influence on African thought after late antiquity has been understudied. That said, there are a few points of documented direct influence that speak to the influence of Augustine's views on the advocacy of study and debate in the quest for truth in Africa. These points are important to remember because they demonstrate how Augustinian hope led directly to dialogue and debate rather than force and violence.

One example is that of Fulgentius of Ruspe, born in 468 under Vandal rule in North Africa and persecuted for his commitment to catholic Christianity. He was such an advocate of Augustine that he was known as "Augustinus breviatus," or little Augustine. In his writing *To Monimus* he demonstrated a commitment to Augustine's position that Christ gives wisdom:

> I do not cease to ask from our True Master of the House and Teacher to deign to teach me through the words of his Scriptures, through the conversations of my brothers and fellow students, or even through the interior and sweeter teaching of his inspiration (in which without the sound of the sermon and without the elements of letters the truth is so sweetly and secretly spoken) so that I can propose and I can assert that in my propositions and assertions I always adhere to the truth (which neither deceives nor is deceived) and I always am found obeying and agreeing.[2]

Fulgentius's commitment to his belief that Christ is the true teacher who does not deceive grounded his vocation as a master of debate. Fulgentius was considered a leading voice in dialogues and debate for catholic Christians.[3]

Similarly, Facundus of Hermiane, a bishop in what is now Tunisia, considered Augustine to be a model bishop and theologian because he insisted on having dialogue with those who disagreed with him rather than condemning them. Facundus believed that Augustine's use of friendly

---

2. Fulgentius, *Ad Monimum* I.iv.2: "Quapropter noc ab illo vero Domino ac Magistro nostro postulare non desino, ut ea me, sive per eloquia scripturarum suarum, seu per serminocinationem fratum condiscipulorumque meorum, sive etiam per inspirationis suae internam suavioremque doctrinam (ubi sine sonis sermonum et sine elementis litterarum eo dulcius quo secretius veritas loquitur) ea me docere dignetur, quae sic proponam, sic asseram, ut in propositionibus atque assertionibus meis, veritati (quae nec fallit, nec fallitur) semper inhaerum, semper obediens consentiensque reperiar."

3. See Ombretta, "Fulgentius of Ruspe," 274–76.

conversation brought about far greater unity in the church than the use of force or punishment. Importantly, Facundus saw that it was necessary to have real humility concerning one's own knowledge in order to truly pursue such conversation.[4]

The influence of Augustine on later North Africans who lived in the era of Byzantine rule and in the time of Arab reign is not well document-ed.[5] But it is worth remembering that North Africa remained a center of the liberal arts and natural sciences during these time periods. Whether or not the commitment to higher education and inquiry can be linked to the acceptance or even knowledge of Augustine's epistemology cannot be answered by current scholarship. However, it is documented that late antique Africans who left Africa for Europe brought their views of Au-gustine with them. For example, Julianus Pomerius, a North African who came to Provence, became a teacher to the Bishop of Arles. There, he wrote an influential handbook for bishops and pastors about the importance of contemplation and preaching.[6] Moreover, it is widely acknowledged that when the Moors in Spain rekindled European interest in the liberal arts and sciences, European scholars used Augustinian trust in the divine na-ture of Truth to advocate for the study of Arab science. This shall be seen in the section on Thomas Aquinas. Thus, Augustinian epistemology can be acknowledged as part of the foundation for the conversation between Europeans and Africans in the medieval period.

Contemporary post-colonial African philosophy by and large ignores Augustine. But it is worth noting that African-American thinkers hailed Augustine as one of "the most illustrious lights of the ancient church"[7] throughout the nineteenth century.[8] Interestingly, Harriet Beecher Stowe said of Sojourner Truth that there was something obviously African about the way she spoke and debated: "I cannot but think that Sojourner with the same culture might have spoken words as eloquent and undying as those of the African Saint Augustine or Tertullian."[9] While the nineteenth-century

---

4. See Petri, "Facundus of Hermiane," 969–70.

5. See Wilhite, "Augustine in Black and African Theology," 126–33.

6. See Leyser, "'Julianus' Pomerius," 1241–42.

7. Garnet quoted in Wilhite, "Augustine in Black and African Theology," 127.

8. See Wilhite, "Augustine in Black and African Theology," 127. For a contemporary look at African-American philosophy done in the Augustinian tradition, see Williams, *Christian Realism and the Ephesian Suggestion*, 238: "The essential self in this Christian context has always been construed to be a social self in communion with God; thus in Thurman and King, the self in its essence was more than a rational decision-maker—it was a self in community."

9. Stowe, "Sojourner Truth."

American tendency to link Augustine to African Americans was mostly based on race, it is worth noting the common theological and philosophical points as well. Indeed, Sojourner Truth was not just a great orator like Augustine, she shared the same trust that Christ was her teacher. She claimed she received her name directly from Christ.

> My name was Isabella; but when I left the house of bondage, I left everything behind. I wa'n't goin' to keep nothin' of Egypt on me, an' so I went to the Lord an' asked him to give me a new name. And the Lord gave me Sojourner, because I was to travel up an' down the land, showin' the people their sins, an' bein' a sign unto them. Afterward I told the Lord I wanted another name, 'cause everybody else had two names; and the Lord gave me Truth, because I was to declare the truth to the people.[10]

Whether or not Sojourner Truth had ever been told about Augustine's works[11] would not have been important to Augustine, himself. He would have been more interested that she had learned from her own lived experience that God has a friendly heart, rescuing those in bondage to error both through interior sight and through good preaching. Her trust in Jesus's friendly heart gave her the hope necessary to give speeches at conventions across the nation about abolition and women's suffrage for all forty years after she escaped slavery in 1843 until her death in 1883.

Women and Women's Philosophy

That Sojourner Truth would claim that Wisdom would choose a woman to spread the words of truth would not have surprised Augustine. There is a prejudice amongst some contemporary scholars that Augustine held a patriarchal philosophical view; however, the writings of Augustine were instrumental in encouraging antique, medieval, and modern women to engage in philosophy. Of course, it is accurate to say that as a political writer Augustine did not directly challenge the patriarchal structures of Roman and African society even though he acknowledged the plights of women in that society. At best, he praised and encouraged women, like his mother, who used submission, patience, and rhetorical skill to subvert the

10. Truth, *Narrative of Sojourner Truth,* 111.

11. Truth's first and last masters were Dutch Reformed, and the family with whom she stayed when she escaped was also of Dutch Reformed roots, although they had become Quakers. She herself joined the African Methodist Episcopal Church. She was well versed in Scripture and protestant Christian teachings. Thus, it is not impossible that Truth did know about Augustine and his theology.

abusive authority of men.[12] At worst, he claimed that female subjection to men was part of the post-Eden world order[13] and told women directly that they simply had to submit to their husband's wills.[14] But in the philosophical milieu, Augustine often treated women as equals. Moreover, his views were seen as especially liberating to philosophical women in his own era, the medieval era, and early modernity.

To begin in Augustine's own era, the young Augustine included his mother in most of his early dialogues and told her that her philosophy, her relationship with Wisdom, was important to him.[15] The older Augustine, the priest and bishop, also encouraged women to do philosophy. Nineteen of the existent letters of Augustine were written to women. Interestingly, it was to a convent of women that Augustine wrote the letter of advice on living peacefully in community that later became codified as the Rule

12. See Conf. IX.ix.19, where Augustine not only praised Monica for her ability to change Patricius's mind peacefully but also gave advice to women who wished to do likewise. It should be noted that in Ord. I.xi.32–33, Augustine portrayed his mother's humility as Christlike and the proud arrogance of the men in the dialogue as childish. This subversion of virtues is taken seriously by Hildegard of Bingen, who also said feminine submission is more divine than manly pride.

13. See DGM, II.xix.29: "dictum est: Erit tibi conversio ad virum tuum, et ipse tui dominabitur." (It is said: Your conversion will be towards your man and he will dominate you.)

14. See Epis. 262, "To Ecdicia" (395). This letter was written to a woman who took a vow of chastity and almsgiving, two vows Augustine praised, without her husband's consent. Her husband did join her in the vow of chastity for some time but then broke his vow with an affair with another woman. In answer to her complaint about this which was addressed to Augustine in a previous letter, Augustine asserted that she should have yielded to her husband's requests because "the wife has no power of her own body, but the man has this power." (*Uxor non habet potestatem corporis sui, sed vir*) Importantly, he also insisted "and in like manner the man has no power of his own body but the woman has this power." (*similiter autem et vir non habet potestatem corporis sui, sed mulier*). However, Augustine explained that there is a hierarchy of power between men and women. Thus, he asserted, she had no right to give all her gold away as alms without her husband's consent, "since the married woman is not allowed to say: 'I do what I want with my property,' since she is not her own, but belongs to her head, that is to her man." (*ubi mulierem coniugatam non licet dicere: "Facio quod volo de meo"; cum et ipsa non sit sua, sed capitis sui, hoc est viri sui.*) He also explained that "if any course of action appears to be better to you" (*si quid tibi forte melius videretur*) she should "suggest it respectfully to the man, following obediently his authority as he is your head" (*suggereres viro reverenter, eiusdemque auctoritatem tamquam tui capitis sequereris obedienter*) so that common sense and peace could then rule. Augustine's confidence in this letter that men will listen to the calm reason of women is also seen in Conf. IX.ix.19.

15. See Ord. I.xi.31. For an analysis of Monica and Augustine's philosophical relationship, see Conybeare, *Irrational Augustine*, 61–138.

for Augustinian Monks.[16] Augustine's letters to individual women were often philosophical in nature and demonstrated that Augustine expected women to engage in philosophical and theological debate. For example, in a letter to Proba, a wealthy woman who had asked Augustine about prayer, he quoted Cicero in order to admonish her to the study of philosophy. He claimed that philosophy would help her determine what it was fitting for her to desire. This she needed to know so that she could pray correctly for what would bring happiness for herself and others.[17] Moreover, in a letter to Maxima, a woman who was concerned that many in her province were in error, Augustine expressed delight that she recognized their errors and wished to confront them in debate. He encouraged her to be as compassionate as a dove and as wise as a serpent as she strove to teach those in error. He promised to send copies of any of his books that she felt might be helpful to her in the debates.[18]

Augustine's trust in women's ability to pursue philosophical debate came directly from his trust in Wisdom's illumination.[19] This is seen in a letter to Paulina, who specifically asked a question about epistemology. To this woman, he wrote fifty-seven chapters in an attempt to answer her difficult question about whether God could be seen by bodily eyes, even while acknowledging that she should not trust his opinion as people "make more progress by thinking and praying than by reading and listening [to him]."[20] Augustine insisted that Paulina ought to consult Scripture and the "truth that is demonstrated more internally."[21] Then, he continued to write what

16. See Epis. 211 (423–424). While there is no title in the address, historians believe the letter was sent to sisters in a convent founded in Hippo.

17. See Epis. 130.5.10, "To Proba" (412): "quidam eorum vir eloquentissimus ait: Ecce autem alii non philosophi quidem, sed prompti tamen ad disputandum, omnes aiunt esse beatos qui vivunt ut ipsi velint. Falsum id quidem: velle enim quod non deceat, idem ipsum miserrimum; nec tam miserum est non adipisci quod velis, quam adipisci velle quod non oporteat. Quid tibi videtur? haec verba nonne ab ipsa veritate per quemlibet hominem dicta sunt." (For the most eloquent man of these [philosophers] says: 'Look however at these others who are not philosophers nevertheless are taken with disputation, they say that all those are happy who live as they wish. This is false, for indeed, to wish for what is not fitting can be most miserable; it is not miserable to not obtain what you wish if what you wish to obtain is not appropriate.' How does this seem to you? Were these words not said by Truth herself through the speech of a person? Truth is spoken through a person?)

18. See Epis. 264, "To Maxima" (395).

19. Se BV ii.10, where he claims that Monica's insight comes from a divine source (*divino fonte*).

20. Epis. 147.1.1, "To Paulina" (413–414): "plus cogitando et orando proficiunt, quam legendo et audiendo."

21. Epis. 147.1.2, "To Paulina" (413–414): "aut interius demonstranti veritati."

amounted to a long disputation with himself about how to reconcile two of his most important philosophical premises: that God must be considered incorporeal rather than material and that Jesus is God in the flesh—a human figure, held in Mary's arms, who was seen by many people during the span of his life and death. Augustine, in this letter, also acknowledged the accounts of the Divine being made manifest to Adam, Eve, Cain, Abraham, Sarah, Jacob, Moses, and many others throughout the Old Testament. Throughout the letter, he insisted that Scripture can be trusted as an account of empirical evidence observed by human beings with their senses. "Indeed, these were done in bodily ways, and certainly could have been seen through the body if we had been there, but now, however, they are not present."[22] Therefore, because these things were not present *to him*, he had to believe these things on faith, which relies on an interior sight rather than the sight of bodily eyes. His disputation continued. On one hand, he asserted that God can be seen by those with a clean heart. But on the other hand, he acknowledged that Genesis proclaimed that God was seen face to face by the wrestler, Jacob, and even by the first murderer, Cain. The Book of Job proclaimed even the Devil himself saw and spoke to God. Thus, finally, Augustine explained his solution to the paradox by proclaiming that all knowledge of God and Truth comes only by the power of God. "No, it is not in our power to see but in his power to appear."[23] The rest of the letter, however, is an admission that this solution does not solve the metaphysical problem about how an incorporeal God can be seen by bodily eyes. This letter, while it did not provide a solution to Paulina's metaphysical quandary, did demonstrate an important epistemological principle made frequently by Augustine: namely that all knowledge and vision of the Truth comes from the Truth itself. This insight meant that women as well as men could do philosophy, for it is not the philosopher but Wisdom who makes knowledge possible.

The activity of Wisdom is also the foundation of a letter to Florentina, a woman whose studies had been noticed by Augustine. Her parents had requested that he write to her because she longed to ask him certain questions. Rather than writing to her as a teacher, however, Augustine insisted that "often in the official duty of sharing, there is a reward of receiving."[24] He suggested to her that in the process of their dialogue, "You may come to know

---

22. Epis. 147.1.6, "To Paulina" (413–414): "Haec enim etiam corporaliter facta sunt, et videri per corpus, si tunc adessemus, utique potuerunt: nunc autem non adsunt."

23. Epis. 147.6.18, "To Paulina" (413–414): "Neque enim in potestate nostra est videre, sed in potestate illius apparere."

24. Epis. 266.1, "To Florentina" (395): "nam saepe officium impertiendi meritum est accipiendi."

about this thing which neither of us know."[25] Thus, Augustine insisted that he was not going to be her teacher, for his Teacher and hers was Christ. And he warned her not to have a false humility before him pretending that she did not know what she knew. He assured her, "You must know that the less you need to learn anything from me or from any person anywhere, the more certainly, more solidly, and more sanely do I rejoice in your faith, hope and delight."[26] Profoundly, he ended his letter telling her that she ought to

> ask what you will so that I may not be superfluous to you by teaching you to recognize what you know, but nevertheless you must hold most firmly that even though you may be able to learn something helpful through me, He will teach you who is the interior Teacher to the interior person. He will show you in your heart what is true, as it is said, "Neither the one who plants nor the one who irrigates does anything, but it is God who gives growth."[27]

Augustine's trust in Wisdom's friendly heart allowed him to recognize women as philosophers and to encourage them in their pursuit. This Augustinian hope for women—that they could pursue wisdom—was established anew in the European middle ages by Hildegard of Bingen. Hildegard, a twelfth-century German theologian, philosopher, scientist, musician, and artist, was according to legend first a precocious child who was told by her nurse that she needed to hide her unusual intellectual talents as they could be dangerous for a woman. Tithed to a local convent at the age of seven or eight, Hildegard was given a religious and scientific education at the abbey of Disibodenberg where she likely was exposed directly to the works of Augustine. Whether or not she read these works herself or simply heard about them, her famous description of her illumination by God bears a striking resemblance to Augustine's account of his experience of the Truth shining above the eyes of his soul. Hildegard wrote, "A burning light coming from the open heavens poured into my whole cerebrum, and it inflamed my whole heart and my chest like a flame which does not burn but generates heat, just as the sun generates heat in something over which it sends its

25. Epis. 266.1, "To Florentina" (395): "noveris pro hac ipsa re quam pariter nescimus."

26. Epis. 266.4, "To Florentina" (395): "Proinde tanto me certius, tanto solidius, tanto sanius gaudere scias de fide et spe et dilectione tua, quanto minus indigueris, non tantum a me quidquam discere, sed ab ullo prorsus hominum."

27. Epis. 266.4, "To Florentina" (395): "quaeras quod vis, ne sim superfluus, si conatus fuero docere quod scis: dum tamen firmissime teneas, quod etsi aliquid salubriter per me scire potueris, ille te docebit qui est interioris hominis magister interior, qui in corde tuo tibi ostendit verum esse quod dicitur; quia neque qui plantat est aliquid, neque qui rigat, sed qui incrementum dat Deus."

rays."[28] Suddenly, Hildegard found that she understood the truths contained in Scripture. Hildegard, unlike Augustine, was not immediately grateful for her new way of thinking; she was bewildered because she had been taught that women were forbidden to teach, preach, or write in philosophy on account of their feeble abilities in these areas. For a time, she refused to write or speak about her insights. She, however, was encouraged to write and preach what God who is Truth was teaching her through inward illumination. This encouragement came from several mentors, including Bernard de Clairveaux, an avid reader of Augustine.[29]

At their insistence, Hildegard felt compelled to answer what she saw as a call from God. She began to paint images of her insights and write explanations. As she did so, she put forth a feminine version of Augustinian epistemology to explain how she knew what she knew. She insisted that knowledge is always a gift of grace from the divine, a gift that can be given to men or to women because insight is not accomplished by the individual on her own. Women have a clearer understanding of this, in Hildegard's view, because their nature is generally less clever than that of men. Women, therefore, are more likely to recognize that their knowledge is a gift of God and not an accomplishment of their own merit. Moreover, because society is less likely to attribute a woman's knowledge to her own cleverness, a wise woman more surely can be recognized as being illuminated by the divine Truth and, thus, better able to teach others. In this way, Hildegard subverted the misogynism of her culture as she argued for the divine illumination of women. That women cannot by their own talents access truths only serves to prove that Truth must be teaching women. She used such arguments to encourage other women to write and teach in philosophy and theology as well.[30]

Hildegard's feminine appropriation of Augustine had other philosophical consequences. Like Augustine, she insisted that the most dangerous sin was pride in one's own individual reason,[31] a sin that she linked to the

28. Hildegard, *Scivias* preface 383: "igneum lumen aperto coelo veniens, totum cerebrum meum transtudit, et totum cor totum que pectus meum velut flamma non tamen ardens, sed calens ita inflammavit, ut sol rem aliquam calefacit super quam radios suos immittet."

29. See Bernard of Clairvaux, "Letter to Hildegard": "Congratulamur gratiae Dei, quae in te est. . . . Ceterum ubi interior eruditio est et unctio docens de omnibus, quid nos aut docere possumus aut monere? Rogamus magis et suppliciter postulamus ut nostri memoriam habeas apud Deum et eorum pariter, qui nobis spirituali societate in Domino iuncti sunt." (We rejoice with you in the grace of God which is in you. . . . For the rest, where there is inner erudition and anointment teaching about all things, what can we teach or instruct? We ask and we beg that you remember us with God and also those who are joined with us by spiritual society in the Lord.)

30. See, for example, Hildegard, "Letter to Elisabeth of Schoneau."

31. See Hildegard, "Letter to Elisabeth of Schoneau": "Solus autem homo illum non

fall of Lucifer.[32] As a contrast, Hildegard held up the humble trust of Eve, whom Hildegard held blameless in the expulsion from Eden, claiming that the Devil used what was best in Eve—her trust in her community members—against her.[33] Hildegard, like Augustine, insisted that human beings are social animals who pursue Truth in community. She held up friendly faith in others as an important virtue and stressed the dependence of the human being on the environment of her earthly home. Against the gnostics of her age, the Cathars, she made arguments about the goodness of the earth, the importance of taking care of the bodies of the poor and the sick, and the relevance of using music and rhetoric in teaching and preaching the Word so that it can delight human ears. In the twelfth century, Hildegard's well regarded reputation forced European medieval society to reconsider the role of women in intellectual pursuits. Hildegard's appropriation of Augustinian arguments helped her dispute the impossibility of a wise woman.

In early modernity, literacy among women increased throughout Europe, in part because of Martin Luther's insistence that all Christians be able to read the Bible. Importantly, these women, in addition to reading Scripture, also read Augustine.[34] Recovered journals of European women from the sixteenth and early seventeenth century contain numerous references to Augustine's writings, and women's private libraries frequently contained a number of Augustine's texts. Indeed, the *Confessions* became a model of spiritual autobiography which many women of this era imitated.[35] Importantly, these women often resonated with Augustine's humility, insisting that "it is not in my owne power to doe good unless thou enable me."[36] This humility in modern women, which was not always present in modern men, was nourished by Augustine's insistence on the gracious friendship of Truth

---

cognovit. Nam cum Deus magnam scientiam homini paret, homo in animo suo se erexit, et se a Deo avertit. Deus omnium, illum sic inspexerat, quod cuncta opera sua in illo perficeret. Sed antiquus deceptor illum fefellit, et crimine inobedientiae illum infecit cum delectatione incongrui venti, dum plus quaereret quam deberet. Ah! o vae!" (Alone, however the human did not recognize him. For when God prepared great knowledge for the human, the human pumped up his own soul himself and turned himself from God. God of all, inspected him, that he might perfect all his works in him. But the ancient deceiver tricked him and infected him with the crime of disobedience and delight in the unstable wind, when he questioned more than he ought. Oh Woe!)

32. Hildegard, *Scivias* I.II.389: "Lucifer qui ob superbiam suam de coelesti Gloria ejectus est." (Lucifer who by his pride was ejected from the Gloria of heaven.)

33. For Hildegard's entire account of the expulsion from Eden, see Hildegard, *Scivias* I.II.

34. See Molekamp, "Women Readers," 1920–22.

35. See, for example, Clifford, *Diary of Anne Clifford 1616–1619*; Hoby, *Diary of Lady Margaret Hoby (1599–1605)*; Isham, *My Booke of Rememberance.*

36. Isham quoted in Molekamp, "Women Readers," 1921.

that was available to all who sought relationship with her. Importantly, while few secular contemporary feminists quote Augustine regularly, Augustine's relational understanding of both the self and Truth bears striking similarity to what some call "feminist epistemology."

Thomas, Thomism, and Roman Catholicism

Within the Roman Catholic tradition there are many who have argued that the epistemology of Thomas Aquinas broke significantly with that of Augustine. And there are, of course, many excellent books available that discuss both the use of Augustine's ideas by Thomas Aquinas and the key differences in their viewpoints. In contrast, this section does not articulate the intricacies of Thomas's epistemology and his conception of Christian philosophy in comparison with that of the African Doctor. Rather, this section simply emphasizes in Thomas's work that which was in common with Augustine, namely his foundational trust in God's friendly heart.

Thomas Aquinas is a key figure in Western philosophy. He is often considered the most important authority in the Roman Catholic Intellectual Tradition. In great part this was because he was a successful proponent of the liberal arts tradition that Augustine hoped to see remain vibrant in Christianity. Thomas is particularly significant in that he successfully argued to the European Christian community that they must take seriously the ideas and works of scholars outside the Christian tradition, especially the works of Aristotle, Maimonides, and many Muslim scientists and philosophers. He advocated to European Christians that they must read and engage with both those thinkers who agree with their positions and also those thinkers who do not agree, for all those who look for the truth can be of help to each other.[37] In so doing, he advocated for a fundamental trust in 'the community of wisdom seekers, a trust that Augustine also shared and preached, a trust that was grounded in Truth's friendly heart. By advocating for this trust and the dialogue that this trust inspires, Thomas helped a

---

37. See Thomas Aquinas, *Sententia Metaphysicae* II.i.1 n.16: "Et ideo dicit, quod iustum est gratiam habere non solum his, quos quis existimat veritatem invenisse, quorum opinionibus aliquis communicat sequendo eas; sed eitam illis, qui superficialiter locuti sunt ad veritatem investigandam, licit eorum opinions non sequamur; quia isti etiam aliquid conferunt nobis. Praestiterunt enim nobis quoddam exercitium circa inquisitionem veritatis." (That is, it is right that we should be grateful not only for those with whom we think we have found truth and with whose opinions we agree and follow, but also with those who spoke superficially in their investigation of truth so that we do not follow their opinions, for they too conferred their other opinions to us. Indeed, they have presented to us their exercises about their inquiry into truth.)

fledgling European intellectual tradition expand and thrive. Subsequently, later thinkers have used his arguments when they wished to call for dialogue amongst diverse people. As a prominent example, the 1879 edition of the *Summa Theologica* begins with an encyclical from Pope Leo XIII addressing all the patriarchs, primates, archbishops, and bishops of the Roman Catholic world to read Thomas's work in order that they might look again at the importance of doing philosophy.[38] This was reprinted in the 1920 edition of the *Summa*, which also included two new points of canon law issued by Pope Benedict XV requiring all religious to study at least two years of philosophy and four years of theology following Thomas's method.[39] More recently, Pope John Paul II's 1998 encyclical *Faith and Reason* (*Fides et Ratio*) used references to both Thomas and Augustine to argue for renewed hope in dialogue and the study of philosophy.

To begin, while Thomas was a very different type of writer than Augustine, he recognized the same divine friendly heartedness. Indeed, it is worth noting that Thomas's explanation of *misericordia* in the *Summa* gives a strong argument for the English translation of the term as "friendly heartedness." Thomas defined *misericordia* as compassion for another's suffering[40] and claimed that it arises

> through a union of affection, which arises through love. For indeed one who is loving looks upon a friend as another self, and looks and counts the friend's hurt as if it was his own. And he grieves for his friend's hurt as though for his own. And this is why the philosopher in the Ethics Book IX put forth that between friends there is the sharing of grief in friendship. And the apostle says, in Romans 12, to rejoice with those who rejoice and to cry with those who cry.[41]

Importantly, Thomas noted that this is not a supreme virtue in human beings because it is most properly attributed to God who offers *misericordia* (a friendly heart) to human beings, although people should also try always

38. See Leo XIII, "Encyclical Letter," ix–xxxiii.

39. See Benedict XV, "New Codex of Canon Law," xxxiii.

40. Thomas Aquinas, *Summa Theologica* II-II q.30 a.2 co: "Respondeo dicendum quod, cum misericordia sit compassion super miseria aliena." (I respond saying that, since misericordia is compassion for the suffering of another.)

41. Thomas Aquinas, *Summa Theologica* II-II q.30 a.2 co: "Uno modo, secundum unionem affectus, quod fit per amorem. Quia enim amans reputat amicum tanquam seipsum, malum impius reputat tanquam suum malum, et ideo dolet de malo amici sicut de suo. Et inde est quod philosophus, in IX Ethic., inter alia amicabilia point hoc quod est condolere amico. Et apostolus dicit, ad Rom. XII, gaudere cum gaudentibus, flere cum flentibus."

to relate to their neighbors with a friendly heart.[42] Moreover, Thomas indicated that Christians know that God is their friend because Christ says
so when he tells his disciples "as it says in John 15, 'I no longer call you
servants, but my friends.'"[43] Like Augustine, Thomas noted that the believer
only knows of this friendship because the divine friend reveals it. The oft
quoted verse from Thomas's Eucharistic hymn *I adore you, God* (*Adoro te,
Deus*) reminds the philosopher as well as the congregant that it is Truth
who speaks truths to people:

> What God's Son has said, I believe is true;
>
> Truth spoken by the Word, nothing is more true.[44]

Of course, it must be admitted, Thomas spoke more about friendship
with God in his discussions on ethics than those concerning epistemology.
That said, there is a recognition evident in the writings of Thomas that the
philosopher comes to know about God who is Truth only through the help
of grace. He wrote,

> I respond saying that the cognition of God that is had by us
> through grace is more perfect than that which is had by natu-
> ral reason. This is proved thus. Indeed, the cognition that we
> have through natural reason contains two things: images de-
> rived from sensible objects; and the natural intelligible light, by
> the virtue of which we abstract from these images intelligible
> conceptions. And in both of these, human cognition is helped
> by the revelation of grace. Now the natural intellectual light is
> activated by the infusion of gratuitous light.[45]

Certainly, this passage is of a different tone than Augustine's passionate
addresses to Truth herself—that she might help him lest he know nothing
about anything without her aid. Yet the reader must note that Thomas insisted that God provides both the universally available natural light of truth
and the light of grace.

42. See Thomas Aquinas, *Summa Theologica* II-II q.30 a.4.

43. John 15:15 quoted in *Summa Theologica* II-II q.23 a.1: "Ioan. XV dicitur, iam
non dicam vos servos, sed amicos meos."

44. Thomas Aquinas, "Hymn 98": "Credo quidquid dixit Dei filius, Nihil veritatis
verbo verius" (I believe anything said by God's Son, nothing is more true than the Truth
of the Word)

45. Thomas Aquinas, *Summa Theologica* I q.12 a.13: "Respondeo dicendum quod
per gratiam perfectior cognitio de Deo habetur a nobis, quam per rationem naturalem.
Quod sic patet. Cognitio enim quam per naturalem rationem habemus, duo requirit:
scilicet, phantasmata ex sensibilibus accepta, et lumen naturale intelligibile, cuius vir-
tute intelligibiles conceptiones ab eis abstrahimus. Et quantum ad utrumque, iuvatur
humana cognitio per revelationem gratiae. Nam et lumen naturale intellectus conforta-
tur per infusionem luminis gratuiti."

Importantly, his insistence on the universal light hoped to inspire scientists of his day to investigate the natural world with rigor. Unfortunately, some later theologians clung to Thomas's appropriation of Aristotle's biology and physics rather than to his Augustinian epistemological hope. Unfortunately, these later theologians condemned women who refuted Aristotle's biological categorizations of women and scientists who refuted Aristotle's physics. But it is interesting that much later, Galileo, when he first was condemned by the Roman Catholic church, turned to Augustine's writings to justify his work. Indeed, Galileo quoted Augustine in his *Letter to the Grand Duchess Christina* and then insisted that the God who created human beings with senses, reason, and intellect would not expect human beings to forego their use.[46] Galileo had found in Augustine the same message that Thomas had: the creator had made an intelligible world and had constructed human beings with the senses and reason so that they might make sense of it. This did not rescue Galileo's work in his own time from condemnation; he was put under house arrest and forced to recant his *Dialogue Concerning the Two Chief World Systems.* But 350 years later, when the Vatican officially recognized his condemnation as an error, Galileo's commitment to the pursuit of knowledge was acknowledged. While neither Thomas nor Galileo spoke as intimately about their relationship with Wisdom as Augustine had, they both grounded their hope in knowing Truth on God's desire that human beings know truth.

Importantly, this hope ought not lead to arrogance but humility. It is when it leads to arrogance in one's own previous knowledge that this hope becomes dangerously anti-philosophical. Indeed, Pope Leo XIII admonished Roman Catholics to read Thomas's *Summa* because he found that his work helped to beat back a dangerous pride in individual reason that had grown during the Enlightenment.[47] Thomas, like Augustine, insisted that people accept that they must learn from each other and only by the help of God. More recently, Bishop Robert Barron made a similar point when he advocated that contemporary people become more like Thomas in their public discourse. Barron reminded his readers that Thomas wrote the *Summa* as if it were a public disputation with all the great minds he knew in both his past and present. Thomas asked questions and then gave the disparate answers of Augustine, Aristotle, Plato, Cicero, Maimonides, and many others from diverse religious traditions as well as answers he found in Scripture. Thomas was charitable in his reading of each of the figures he quoted, even when he made a counter argument. Barron explained that this is a good model for all public argument and discussion. He urged his

46. See Galileo, "Letter to the Grand Duchess," 5.
47. See Leo XIII, "Encyclical Letter," xxix.

readers to imitate Thomas by listening to others, being charitable in inter-
preting their views, and arguing logically and civilly.[48] While Barron did
not say so explicitly, imitating this style requires a trust that Truth can be
found through discussion and argument, for no one should fear listening
to others if the Truth wills to be known. Indeed, Barron did make this
argument implicitly by shaming post-modern philosophers who, in his
opinion, lack such faith, evidenced by their skeptical refusal to assent to
any conclusion. Moreover, Barron suggested that only such faith can provide the truly comforting and safe space that many contemporary students
desire when having difficult conversations.

The most recent formal Roman Catholic teaching concerning philosophy was presented in Pope John Paul II's Encyclical *Fides et Ratio*. John
Paul II, a professional philosopher before becoming a cardinal and then
pope, began this document with a call to all readers to remember philosophy's original vocation to pursue the innate desire for Truth that is in every
human heart.[49] The document presents philosophy as a global pursuit of
Truth, pursued in all the nations and all the eras of human history. The pope
made clear that the philosopher ought to be in conversation with thinkers from different creeds and locations than her own. This need for global
relationships is key as the document was issued to address the skepticism
that had arisen from modern Western philosophy and its dependence on
an individual using reason on her own. The document stresses the need to
trust others. The pope considered the modern focus on the individual to be
a view inspired by "the blindness of pride" which "deceived our first parents
into thinking themselves sovereign and autonomous, and into thinking
that they could ignore the knowledge which comes from God"[50] as well
as the knowledge that comes from trust in our human communities. The
pope stressed the social nature of the human being, saying, "Human beings
are not made to live alone."[51] The encyclical stresses that it is important
that "we entrust ourselves to the knowledge acquired by other people,"[52]
and claims "friendship as one of the most appropriate contexts for sound
philosophical enquiry."[53] John Paul II supported the method of faith seeking understanding by explaining that

---

48. Barron, "Thomas Aquinas."

49. John Paul II, "Fides et Ratio" 3.

50. John Paul II, "Fides et Ratio" 22.

51. John Paul II, "Fides et Ratio" 31.

52. John Paul II, "Fides et Ratio" 32.

53. John Paul II, "Fides et Ratio" 33.

belief is often humanly richer than mere evidence, because it involves an interpersonal relationship and brings into play not only a person's capacity to know but also the deeper capacity to entrust oneself to others, to enter into a relationship with them which is intimate and enduring.[54]

Importantly, the pope also claimed the hope of the philosopher is grounded in relationship with Wisdom, who is revealed through the Incarnation.[55] As a whole, the document is a rousing letter, calling together insights from a great number of diverse scholars and urging readers to philosophy, to the friendly relationship with the Wisdom who grounds and grows all human relationships.[56]

Thomas Aquinas's teachings are often considered the heart of the Roman Catholic Intellectual tradition today. But Thomas, like Augustine, did not advocate that others rely on his doctrines but on the friendly heart of Truth as their foundation. Etienne Gilson, a philosopher who proudly labeled himself as a Thomist throughout his life, explained in his short book *Philosophy and Incarnation According to Saint Augustine* that without Augustine's understanding of God's grace, the philosopher must despair of knowing her world:

> God alone has saved Augustine of despair, because the Christian God is at the same time the One who is, the One who creates, and the One who saves. Philosophy is not unable to recognize the one who is and even the one who creates. But the one who saves remains for her a mystery that renders the world intelligible.[57]

In other words, a philosopher can only understand her world if the maker of that world gives her help.

---

54. John Paul II, "Fides et Ratio" 32.

55. See John Paul II, "Fides et Ratio" 12: "Through this Revelation, men and women are offered the ultimate truth about their own life and about the goal of history." See also 33: "Moving beyond the stage of simple believing, Christian faith immerses human beings in the order of grace, which enables them to share in the mystery of Christ, which in turn offers them a true and coherent knowledge of the Triune God. In Jesus Christ, who is the Truth, faith recognizes the ultimate appeal to humanity, an appeal made in order that what we experience as desire and nostalgia may come to its fulfilment."

56. For a detailed explanation of *Fides et Ratio* philosophy about relationships, see Gardiner, "Entrusting Ourselves," 337–45.

57. Gilson, *Philosophie et Incarnation selon Saint Augustin*, 54–55: "Dieu seul a sauvé Augustin de ce désespoir, parce que le Dieu chrétien est à la fois Celui qui est, Celui qui crée et Celui qui sauvé. La philosophie n'est pas sans connaître celui qui est et même celui que crée. Mais celui qui suave reste pour elle un mystère seul rend le monde intelligible."

Chapter 7

The Influence of Hope

Augustine's Epistemology and Later Philosophy,
Part II

Martin Luther and Lutheranism

IF IT IS TRUE, as Pope Leo XIII said, that "reason can now hardly rise higher than she rose, borne up in the flight of Thomas,"[1] then a cynic could claim that reason could hardly have fallen lower than when she was condemned by Luther as "the devil's bride and most lovely mistress."[2] It might seem impossible that the the the epistemologies of Thomism and Lutheranism have a common root. But, indeed, they share a grounding in Augustine's foundational trust that humans come to know only through relationship with the Truth herself. This is not to say that Thomas and Luther shared much in common in regard to philosophical method. There are enormous differences between them. Scholars have been right to discuss these differences and how these differences have led to divergent paths in theology, philosophy, and science. That said, these two intellectual giants shared a foundational trust that the Truth, who does not deceive, works with human beings as embodied social animals who learn from empirical evidence and conversation through the help of the natural and gracious light of Truth herself.

Scholars have analyzed the relationship between Augustine's writings and the work of Martin Luther for the last five hundred years with particular emphasis on the Augustinian influence in Luther's doctrine of justification. Importantly, Luther, too, was interested in this relationship. He often noted where he found himself directly in line with Augustine and where, in a few instances, he felt that Augustine was not useful. However, the influence of Augustine on Luther's understanding of philosophy has been vastly understudied. Perhaps this is because at first glance Augustine and the Augustinian

---

1. Leo XIII, "Encyclical Letter," xxiv.

2. Luther, "Predigt am 2. Sonntag nach Epiphonia" (WA 51:126): "aber des Teufels Braut, ratio, die schöne Metze."

monk seem to have opposing views. Augustine, who found philosophy to be the friendly love of wisdom and, as such, a friendly relationship with Christ, would likely have been shocked to hear Luther's claim that philosophy was "the woman who should be quiet in church."[3] Furthermore, Augustine, who rushed to the bosom of philosophy to find everything that could move him when he was frightened or in doubt,[4] would likely have been confused to hear that Luther announced that "we say that philosophy knows nothing at all about the human being."[5] For many scholars, these differences closed the case on Augustine's influence on Luther's view of philosophy and epistemology. Augustine was a philosopher; Luther a theologian. Augustine favored believing in order to understand; Luther insisted on faith alone.

On one hand, it is a fair assessment to claim that Augustine's view of philosophy as a passionate love affair with Wisdom differs greatly from Luther's understanding of philosophy as the secular discipline used to analyze sentences and justify one's self, a discipline he found easily corrupted.[6] On the other hand, this assessment is only fair at the most superficial level of their uses of the word philosophy. For the kind of philosophy that Luther disparaged was the same kind of philosophy that Augustine also pushed aside. Indeed, Luther himself qualified that the type of philosophy that knows nothing about human beings is a specific type of Aristotelian philosophy also ignored by Augustine. He wrote,

> Aristotle proposes a prime mover. He concludes that everything is done by the prime mover with interior cooperation, and therefore he dreams that the prime mover acts as a nursemaid who moves the cradle of a child, yet admires herself. So does Aristotle condemn us. In sum, philosophers know nothing of God the creator and the human being made of a glob of earth. Augustine says that he himself found all things in the Platonic books, except this one thing that the Word was made flesh. But

---

3. Luther, "Die Disputation de Sententia" (WA 39.2:4): "Sed ubiubi impingit vel forma syllogistica vel ratio philosophica, dicendum est ei illud Pauli: Mulier in Ecclesia taceat." (But wherever the syllogistic form or philosophical reason impinges, the saying of Paul must be applied: The woman should be quiet in church.) See 1 Cor 14:34.

4. See CA II.ii.3

5. Luther, "Die Disputation de Homine" (WA 39.1:179): "Non dicimus, quod philosophia nihil omnino sciat de homine."

6. Luther, "Die Disputation de Homine" (WA 39.1:180): "Diabolus regnat in optimis etiam virtutibus. Philosophia est prudential carnis inimical Deo. Haec est laus philosophiae." (The Diabolic One reigns even in the best virtues. Philosophy is the prudence of the flesh which is hostile to God. This is praise of philosophy.)

Hermegistus composed that book of Plato and stole it all from
the Gospel of John.[7]

In other words, Luther insisted that Augustine found Plato to be a help to
his understanding of himself or his God, not Aristotle. Moreover, Luther
claimed that Augustine's Platonism truly came only from the Gospel of
John, which declared in words proclaimed by the Word that the one who is
the Truth came out of love to dwell with human beings. Indeed, Augustine
himself insisted that the fundamental core of his philosophy was his relationship with Truth, who became incarnate. Augustine wrote that this was
missing in the books of the Platonists.[8]

Additionally, while Thomas Aquinas did not find Aristotle's philosophy antithetical to Augustine's and wrote convincing arguments for the
benefits of synthesizing their views, Luther was right to note that Augustine
himself did reject Aristotle after a brief encounter with the Greek philosopher's work. In the *Confessions,* Augustine declared that the philosophy of
Aristotle, insofar as he knew it, was of no benefit to him:

> And what benefit was produced for me around the year I was
> twenty, when Aristotle's work came into my hands? I read this
> alone and understood it by myself, this work which is called
> the *Ten Categories.* . . . The meaning of the book seemed clear
> enough to me. It was speaking about substance . . . and its quali-
> ties. . . . How did this profit me when I tried to understand you,
> my God, who are wonderful, simple, and unchangeable, and
> thought I could comprehend anything by using these ten cat-
> egories? As if you are a substance, and magnitude and beauty
> were your attributes? . . . Indeed, it was false how I understood
> you, it was not truth. It was a figment of my misery, not a firm
> image of your beatitude.[9]

7. Luther, "Die Disputation de Homine" (WA 39.1:179–80): "Aristoteles facit primum mobile vel movens. Concludit inde omnia interiore cooperante primo movente
fieri, et ita somniat, quod primum movens sic agat, ut ancilla, quae cunas pueri movet,
se tamen intuetur. Sic condemnat nos Aristoteles. In summa, philosophi nihil sciunt de
creatore deo et homine de gleba terrae facto. Augustinus ait, se omnia invenisse in Pla-
tonicis libris, nisi hoc unum, quod verbum caro factum sit. Sed Hermegistus composuit
istum librum Platonis et omnia surripuit ex Ioannis evangelio."

8. See Conf. VII.ix.14.

9. Conf. IV.xvi.28–29: "Et quid mihi proderat, quod annos natus ferme viginti, cum
in manus meas venissent Aristotelica quaedam, quas appaellant decem categorias[?] . . .
et satis aperte mihi videbantur loquentes de substantiis, . . . et quae in illis essent, . . .
Quid hoc mihi proderat, quando et oberat, cum etiam te, deus meus, mirabiliter simpli-
cem atque incommutabilem, illis decem praedicamentis putans quidquid esset omnino
comprehensum, sic intelligere conarer, quasi et tu subiectum esses magnitudini tuae aut

Augustine did not think that the analysis of substances into categories could help someone understand themselves or God. But this analysis was not what Augustine meant by philosophy. What Augustine meant by philosophy was a relationship with Wisdom, initiated by Wisdom, who taught humans that they were created and loved by Wisdom in the world. This relationship that begins by hearing the Word, Luther was more likely to call theology.[10] But despite that difference in vocabulary, the point in common is that both agreed that human beings are always in relationship with the Truth they seek and that this relationship grounds the hope they have of understanding themselves and their world.

This is where the reader finds that Luther and Augustine had a similar view about the quest for knowledge of one's self and God. Luther fully embraced Augustine's view that "the human being does not have the power to see, but Truth has the power to appear."[11] For Luther, as for Augustine, true insight came from the friendly heart of Christ. This is seen in Luther's account of his conversion experience. Like Augustine, Luther was a trained academic with obvious intellectual talent that matched his passion for learning. Yet like Augustine—and like Hildegard—Luther had the experience that real insight did not come from his desire, his talent, or his skill but from the merciful action of God. This is seen in Luther's account of his Reformation breakthrough:

> Meanwhile, during that year I returned to interpret the Psalter anew seeing as I was more exercised for the task after I had lectured in the school on Saint Paul's epistles to the Romans, to the Galatians, and the one which is to the Hebrews. I was captivated with a wonderful ardor for understanding Paul in the Epistle to the Romans. So it was not frigid blood around the heart, but one bit of vocabulary which was in Romans 1:17, that obstructed the path. "In it the Justice of God is revealed." Indeed, I hated the phrase that is "Justice of God" which by use and custom I was taught by all the teachers to understand philosophically as formal or active justice (as they called it) as God is just and punishes the unjust sinner. . . . Thus, with a fierce and troubled conscience, I beat nevertheless importunately upon Paul at that place, most ardently desiring to know what St. Paul wanted. At last, *by the mercy of God*, meditating day

---

pulchritudini, ut illa essent in te quasi in subiecto, . . . ? falsitas enim erat, quam de te cogitabam, non veritas, et figmenta miseriae meae, non firmamenta beatitudinis tuae."

10. See Luther, "Die Disputation de Sententia" (WA 39.2:4).

11. Epis. 147.6.18, "To Paulina" (413–414): "Neque enim in potestate nostra est videre, sed in potestate illius apparere."

and night, I attended to the connection of the words, namely, "In it the justice of God is revealed, as it is written, 'The one who is justified by faith lives." I began to understand the justice of God, that by which the justified lives by a gift of God, namely by faith. And this is the meaning: the justice of God is revealed by the Gospel, it is passive. *The friendly hearted God makes us just through faith,* exactly as it is written: "The one who is justified through faith lives." Here I felt that I was reborn and had entered paradise itself through an open gate. There, *a totally other face of the entire Scripture appeared to me.*[12]

Luther says that God made this manifest to him as he read Scripture, but he was happy to find that Augustine had a similar revelation that he had explained in *On the Spirit and the Letter,* where he wrote, "By the law we fear God, by faith we hope in God."[13] Thus, Luther's preaching sounded like a command of Augustine, "flee through faith to the friendly heart of God."[14]

Importantly, Luther's Reformation breakthrough is commonly considered to be about justification only, not epistemology. Luther was speaking about how a person can become just, not wise. But much can be learned about Luther's epistemology in analyzing how he came to know that he was justified by faith. What he learned from Scripture, what he read through the lens of faith given by Christ, was that the human being does not become justified by doing just acts. In other words, justice is not actively achieved or earned. Rather, God calls the sinner just. Because God is in relationship with the sinner, the sinner is justified by God's promise of friendship in the same way that a bride gains the title and merits of

12. Luther, "Vorrede zum ersten Bande" (WA 54:185–86) (emphasis added). "Interim eo anno iam redieram ad Psalterium denuo interpretandum, fretus eo, quod exercitatior essem, postquam S. Pauli Epistolas ad Romanos, ad Galatas, et eam, quae est ad Ebraeos, tractassem in scholis. Miro certe ardore captus fueram cognoscendi Pauli in epistola ad Rom., sed obstiterat hactenus non frigidus circum praecordia sanguis, sed unicum vocabulum, quod est Cap. 1: Iustitia Dei revelatur in illo. Oderam enim vocabulum istud 'Iustitia Dei,' quod usu et consuetudine omnium doctorum doctus eram philosophice intelligere de iustitia (ut vocant) formali seu activa, qua Deus est iustus, et peccatores iniustosque punit . . . ita saeva et perturbata conscientia, pulsabam tamen importunus eo loco Paulum, ardentissime sitiens scire, quid S. Paulus vellet.Donec miserente Deo meditabundus dies et noctes connexionem verborum attenderem, nempe: Iustitia Dei revelatur in illo, sicut scriptum est: Iustus ex fide vivit, ibi iustitiam Dei coepi intelligere eam, qua iustus dono Dei vivit, nempe ex fide, et esse hanc sententiam, revelari per euangelium iustitiam Dei, scilicet passivam, qua nos Deus misericors iustificat per fidem, sicut scriptum est: Iustus ex fide vivit. Hic me prorsus renatum esse sensi, et apertis portis in ipsam paradisum intrasse. Ibi continuo alia mihi facies totius scripturae apparuit."

13. SL xxix.51: "Ex lege timemus Deum, ex fide speramus in Deum."

14. SL xxix.51: "per fidem confugiat ad misericordiam Dei."

her husband in legal marriage.[15] The words of the marriage contract have the authority to change the status of the bride. The words of the Word's promise have the authority to change the status of the sinner. But because there is no outward change in the bride, her status depends on her faith and society's faith in the contract. So, too, the sinner must believe in the relationship with God in order to know herself justified. Luther was clear that God's contract with the sinner is real whether the sinner recognizes it or not. Hence, Luther argued for infant baptism because the faith of the child is not necessary for the efficacy of God's Word. Also, Luther insisted on the real presence of Christ in the Eucharist, which is not dependent on the faith of the believer but again on the promise of the Word. But Luther also acknowledged that for the person *to know* that she is justified, that her baptism was efficacious, and that Christ is present in her communion bread, she must *have faith* that Christ is not a deceiver.

In this way, Luther's use of the word faith must be considered a bit differently than Augustine's use. Faith, for Luther, is not just a belief in any hypothesis that one wants to explore in order to understand. Luther did not use the word *fides* as a universal term, as if it meant the same thing in theology as it meant in a scientific, political, or philosophical context, like Augustine did. Moreover, Luther did not apologize for Christian faith by claiming it is akin to the same kind of trust in authority that humans require as social animals in order to acquire any knowledge. Faith, for Luther, when he says that humans are justified by faith, is a very specific trust in the friendly heart of God who does not lie. But importantly, this trust is a gift of Truth, a trust that is so sure that it is not a hypothesis but a bond that the Truth uses to capture the soul. Luther understood that Augustine had claimed that Truth captures the soul so that it knows truth, and he claimed that this is similar to how the Spirit of Truth captures the soul so that it knows by faith that she is justified. Luther insisted that in this he agreed with Augustine. Luther explained in *On the Babylonian Captivity of the Church*:

> But as Augustine says in another place, the soul is captured by Truth herself so that through her it can judge most certainly about all things; but it cannot judge the Truth, but is compelled to say with unerring certainty that this is the truth. For example, the mind pronounces with unerring certainty that three and seven are ten; and yet it cannot give a reason why this is true when it cannot deny that it is true. It is clearly taken captive by the Truth; and rather than judging the Truth, it is itself

15. Luther, "Tractatus de libertate christiana" (WA 7:54): "Quod animam copulat cum Christo, sicut sponsam cum sponso." (That the soul is united with Christ, as a bride is to a groom.)

judged by her. There is such a mind also in the church, when under the enlightenment of the Spirit, she judges and approves doctrines; she is unable to prove it and yet is most certain of having it. For as among philosophers nobody judges the general concepts, but all are judged through them, so it is among us with the sense of the Spirit, who judges everything and is judged by no one, as the Apostle says.[16]

Here is where the reader can see that Luther's emphasis on justification by faith is related both to Augustine's views of justification and epistemology. Both the African Doctor of Grace and the German Reformer believed that human beings come to understand themselves as justified only through the actions taken by Truth herself. Moreover, both agreed that the human being is a physical creature who accesses the world only through sense experience. Yet that sense experience only makes sense because of the inner working of Truth on the mind. The human being does not derive her understanding of math from sense experience. She applies the understanding of math, which she knows because of the inner workings of Truth, who enlightens her mind, to the world in order to make sense of sense data. As Augustine says, the concept of "oneness" cannot be found in sense experience, but by using that concept of "oneness," the human being can count physical objects and add one and two and three and four to determine ten.[17] While this sounds like a complicated epistemological argument, the important point for both Augustine and Luther was much less about providing a systematic epistemology than about providing the foundation for hope in bold inquiry. Indeed, because of their faith in the friendly heart of Truth that actively and personally engages every human mind, both Augustine and Luther, like Hildegard and Thomas, believed in free inquiry in the sciences through empiricism and trust in the power of words shared in preaching, teaching, dialogue, and debate.

---

16. Luther, "De Captivitate Babylonica Ecclesiae" (WA 6:561): "Sed, sicut alibi dicit Augustinus, veritate ipsa sic capitur anima, ut per eam de omnibus certissime iudicare possit, sed veritatem iudicare non possit, dicere autem cogatur infallibili certitudine, hanc esse veritatem. Exempli gratia, Mens infallibili certitudine pronunciat, iii et vii esse decem, et tamen rationem reddere non potest, cur id verum sit, cum negare non possit verum esse, capta scilicet ipsa et iudice veritate indicate magis quam indicans. Talis est et in Ecclesia sensus, illustrante spiritu, in iudicandis et approbandis doctrinis, quem demonstrare non potest et tamen certissimum habet. Sicut enim apud philosophus de communibus conceptionibus nemo iudicat, sed omnes per eas iudicantur, ita apud nos de sensu spiritus est, qui iudicat omnes et a nemine iudicatur ut Apostobis." See LA II.viii.22–23.

17. See LA II.viii.22–23.

First, Luther and later Lutherans advocated for the bold use of empiricism in the natural sciences. While Luther did not find Augustine's commentaries on Genesis to be helpful for his own exegesis,[18] Luther's support for science came from his Augustinian epistemology, which was grounded in the Scriptural promise of the Truth made incarnate. As Luther explained in his *Lectures on Genesis*:

> The human being measures heaven and all the heavenly bodies. Here gleams a spark of eternal life, as the human being naturally exercises the cognition of these natural things. This care, indeed, indicates that human beings were not created to live always in this lowest level of the orbits but to take possession of heaven, because in this life they admire and busy themselves with the study and care of heavenly things.[19]

Moreover, Luther reminded his listeners that scientific knowledge ought to be used in medicine, agriculture, politics, and civic law to help humans find ways to better serve their neighbors. Thus, flourishing human society needs scientists. Scientists provide a different type of knowledge than theologians, but both are necessary in human society.[20] That said, Luther did insist on limits to the trust that should be put in scientific theories. These

---

18. See Luther, *Genesisvorlesung* (WA 42:4): "Ac Augustinus mirabiliter ludit in tractatione sex dierum." (Augustine plays wonderful games with these tractates of the six days.) See also Luther, "Predigt am Sonntag Septuagesimä" (WA 41:22): "Nam Ambrosius et Augustinus satis pueriles cogitations habent." (Now Ambrose and Augustine have rather childish thoughts.)

19. Luther, *Genesisvorlesung* (WA 42:34): "homo coelum et omnia coeli corpora metitur. Quare hic emicat scintilla aeternae viae, quod homo naturaliter exercetur in illa naturae cognitione. Significat enim cura illa homines non eo conditos, ut in hac infima orbis parte semper vivant, sed ut coelum possideant, quod in hac vita admirantur et occupantur studio et cura coelestium rerum."

20. Luther, *Genesisvorlesung* (WA 42:35–36): "Quod igitur Astronomus sphaeras, auges, epiciclos appellat, recte facit, licet enim id in sua professione, ut commodious alios doceat. Econtra Spiritus sanctus et scriptura sacra illas appellationes nesciunt et totum hoc, quod supra nos est, vocant coelum. Nec debet id reprehendi ab Astronomo, sed uterque loquatur suis terminis. . . . sed iuvet potius alia aliam et praebeant mutuas operas. Sicut artifices faciunt, ut convservetur tota civitas, quae (sicut Aristotles inquit) non potest consituti ex medico et medico, sed ex medico et agricola." (An astronomer, therefore, does right when he calls things "spheres," "apsides," and "epicycles," as this is appropriate in his profession so that he teaches others with common terms. By way of contrast, the holy spirit and holy scripture know nothing about that way of speaking and call the entire area above us "heaven." An astronomer ought not find fault with this, but each should speak in his own terms. . . . But one should more easily help the other, and they should put forward their mutual works. Just as artisans do to maintain the whole city, which [as Aristotle says] cannot be composed of a physican and a physican but of a physican and a farmer.) See Aristotle, *Nicomachean Ethics* V.5.

should be trusted insofar as they are useful and appear to correspond with the data of the senses. But because human beings are always susceptible to self-interest and self-deception, these theories should be re-evaluated constantly. And the reader of Luther's commentary on Genesis will note how right Luther was to assert that scientists must always reevaluate their claims as she reads how earnestly Luther explained medieval scientific theories that have now been replaced by contemporary theories. Most importantly, Luther insisted that secular theories could never be expected to tell people about their fundamental value, which could be only known through faith in the loving promise of God who bestows all value and calls the sinner justified by Christ's love.

The influence of Luther's understanding of science can be seen as significant in the history of science. For example, Andreas Osiander, a Lutheran pastor and friend of Luther, wrote a foreword to Copernicus's *On the Revolutions of the Heavens* that was published with Luther's permission. There, Osiander explained why those interested in cosmology should read Copernicus:

> For it is the duty of an astronomer to compose the history of the celestial motions through careful and expert study. Then he must conceive and devise the causes of these motions or hypotheses about them. Since he cannot in any way attain to the true causes, he will adopt whatever suppositions enable the motions to be computed correctly from the principles of geometry for the future as well as for the past. The present author [Copernicus] has performed both these duties excellently. . . . The philosopher will perhaps rather seek the semblance of the truth. But neither of them will understand or state anything certain, unless it has been divinely revealed to him. Therefore, alongside the ancient hypotheses, which are no more probable, let us permit these new hypotheses also to become known, especially since they are admirable as well as simple and bring with them a huge treasure of very skillful observations. So far as hypotheses are concerned, let no one expect anything certain from astronomy, which cannot furnish it, lest he accept as the truth ideas conceived for another purpose, and depart from this study a greater fool than when he entered it. Farewell.[21]

21. Osiander, "Ad Lectorem": "Est enim Astronomi propium, historiam motuum coele stium diligenti & artificiosa obseruatione colligere. Deinde causas earundem, seu hypotheses, cum ueras assequi nulla ratione possit, qualescunque excogitare & confingere, quibus suppositis, idem motus, ex Geometriae principiis, tam in futuru quam in praeteritu recte possint calculari. Horu aute utrimque egregie praestitit hic artifex. . . . Philosophus fortasse, ueri similitudinem magis regis requiret, neuter tamen quicquam

Osiander claimed that scientists should use empirical evidence and mathematics to create the simplest hypothesis that best explains the empirical data. This scientific hypothesis, however, should not be considered theologically certain. The cosmology of Copernicus does not tell the human being something about her value or her relationship with God. This was an important distinction as many readers of Copernicus were worried that his cosmology had theological consequences about the place of human beings in relationship to God. As seen in Luther's quote from his Lectures on Genesis,[22] most medievals considered the Earth's location at the center of the universe to be the lowest in the cosmos, making Copernicus's claim that the Earth was above the sun a dangerously arrogant position. Osiander's preface reminded readers of both the practical need to do physics well and the irrelevance of physics for theology. But most importantly, Osiander repeated the Augustinian epistemology that grounds all bold investigation. Human beings only understand anything certain *if the divine reveals it*. It is too bold to claim that the love of physics and the bold inquiry in astronomy done in Lutheran nations such as Denmark owe everything to a conscious trust in Augustinian epistemology that made them fearless to create new hypotheses. But it is worth noting that Lutheran scientists at Lutheran Universities, from Kepler to Bohr, boldly reformed and revolutionized the study of physics again and again.

Of course, Luther's personal appreciation for natural science paled in comparison to his appreciation for rhetoric, dialogue, and debate. Luther believed strongly in the possibility of human words to contain the fullness of truth. Here, the reader can see a common legacy from Augustine in the insistence on the importance of words. Hildegard, Thomas, Luther, and those who canonized their works held in common a philosophy of language that encouraged commitment to dialogue and debate. They believed that human words can hold the fullness of the Word. As Luther said in his debate against the Radical Reformers, Christ is made manifest to human beings in human words that can be shared. "I preach the gospel of Christ, and with my bodily voice I bring you Christ into your heart, so that you may form

---

certi compraehedet, aut tradet, nisi diuinitus illi reuelatum fuerit. Sinamus igitur & has nouas hypotheses, inter ueteres, nihilo uerisimiliores inno tescere, praefereim cum admiribiles simul, & faciles sint ingen temoque thesaurum, doctissimarum observationum secum aduehant. Neque quisquam, quod ad hypotheses attinet, quicqua certi ab Astronomia expectet, cum ipsa nihil tale praestare que at, ne si in alium usum conficta pro ueris arripiat, stultior ab hac disciplina discedat, quam accesserit. Vale."

22. See Luther, *Genesisvorlesung* (WA 42:34): "in hac infima orbis." (in this lowest orb.)

him within yourself."[23] Luther, like Augustine, was certain that Truth could be expressed in human language. Luther, the law student turned monk, was a professor who flourished in public disputation, a pastor who stressed the importance of preaching, and a friend who invited both those who agreed and those who disagreed to his table for conversation. He insisted that princes pay for schools so that all children, both boys and girls, could learn to read and write for themselves. His willingness to speak openly and debate publicly came from his fundamental trust that the Truth was in relationship with speakers and listeners. This was seen in his initial stance at the Diet of Worms when, after stating his core beliefs, he declared that he was willing to listen to anyone who could use the words of Scripture or clear reason to convince him otherwise. Luther, for all his bombast, trusted words and encouraged debate, formal disputation, and casual table talk.

Except, of course, there were times when Luther, like almost every person, failed to trust words. Phillip Cary makes a good argument that when Luther, at the end of his life, threatened that someone should take away the free speech of Jews, he showed a marked failure to follow his own theology and his own ethic to love his neighbor. Indeed, Cary, like others, points accurately to the fact that Luther's earlier writing *That Jesus Christ Was a Jew* was far more faithful to his theology. In that work, Luther reminded his reader that Christ was Jewish; while all Gentiles, such as native Germans, were alien to Christ, Jews are his blood relatives. Luther advocated for friendly conversations between Jews and Christians, denouncing the cruelty of Christians against Jews and reminding them to be grateful that the Jews had been kind to them in earlier centuries.[24]

As Luther aged, his commitment to friendly conversation did not cease. He continued to invite both friends and enemies to his table. While in places his writing was caustic against those who disagreed with him, he never failed to try to answer questions or debate publically. Yet in his writings he declared that some of those who disagreed with him actually recognized the truth of his words but consciously lied and denounced that truth. Luther put Roman Catholics, Anabaptists, and Jews in this category of people who lied against their own consciences, although it is unclear that he ever actually debated any Jewish theologians. In one writing, as an old man, Luther declared that Jews should be deprived of their freedom of speech and freedom of worship.[25] Phillip Cary is not the only recent scholar

23. Luther, "Sermon von dem Sacrament" (WA 19:488): "Item ich predige das Evangelion von Christo und mit der leiblichen stim bringe ich dir Christum ins hertz, das du ihn in dich bildest."

24. See Luther, "Daß Jesus Christus ein geborner Jude" (WA 11:314–36).

25. See Luther, "Von den Jüden und ihren Lügen" (WA 53:412–552).

to point out that Luther went horribly wrong in this writing. Cary claimed Luther exhibited "most obviously a failure to love."[26] And while that is most certainly true, the root of Luther's sin was due to what he believed was always the root of sin, a failure to trust God and God's promises. What comes across as tremendous arrogance on the part of the elderly Luther is actually, according to Cary, at root, a lack of confidence, a "fear of those whose words threaten his own grasp on the Word of God."[27] Somehow, Luther, who poetically pronounced that not even the Devil could wrench a person from the grasp of Christ in his famous hymn "A Mighty Fortress," suddenly wrote as if maybe a freely speaking Jew or Anabaptist could do what the Devil could not. Luther had earlier claimed that there was no need to prohibit the free speech of any person of any creed, not even if such a person was deliberately lying, for Christ is stronger than any deceiver. Luther had told Germans to read for themselves the Scripture and trust that even children could understand it with the help of Christ. Indeed, Luther told Christians they ought to read the Koran and have no fear of a Muslim invasion.[28] Cary's opinion is that the "deepest problems in Luther's theology . . . arise when his hope fails. . . . Hope opens us to the possibility that our opponents are not enemies but potential friends who have good things to give us, even when their words loosen our grasp on the meaning of God's words."[29] Without this hope, Luther lost the courage to advocate for the necessary Augustinian humility that belief needs to seek further understanding. This hope is essential to keep a person from blind faith and gnosticism, the idea that there is an esoteric truth, which cannot stand up to questioning. Luther was indignant because he believed that the teachings of the Radical Reformers and the Jews might lead people away from Christ. But Luther's idea that human beings should limit the freedom of others in order to help Christ win the battle was at odds with his central theological hope that faith is a gift of God. As Augustine had insisted, it is not in our power to see the Truth, but it is in Truth's power to appear. Those who trust in Truth can always keep the conversation open.

Luther's failure to write with a message of hope at various points in his old age points to an important question about Augustine's epistemology. It must be acknowledged that human discourse often does not bring unity. Worse, it must be acknowledged that a person can even misunderstand his own teachings. This might seem like a convincing counterargument to

---

26. Cary, *Meaning of Protestant Theology*, 235.

27. Cary, *Meaning of Protestant Theology*, 235.

28. See Luther, "Vorrede zu Theodor Bibliianders Koranausgabe" (WA 53:569–72).

29. Cary, *Meaning of Protestant Theology*, 236.

the claim that the Truth is always working in friendly relationship with the seeker of Truth. Yet it is not. For Luther, Christ is present even in the suffering of the cross, even in the darkness of death, and even in the despair of the descent into Hell. Luther proclaimed that Christ is present even in the darkness where faith cannot see.[30] Luther, like Augustine and like Monica, insisted that whether or not the seeker of Truth is able to believe in her relationship with Truth, that relationship is real.[31] And the promise is that the Truth will win. While Luther faltered in his own trust in that promise, and while oftentimes debates, dialogues, and private moments of contemplation do not bring unity of understanding, that does not undermine the promise. Of course, the issue is tricky. Indeed, Augustine, Luther, and Calvin were all tempted towards considering doctrines of predestination to try to understand why some people persist in error. Augustine and Luther ultimately decided that preaching a doctrine of predestination would only serve to undermine faith in God's promise of constant friendly presence, a promise that they believed was true even if they could not understand completely the entanglement of the relationship between the human will and God's love. They had to trust the promise of Christ's friendly heart, and they refused to give an answer to why some people seemed unable to have that trust. Augustine at his best claimed that error, like sin, is simply part of the human condition post-Eden. Rather than despair at the reality of error, one must rejoice in the experiences of liberation from error and know that even when one was floundering in doubt, the Truth is present, although unseen. Clinging to this hope allows one to boldly and humbly keep inquiry and dialogue open in community.

Importantly, later Lutheran philosophers demonstrated this type of humble and bold community inquiry, especially during the Enlightenment, when other philosophers suggested that philosophy could be done by a solitary thinker with reason and empiricism alone. For example, the protestant princess Elisabeth of Bohemia, cultivating a friendship with Descartes, was his most serious interlocutor, pressing them both to learn and grow from each other. Elisabeth saw friendship as the foundation of philosophical inquiry and later befriended the Lutheran Leibniz, whose metaphysics

30. Luther, *Genesisvorlesung* (WA 43:392): "Ideoque in mundo apparet nihil esse fallacius verbo Dei et fidei, nihil vanius spe promissionis. Denique nihil magis nihil esse videtur, quam Deus ipse. Haec igitur est scientia sanctorum et mysterium absconditum a sapientibus et revelatum parvulis." (In this way, nothing in the world seems more fallacious than the word of God and faith, nothing more empty than hope in the promise. Then, nothing seems to be more nothing than God himself. Here, then, is the knowledge of saints that is a hidden mystery to the wise and revealed to the little ones.)

31. See BV iii.19–21, where Monica explains how the human being is never without God even when one is clearly not happy or even aware of God.

claimed that the human mind was nothing but relationship with God and the world. More than a century of Enlightenment philosophy later, Hegel's influential "Lord/Bondsman Dialectic" proclaimed that the Truth demonstrated herself only through the intellectual and physical debate of human competition. Kierkegaard cleanly put this dialectic back in its Augustinian context, restating Augustine's position that the only teacher of Truth is the Teacher who works through human beings who are for each other occasions for new understanding. Contemporary philosophers who are considering the relational understanding of Truth, such as Judith Butler, rely heavily on these Lutheran Augustinian thinkers' relational thinking, especially Hegel. For example, Butler insists that human beings exist, become, and learn only in an entangled relationship with each other. She wrote, "True subjectivity comes to flourish only in communities that provide for reciprocal recognition for we do not come to ourselves through work alone, but through the acknowledging look of the Other who confirms us."[32] Butler, a Jewish Hegelian and a committed non-violent activist for women, queer people, and the disabled, is America's most known philosopher and a proponent of the notion that human beings are products of their social relationships.[33] She insists that only in community can human beings come to understand new ways of living livable lives together.[34]

Calvin and Calvinism

Although the impact of Thomas and Luther in Christian theology has been well noted, in the United States "Christianity" has often been used broadly as a synonym for Calvinism. Indeed, many of the theological and philosophical commitments of Christians in the US do come from Calvin's way of thinking. As was true with Thomas and Luther, Calvin was consciously aware of his appropriation of Augustine, and the influence of Augustine on Calvin has been regularly noted by scholars. Indeed, Calvin even suggested that his more controversial doctrines, like that of predestination, came from his reading of Augustine. In Calvin's own words, "As for Augustine, he is

32. Butler, *Subjects of Desire*, 58.

33. Butler, *Notes toward a Performative Theory*, 21: "Everyone is dependent on social relations and enduring infrastructure in order to maintain a livable life, so there is no getting rid of that dependency."

34. See Butler, *Notes toward a Performative Theory*, 21–22: "This initiates the possibility of taking apart that individuating and maddening form of responsibility in favor of an ethos of solidarity that would affirm mutual dependency, dependency no workable infrastructures and social networks, and open the way to a form of improvisiation in the course of devising collective and institutional ways of addressing induced precarity."

totally with us, so that if I were to write a confession, it would suffice for me
to compose it from what is taken from his books."[35] While that particular
matter is debatable, Calvin's epistemology is certainly Augustinian, as has
been noted by many reformed philosophers.

Indeed, Calvin began the *Institutes of the Christian Religion* with an
Augustinian understanding of the human self as a self in relationship with
God, a self that can only know itself in terms of that relationship: "In the
first place, no one can contemplate oneself, without immediately turning
his thoughts to regard God. . . . Indeed, we have no strength or firmness
except in that we subsist and are supported in God."[36] Calvin, then, insisted
that the human mind cannot ascend in order to look to God but is dependent on God's willingness to descend to the human being. In Calvin's words,
"How then God, so as not to be without witness, softly invites people so that
they may know him for their benefit."[37] Calvin's account of how God gives
witness of himself is also Augustinian. On one hand, the very fact that human beings can make sense of their world and recognize its beauty is a fact
that bears witness to the majesty of God. On the other hand, revelation in
Scripture and the Incarnation is necessary to provide direct access to Truth
through the word that speaks Truth:

> Thus, there is a singular gift when God, to instruct his church,
> did not use only the mute teachers we have mentioned so that
> we know the works he produces in us, but also he opens his
> own most sacred mouth, not only to make us know and witness
> that we must adore this God but also to make us know that he
> is this one here.[38]

Calvin especially emphasized that human beings come to know about
their relationship with Truth through the study of nature. Augustine, in
the *Confessions*, wrote, "I love you, Sir, with no doubt but with a certain

35. Calvin, "Praedestinatione," 265: "Porro Augustinus ipse adeo totus noster est,
ut si mihi confession scribenda sit, ex eius scriptis contextam proferre, abunde mihi
sufficiat."

36. Calvin, "L'Institution Chrestienne" I.i.1: "Car en premier lieu, nul ne se peut
contempler, qu'incontinent il ne tourne ses sens au regard de Dieu, . . . mesmes que nos
forces et fermeté ne sont autre chose que de subsister et estre appuyez en Deiu."

37. Calvin, "L'Institution Chrestienne" I.v.13: "Combien donc que Dieu ne soit
pas destitute de tesmoins, conviant par ses benefices si doucement les homes a sa
cognoissance."

38. Calvin, "L'Institution Chrestienne" I.vi.1: "Parquoy c'est un don singulier, quand
Dieu pour instruire son Eglise n'use pas seulement de ces maistres muets dont nous
avons parlé, assavoir ses ouvrages qu'il nous produit, mais daigne bien aussi ouvrir
sa bouche sacrée, non seulement pour faire savoir et publier que nous devons adorer
quelque Dieu, mais aussi qu'il est cestuy-la."

conscience; You pierced my heart with your Word and I loved you."[39] But he was quick to add that he also found a call to love God in nature:

> But the sky and the earth and all that is on it, behold how they say to me that I ought to love you. They do not cease to say it to everyone, they are impossible to ignore. From on high, however, you are empathetic to those with whom you empathize, and you present your friendly heart to those to whom you are friendly hearted, otherwise the sky and earth would speak your praise in vain.[40]

Calvin found passages like these especially important. Like Augustine, he asserted that nature speaks truths to all people equally, and that true statements should be admired no matter who proclaims them. Calvin wrote,

> Then, when we see in these secular writers this admirable light of truth that appears in their books, we must remember that the nature of the human person, although spoiled and corrupted in its integrity, nevertheless is clothed and ornamented with many gifts of God. If we recognize the Spirit of God as the unique fountain of truth, we will not condemn the truth, wherever she appears.[41]

For Calvin, as for Augustine, all disciplines that discover truth bear witness to Truth's existence and love for human beings. This is true of physics, dialectics, mathematics, and other disciplines, no matter who does them.[42] As Calvin explained,

> There are infinite signs both in heaven and on earth that testify to his admirable power: not only those secrets of nature that require special study to know, Astronomy, Medicine and all of Physics, but also those which are apparent even to the most rude

---

39. Conf. X.vi.8: "Non dubia sed certa conscientia, domine, amo te: percussisti cor meum verbo tuo, et amavi te."

40. Conf. X.vi.8: "sed et caelum et terra et omnia quae in eis sunt, ecce undique mihi dicunt ut te amem, nec cessant dicere omnibus, ut sint inexcusabiles. altius autem tu misereberis cui misertus eris, et misericordiam praestabis cui misericors fueris: alioquin caelum et terra surdis loquuntur laudes tuas."

41. Calvin, "L'Institution Chrestienne" II.ii.15: "Pourtant, quand nous voyons aux escrivains Payens ceste admirable lumiere de verité, laquelle apparoit en leurs livres, cela nous doit admonnester que la nature de l'homme, combien qu'elle soit descheute de son integrité, et fort corrompue, ne laisse point toutesfois d'estre ornée de beaucoup de dons de Dieu. Si nous recognoissons, l'esprit de Dieu comme une fontaine unique de verité, nous ne contemnerons point la verité par tout où elle apparoistra."

42. See Calvin, "L'Institution Chrestienne" II.ii.16.

and idiotic person who recognizes them, as they cannot open their eyes without being aware of this testimony.[43]

Importantly, this is both because the beauty of creation commands that the observer recognize the wonderful art of the creator[44] and because the mind's very powers of observation and contemplation demonstrate that "there is a God who wants to have us look at him. . . . For nothing is more confused and unreasonable than to enjoy the precious things that show us divinity and then to overlook the Author who presents them to us."[45] The two-fold realization is important because, like Augustine, Calvin believed that the God who is Truth is personally interested in human beings. He was not a deist who believed that nature gave evidence of a Divine Creator but this Divine Creator was no longer invested in creation. Calvin believed that this Creator was actively engaged in human life, overcoming error to help people understand truth.

This is not to say that Calvin believed that human access to Truth was without fetters. Calvin was no naïve realist. Interestingly, his views in their complexity come to fruition in the skeptical philosophy of David Hume, a Scottish Enlightenment thinker who was raised in the Calvinist tradition. For example, Calvin expected that science attested to a magnificent creator. "Look, but it is to make a diabolic point to suggest that the world, which was created as a spectacle of the glory of God, must be its own creator."[46] Surely, such could have been a declaration uttered by Hume's character Cleanthes, a proponent of natural theology, in Hume's posthumously published *Dialogues Concerning Natural Religion*. But Calvin's next claim in this passage sounds more like the comments of the orthodox Demea and even the skeptical Philo in that same dialogue: "It is a bad and pernicious thing in matters so grand that one must proceed with total sobriety, to envelop the majesty of God in the inferior course of his works."[47] Calvin insisted

43. Calvin, "L'Institution Chrestienne" I.v.2: "Il y a des enseignemens infinis tant au ciel qu'en la terre pour nous testifier sa puissance admirable; ie ne dy pas seulement des secrets de nature qui requirent estude special, et savoir d'Astrologie, de Medecine et de toute la Physique, mais i'enten de ceux qui sont si apparens que les plus rudes et idiots y cognoiseent assez: en sort qu'ils ne peuvent ourvrir les yeux qu'ils n'en soyent tesmoins."

44. See Calvin, "L'Institution Chrestienne" I.v.2.

45. Calvin, "L'Institution Chrestienne" I.v.5: "un seul Dieu qui gouverne tellement toutes natures qu'il veut que nous regardions á luy. . . . qu'il n'y a rien plus confus ne desraisonable, que de iouir des graces si precieuses qui monstrent en nous quelque divinité, et mesprise l'autheur duquel nous les tenon."

46. Calvin, "L'Institution Chrestienne" I.v.5: "Voire, mais c'est pour revenir á un poinet diabolique assavoir que le monde, qui a esté creé pour spectacle de la gloire de Dieu, soit luy mesme son createur."

47. Calvin, "L'Institution Chrestienne" I.v.5: "c'est une chose mauvaise et pernicieuse

that science could not give the true goals and causes of natural things as Aristotle might have hoped.[48] And he insisted that human thinkers admit that the short span of their lives meant that what they could know of the reality of the world is akin to how much a traveler caught in a dark night knows of a field during a lightning flash.[49] What human beings do know thus attests to the grace of God, who actively teaches through the movement of the Holy Spirit. For Calvin, all people are totally blind and completely in darkness without the light of the Spirit.[50] Thus, Calvin noted how important it is for philosophers to remember Augustine, who so often said: "We ought to glory in nothing, because nothing is ours."[51]

Indeed, while some historians of ideas consider Enlightenment thinking and William Paley's theory by design as consequences of Calvinist epistemology, the great skeptic David Hume is also a vehicle of Calvin's Augustinianism. Hume questioned the Enlightenment's overabundant optimism about the possibilities for the human mind to find Wisdom on its own. In contrast, Hume wrote the *Dialogues Concerning Natural Religion*, insisting that inquiry into such matters required a community in dialogue together. The prefatory letter to the dialogue suggests the same hypothesis that marked many of Augustine's early writings, namely that the form of dialogue "can unite the two greatest and purest pleasures of human life, study and the company of others."[52] And Philo's conclusion also appears to be Augustinian:

> But believe me, Cleanthes, the most natural feeling that a well-disposed mind will have on this occasion is a longing desire and expectation that God will be pleased to remove or at least to lessen this profound ignorance, by giving mankind some particular revelation, *revealing* the nature, attributes, and operations of the divine object of our faith. A person who has a sound sense of the imperfections of natural reason will eagerly fly to revealed truth, while the haughty dogmatist, persuaded that he can erect a complete system of theology with no help but that of philosophy, will disdain any further aid and will reject this help

---

en choses si grandes, et ou on doit proceder en toute sobrieté, d'enveloper la maiesté de Dieu avec le cours inferieur de ses oeuvres."

48. See Calvin, "L'Institution Chrestienne" I.xvi.9.

49. See Calvin, "L'Institution Chrestienne" II.ii.18.

50. See Calvin, "L'Institution Chrestienne" II.ii.21.

51. Calvin, "L'Institution Chrestienne" II.ii.9: "Il ne nous faut en rien glorifier, car il n'y a nul bien qui soit nostre."

52. Hume, *Dialogues Concerning Natural Religion*, "Letter from Pamphilus to Hermippus," 1.

> from the outside. To be a philosophical sceptic is, in a man of
> letters, the first and most essential step towards being a sound,
> believing Christian.[53]

Hume's Philo refused to accept that his own intellect can discover the nature of his self and his God. And while Demea and Cleanthes both cringed at the suggestion that Christian faith be adopted out of a fear of skeptical nihilism, Augustine's *Confessions* made a similar argument. Augustine insisted on the importance of recognizing how little can be known by clear reason alone in order that the philosopher might recognize the graceful help of Truth in knowing what she does know. Hume's humility about the potential of human reason does not mean that Hume was a faithful Christian, but it does point to his understanding of Calvin and Augustine.

Calvin emphasized the importance of this humility as often as he emphasized how clearly God's Truth is evident in the world. As a result, Calvin's Augustinianism had a double influence on philosophers that grew up in Calvinist traditions. On one hand, many Calvinist members of the Enlightenment, especially the Scottish Enlightenment, had a profound optimism about the possibilities of human knowledge through empiricism and reason. Likewise, contemporary Calvinist, or reformed, philosophers often expect that natural science can provide truths that are compatible with Scripture. Alvin Plantinga might be the most recognizable example of a Calvinist philosopher who expects fruitful interplay between faith and reason, between Christianity and science. His "reformed epistemology" seeks to inspire others to a re-commitment to empiricism, which he claims leads to a recognition of an intelligent designer. On the other hand, skeptics like David Hume and the twentieth-century reformed philosopher and theologian Reinhold Niebuhr were more likely to emphasize the inability of a human being to know God or any truths on her own. Importantly, both types of Calvinist philosophers bear the mark of Augustine's epistemology; both insist on the importance of conversation and dialogue.

Descartes and Modern Philosophy

Of course, Calvin was not the only vehicle for Augustine's influence on Enlightenment thinkers. The reader must consider the legacy of Rene Descartes, who is often named as the father of modern philosophy. Descartes was a French Roman Catholic but not a Thomist. He saw himself as the father of a new method that he hoped would replace Augustine's method of believing

---

53. Hume, *Dialogues Concerning Natural Religion*, Part 12, 62.

in order to understand, a method that he thought anchored the European university to past mistakes. Descartes wanted a new method that did not rely on past authority but rather was rooted on clear and certain foundations. The first step in his method was that the philosopher strip away all propositions that she believed on authority or faith in order to begin her pursuit of new knowledge, with firm foundations demonstrated clearly and distinctly.[54] Many contemporary Thomists, Lutherans, and Calvinists see Descartes, rightly, as an obvious opponent of Augustine. However, while Descartes absolutely attempted to build a new method for philosophy in *Discourse on Method* and *Twelve Rules of Mind* that relies only on the use of discursive reason, the *foundation* for that philosophical method is still obviously Augustinian. Indeed, the *Meditations on First Philosophy* bears a striking resemblance to Augustine's *Soliloquies*. Like Augustine, Descartes using reason alone found himself unable to find any clear and distinct truth that he could not doubt until, like Augustine, he recognized that he could not doubt his ability to doubt.[55] The fundamental truth that he knew that he could doubt and that he knew he could be deceived led Descartes to recognize that he knew something, namely that he existed as a being who could doubt, be deceived, and think.[56] Thus, he recognized that there is a truth he knew. His foundation is that because he knew one truth, he knew that Truth is accessible. Like Augustine, he immediately turned to the idea of a perfect, non-deceiving God who created him in order to explain how it could be that he exists as a being who has such an idea. The foundational hope that Descartes had for philosophy is the same as Augustine's—his trust that God created him with a mind that can understand truths. Descartes's God is not as friendly hearted as Augustine's, but he did see that the God who is no deceiver was his guard against both gnosticism and nihilistic skepticism.

54. See, for example, the first sentences of Descartes's *Meditations*, where he guides the reader through his own process with his method: "Animadverti jam ante aliquot annos quàm multa, ineunte aetate, falsa pro veris admiserim, & quàm dubia sint quaecunque istis postea superextruxi, ac proinde funditus omnia semel in vitâ esse evertenda, atque a primis fundamentis denuo inchoandum, si quid aliquando firmum & mansurum cupiam in scientiis stabilire." (It has now been some years since I determined how many false things I had taken for true since my earliest youth and how dubitable was everything that I had constructed on this foundation. And from that time I was convinced that once in my life I must overturn everything and begin again from firm foundations, if I desired to establish anything firm and permanent in the sciences.) Descartes, *Meditatio* I.1.

55. Cf. Descartes, *Meditatio* II.1–4; CD xi.26.

56. Descartes, *Meditatio* II.3: "Imo certe ego eram, si quid mihi persuasi. . . . Ego sum, ego existo, quoties a me profertur, vel mente concipitur, necessario esse verum." (Then I am certain that I am, if anyone can persuade me. . . . I am, I exist, is necessarily true every time that it is proclaimed or conceived by my mind.)

Importantly, Descartes insisted that he did not rely on Augustine's writings to find this idea. He was not using Augustine as an authority, but he was pleased to find that Augustine agreed with him.[57] To Descartes, the fact that both he and Augustine discovered the same line of argument suggested the universal nature of that path to truth. Interestingly, several historians have discovered that Descartes attributed the very idea of creating a new philosophical method to a series of divinely inspired dreams, suggesting that Descartes, indeed, believed that the divine personally interacted with the philosopher.

To be clear, Descartes's new modern method is certainly not Augustinian. The Cartesian method insists on the use of logic and mathematics in order to evaluate what empirical evidence should be trusted and what authorities should be believed. Augustine would surely have thought that Descartes falsely understood human nature. Descartes assumed the human being to be purely rational, ignoring the social and physical nature of the human being. But it is significant that Descartes's hope was an Augustinian kind of hope—that the Divine was working on the side of the human being who wanted to know truths. The foundation for Descartes's method was his absolute certainty that the God who created him and his world was no deceiver. Thus, when Friedrich Nietzsche wrote of a madman who declared that God was dead, he rightly recognized that this would unchain not only Christian philosophy but also modern and Enlightenment philosophy that was considered secular.[58] Without a fundamental trust in a transcendent Truth that was no deceiver, there could be no friendly relationship with Wisdom; there could be no philosophy.

American Pragmatism

Nietzsche was not the only philosopher to experience post-modern despair concerning the accessibility and even existence of truth. This was a general reaction in academic philosophy to the failure of the modern philosophical method to accomplish what it had set about trying to accomplish. Using logic and mathematical principles to evaluate empirical data in order to create systematic knowledge of human beings and their world did lead to many scientific discoveries and some new social and political practices, but it ultimately could not help human beings answer ultimate questions. Immanuel Kant's *Critique of Pure Reason* devastated certain types of modern philosophical ambitions by arguing that pure reason could not determine the

---

57. See Menn, *Descartes and Augustine*, 66.
58. See Nietzsche, *Die fröhliche Wissenschaft* III.125.

truth value of certain axioms, such as the existence of God or the freedom of the will. Generally, over the course of the nineteenth century and into the early twentieth century, European philosophers began to re-evaluate the modern method of doing philosophy.

But American philosophers seemed to be on a different course. Rather than attempting to discover foundational universal truths, Americans like Ralph Waldo Emerson, Charles Sanders Pierce, and William James were more interested in finding pragmatic lessons. Unconcerned with the attempt to ground their search for meaning in a search for universal truths, these Americans stressed "the dynamic character of selves and structures, the malleability of tradition and the transformative potential in human history."[59] In other words, according to contemporary American philosopher Cornel West, American philosophers evaded modern philosophy's goals and methods. They were not looking for true propositions that were independent of human bias, interest, and value. They were looking for a "'human truth' for us."[60] George Santayana suggested that some of these pragmatists, such as William James, saw modern philosophy as a set of puzzles, a maze created by philosophers that they had to escape.[61] In contrast, American pragmatism was the search for helpful lessons that would guide people in society to better thrive.

Importantly, most of these Americans did not apologize for a foundational belief in a friendly God. But Emerson, Pierce, and James did have appreciation for experiences of divine love or divine purpose that grounded their hope as they pursued self-knowledge. Emerson claimed,

> I cannot, nor can any man, speak precisely of things so sublime, but it seems to me the wit of man, his strength, his grace, his tendency, his art, is the grace and the presence of God. It is beyond explanation. When all is said and done, the rapt saint is found the only logician. Not exhortation, not argument becomes our lips but paeans of joy and praise.[62]

59. West, *American Evasion of Philosophy*, 10.

60. West, *American Evasion of Philosophy*, 65.

61. See Santayana, *Character and Opinion*, 54: "He once said to me: 'What a curse philosophy would be if we couldn't foget all about it!' In other words, philosophy was not to him what it has been to so many, a consolation and sanctuary in a life which would have been unsatisfying without it. . . . Philosophy to him was rather like a maze in which he happened to find himself wandering, and what he was looking for was the way out." See also West, *American Evasion of Philosophy*, 68.

62. Emerson, "Method of Nature," 221, quoted in West, *American Evasion of Philosophy*, 25.

While Emerson's quote is a beautiful poetic articulation, Charles Sanders Pierce wrote more formally in his *Neglected Argument for the Reality of God*, where he explained that the existence of God is more plausible than that God does not exist, for the existence of God is the most plausible explanation for the human ability to make sense out of their experiences.[63] This argument is obviously similar to Augustine's against the academic skeptics. That said, there is little in Pierce to suggest that his understanding of God entailed a personal God who consciously chooses to interact with human beings. In contrast, William James evaded the task of proving that God exists with logic and looked instead into people's personal experiences of the divine. Of course, he looked at the phenomena of religious experiences in order to find what pragmatic lessons these hold for human beings.[64] What he found is that faith in a transcendent being who lovingly heals what the human being cannot heal herself helps people act in healthy minded ways. Yet in the *Varieties of Religious Experience* James built a case that this tenet best fits the phenomenological evidence given by many people who claim to have had religious experiences. Still, James insisted that faithful believers keep conversations open with other types of believers so that they might avoid the trap of unhelpful dogma.

In the late twentieth century, American pragmatism began to unravel. Two of the best known philosophers at that time, W. V. Quine and Richard Rorty, were being interpreted as claiming that there simply is no truth. In 1989, Cornel West, trained at Harvard by these American pragmatists, urged American philosophers and the American public to reconsider the gifts of American pragmatism. Rather than culminating American philosophy in *aporia*, saying that truth is non-existent or inaccessible, West suggested that Americans needed to come together to refine pragmatic ideas in democratic assembly. Still today, West believes that the American pragmatic tradition is built on a hope that individuals can learn from each other in community. As such, West does not advocate that philosophers look for an absolute truth outside of themselves but rather a relational way of being together that is co-created by people in conversation. West, like James, insists on dialogue between people of differing faiths. But interestingly, his insistence on that dialogue seems grounded, as was Augustine's, in his own faith in a loving God who speaks in the world. In 1989, he wrote,

---

63. See Pierce, "Neglected Argument," 434: "The word 'God' so 'capitalized' (as we American say), is the definable proper name, signifying *Ens necessarium*: in my belief Really creator of all three Universes of Experience."

64. For a full account of his position, see James, "Faith and the Right to Believe."

Of course the fundamental philosophical question remains whether the Christian gospel is ultimately true. And as a Christian prophetic pragmatist whose focus is on coping with transient and provisional penultimate matters yet whose hope goes beyond them, I reply in the affirmative, bank my all on it, yet am willing to entertain the possibility in low moments that I may be deluded.[65]

Importantly, faith in this friendly hearted Wisdom requires that the philosopher talk to others who doubt this faith and even remain open to the possibility that the philosopher's faith is deluded. Ultimately, West's type of American pragmatism, like Augustine's Christian philosophy, is grounded in the hope of Wisdom's friendship with human beings. Trust in this love of wisdom allows human beings to use their senses and their reason, to talk together, to trust each other, and to question each other in order to discover and create principles that promote human flourishing.

West is not alone in his Augustinian hope today. Evidence of this hope lies in the many people who sing joyfully the beloved contemporary hymn by Thomas H. Troeger, composed for Duke University's celebration of the work of Waldo Beach, an American Christian ethicist, on the occasion of his retirement in the late 1980s. This hymn, written by a Presbyterian, has been welcomed by a variety of Christian, Unitarian, and non-Christian sects throughout America. In it, Augustine's hope is set to music for Americans as they seek meaning in their lives.

Praise the Source of Faith and Learning

Praise the source of faith and learning that has sparked and stoked the mind

with a passion for discerning how the world has been designed.

Let the sense of wonder flowing from the wonders we survey

keep our faith forever growing and renew our need to pray.

God of wisdom we acknowledge that our science and our art

and the breadth of human knowledge only partial truth impart.

Far beyond our calculation lies a depth we cannot sound

where your purpose for creation and the pulse of life are found.

65. West, *American Evasion of Philosophy*, 233.

May our faith redeem the blunder of believing that our thought
has displaced the grounds for wonder which the ancient prophets taught.

May our learning curb the error which unthinking faith can breed
lest we justify some terror with an antiquated creed.

As two currents in a river fight each other's undertow,
till converging they deliver one coherent steady flow,

blend, O God, our faith and learning till they carve a single course,
till they join as one, returning praise and thanks to you, the Source.[66]

66. Troeger, "Praise the Source of Faith and Learning."

Chapter 8

Beyond Truthiness

Philosophical Pursuit in the Twenty-First Century

> However, if my books, by chance, come into the hands of some reader who seeing my name does not say, "Who is that?" and throw the books aside, but rather with curiosity or an eagerness for study, will enter without contempt for the lowliness of the doorway, they will not be upset to see that I philosophize with you. . . . Your philosophy pleases me very much.[1]

IN DECEMBER OF 386, Augustine, his friends, and his mother set about a dialogue on the most important and difficult philosophical question Augustine faced—the problem of evil. For Augustine, this question was directly linked to the problem of human error. Augustine was not as concerned about what might be termed natural evil; he had been satisfied by the stoic answer that providence rules all things in nature. That which seems like evil or even simply imperfection in nature to a suffering person is, according to Augustine, most likely a problem of that person's self-centered human attitude rather than the result of a true natural disaster.[2] The question for Augustine was more seriously psychological and philosophical. He asked why the parts and will of a flea are so "wonderfully placed and distinguished"[3] while human life is tossed and turned with constantly changing disturbances.[4] He won-

1. Ord. I.xi.32: "Mei autem libri si quorum forte manus tetigerint lectoque meo nomine non dixerint: Iste quis est? codicemque proiecerint, sed vel curiosi vel nimium studiosi contempta vilitate liminis intrare perrexerint, me tecum philosophantem non moleste ferent nec quemquam istorum quorum meis litteris sermo miscetur, fortasse contemnent. . . . philosophia tua mihi plurimum placet."

2. See Ord. I.i.2: "Nihil enim aliud minus eruditis hominibus accidit, qui universam rerum coaptationem atque concentum imbecilla mente complecti et considerare non valentes, si quid eos offenderit." (Nothing indeed is less erudite than that suggested by people who being filled with the mentality of an imbecile do not consider the fittingness of the things in the universe to be valuable if anything offends them.)

3. Ord. I.i.2: "membra pulicis disposita mire atque distincta sunt."

4. Ord. I.i.2: "cum interea humana vita innumerabilium perturbationum inconstantia versetur et fluctuet."

dered why, if God is so good as to order the world perfectly for the flea and
fit the flea so perfectly for the world, there seems to be so much trouble for
human beings, who appear unable to understand themselves or to determine how they ought to act in the world. Augustine's question surely reso-
nates today. Why are human beings, who have such large intellects, unable
to understand themselves and behave so as to fit into the larger providence
of the world and live happy lives? And from his question comes another
question, a question that threatens to undo the entire philosophical project:
Does not their failure to do so require people to admit that human beings
do not have access to necessary truths, to admit that there may not be any
truths at all, to admit the hopelessness of philosophy?

Importantly, Augustine did not find a satisfactory answer to his
question about evil and error. Throughout the dialogue on the topic and
throughout many other works written in the span of his prolific career,
Augustine considered and disputed many different possibilities but was unable to provide a solution that satisfied him. But Augustine did answer the
question about the ramification of error for the possibility of philosophy.
For Augustine, the problem of error did not mean the end of philosophy
or the absence of truth. Indeed, in *On Order*, Augustine—with his friends
and his mother—went through many different hypothetical solutions to the
problem of evil and rejected each of them, yet they ended the disputation
filled "with the joy of it all and much hope."[5]

It is this hope that Augustine has to offer the twenty-first-century
philosopher. In the works of Augustine there are not final answers to all
or even many philosophical questions. The lesson to be learned from Augustine in the twenty-first century is not doctrinal but inspirational. Augustine, in testifying to his own experiences of his relationship with Truth,
encouraged his friends, family, and readers to pursue their own relationship with Truth. To them and to the reader today, Augustine's word is the
same he gave his mother earnestly at the end of the first book of *On Order*,
"Your philosophy pleases me greatly."[6]

Augustinian hope has inspired many different thinkers to create and
discover their own philosophy: Fulgentius and Hildegard, Thomas and
Luther, Calvin and Elizabeth Isham, Descartes and Galileo, Etienne Gilson
and Cornel West. These men and women discovered and created divergent
hypotheses, theorems, ideas, and doctrines. Augustine would have been
encouraged by this, for what interested him was not just his own ideas but
his ideas in conversation with others in the light of Wisdom. While some

5. Ord. II.xx.54: "laetisque omnibus et multum sperantibus."
6. Ord. I.xi.31: "philosophia tua mihi plurimum placet."

philosophers end their works with doctrines and some philosophers end their works in *aporia*, a void of answers, Augustine finished most of his works humbly evangelizing hope in the promise that Truth is in friendly relationship with him and with the reader.[7] Thus, the twenty-first-century reader now must consider not Augustine's views but her own relationship with wisdom, her own philosophy.

Augustinian Advice for Those Who Seek Truth

Of course, there are philosophical ideas advocated by Augustine that are still held as foundational for many thinkers, especially Christian thinkers. Chief among these are his view that the human person is an embodied, social, rational animal who is a creature of God. From this understanding of human nature, the reader can derive the following advice for how to go about pursuing her own philosophy, her own friendly relationship with Wisdom.

Augustine's view that the human person is made of earth and ashes required him to consider humbly the physical and bodily needs of himself and those around him. His philosophical dialogues never failed to break for lunch and dinner, for a hot bath, and for sleep. He recognized that his own ability to hold philosophical conversation was weakened when he strained his voice and his lungs. Moreover, he was well aware that the place and leisure time required for philosophical conversation had to be secured by

---

7. For example, see Doct. IV.xxxi.64: "Ego tamen Deo nostro gratias ago, quod in his quattuor libris non qualis ego essem, cui multa desunt, sed qualis esse debeat qui in doctrina sana, id est Christiana, non solum sibi sed aliis etiam laborare studet, quantulacumque potui facultate disserui." (I nevertheless give thanks to our God that in these four books I was able to explain not the type of person that I am, to whom much is lacking, but the type of person that one ought to be, who tries to work out sane doctrine that is Christian, not for oneself alone but indeed for others.); Ench. I.xxxiii.122: "Sed sit aliquando huius voluminis finis, quod ipse videris utrum Enchiridion vel appellare debeas vel habere." (But the volume is finished, so that you will see whether you ought to call this a *handbook* or hold onto it as such.) See also the end of De *Trinitate*, where Augustine quoted Ecclesiastes 43:27, Trin. XV.xxviii.51: "Multa, inquit, dicimus, et non pervenimus, et consummatio sermonum universa est ipse." (We said many things, and we did not come through, and the last word is "He is the all".); "Domine Deus une, Deus Trinitas, quaecumque dixi in his libris de tuo, agnoscant et tui: si qua de meo, et tu ignosce, et tui." (Sir, One God, Triune God, whatever I said in this book that is about you may they who are yours recognize it as yours, and if I said anything of my own may you and your people ignore it.) For example, see CA III.xx.44: "Quare iam, socii mei, exspectationem vestram, qua me ad respondendum provocabatis, certiore spe mecum ad discendum convertite. Habemus ducem qui nos in ipsa veritatis arcana, Deo iam monstrante, perducat." (Now, my fellows, change your expectations, by which you tried to provoke me to give a response. Convert to a more certain hope of being a student with me. We have a leader who leads us into the mysteries of Truth herself, under God's guidance.)

money given by benefactors who were willing to share with others what they had earned or inherited. In contrast, he criticized the Manicheans for ignoring bodily needs and their elitist beliefs that forbid the giving of bread to the hungry outside of their sect. In general, Augustine suggested, while one fruit of philosophy was to become less concerned with physical discomfort and even to lose one's fear of death,[8] taking care of one's own body and the body of others was imperative for human beings as they searched for wisdom. Taking care of the bodies of others is important because no human being is able to grow in wisdom or even exist on her own, according to Augustine. His understanding of the human being as relational required that he understood that bodies exist together in relationship with their environment and each other. The sun, the earth, the air, and the water are shared in the interaction of human beings. The health of one person's body relates directly to the health and well-being of all.

This, according to Augustine, is also true of the human mind. The human mind does not create and contain its own ideas but rather shares ideas with others through culture, books, and conversations. Just as human beings share air through breathing, human beings share ideas through communicating. The sanity of one person's mind relates directly to the sanity and well-being of all. In order to best navigate and cultivate the ideas of one's community and culture, Augustine had several important suggestions beyond the taking care of bodies.

For one, Augustine, professor of rhetoric that he was, evangelized often for the liberal arts, those disciplines that Greeks and Romans named liberal because they were appropriate for free citizens and because they encouraged free thinking. In Augustine's Roman Empire, the liberal arts were seven in number: Rhetoric, Logic (or Dialectic), Grammar, Arithmetic, Geometry, Astronomy, and Music. Augustine insisted throughout his life that people should seek and encourage others to seek a liberal education because philosophy and the pursuit of true ideas required that one learned to read and write, to listen well and speak clearly, to understand harmony, and to think logically about mathematics, the natural world, and all that one read, heard, and promoted. While he did not want to discourage any person, such as his mother, from doing philosophy if she had not had the benefit of a liberal

---

8. See Ord. I.xi.32: "in ea tantum profeceris, ut iam nec cuiusvis incommodi fortuiti nec ipsius mortis, quod viris doctissimis difficillimum est, horrore terrearis, quam summam philosophiae arcem omnes esse confitentur." (You have become so proficient in this [love of wisdom] that you are not dreadfully afraid of any unfortunate discomfort or even death itself, which is most difficult for the most learned man and is confessed by all to be the highest fortress of philosophy.)

education,[9] he did want to make liberal arts education as widely available as possible. His insistence on this point inspired Europeans—even in the most illiterate eras of the Middle Ages—to keep the liberal disciplines alive if only in monasteries and the studies of the wealthiest nobles.[10]

Next, Augustine insisted that philosophy should be done by and with many different kinds of people, certainly not only among the wealthiest of nobles. This is seen in Augustine's admonition to young women and his own mother that their philosophical pursuits were important to him. Augustine insisted that he had much to learn from everybody. Indeed, he said that often some of the best philosophers were cobblers.[11] And he claimed that he learned a great deal from conversations with his young teenage son.[12] As a priest and as a bishop, Augustine urged his congregants to do philosophy with each other for the good of the whole community. His goal was to encourage others not just to do philosophy for their own sake but also for the sake of communal knowledge. He believed that human beings, as social animals, could only learn in community. The broader and more diverse the community the fuller the conversation.

Thus, Augustine debated with those who disagreed with him in public. From the time Augustine was a young man debating the Manichean Faustus until he was an established bishop debating the Donatists, Crispinus and Emeritus, Augustine believed in the power of public conversation and disputation to reveal error and provide correction. While gnostics proclaim that their knowledge is secret and elect, Augustine believed that all truths are universally accessible. While some Christians were afraid to talk to non-believers or people of other sects lest they be led away from truth into error, Augustine insisted that no interlocutor was to be avoided. Rather than warn people away

9. See Ret. I.iii.2.

10. For more on Augustine's understanding of the liberal arts and the effect of his views on Europe's medieval period, see Marrou, *History of Education in Antiquity*; Abelson, *Seven Liberal Arts*.

11. Ord. I.xi.31: "Doctissimorum autem hominum litterae etiam sutores philosophatos et multo viliora fortunarum genera continent: qui tamen tanta ingenii virtutisque luce fulserunt, ut bona sua cum qualibet huiuscemodi nobilitate nullo modo vellent, etiamsi possent, ulla conditione mutare." (However, the writings of the most learned people include philosophical shoemakers and those with much more vulgar types of fortunes, who nevertheless shone with the light of such genius and virtue that even if they could have done so they would in no way have wanted to exchange their good for that of any of the nobility.)

12. See Conf. IX.vi.14. Augustine claimed that at the age of fifteen, Adeodatus's "genius surpassed many serious and educated men" (ingenio praeveniebat multos graves et doctos viros). Augustine claimed that while he gave nothing to Adeodatus but sin, "I experienced many things about him which were wonderful: his genius was awesome to me" (multa eius alias mirabiliora expertus sum: horrori mihi erat illud ingenium).

from speaking to Manicheans, he debated them in public. Rather than accept that any bishop, whether of Hippo or of Rome, could make declarations that would hold for the entire church, he expected counsels and conversation on every issue, even ones as dangerous as Pelagianism.

Importantly, this did not mean that Augustine expected every person to be able to have a conversation and find the truth clearly and instantly on her own. Again, he believed that human beings needed education in reading, writing, speaking, and thinking in order that they might learn how to detect fallacies and to recognize syllogisms. In general, human beings, even those of great talent and education, needed to do their learning and their discerning in and with community. Even when they were certain that they had found the truth or had rooted out an error, they needed to remain in conversation with their community members to increase their understanding. The greatest danger to a human being as she pursues knowledge is not someone who is ignorant or even a trickster.[13] Rather, the greatest danger is her own pride, which might blind her to the arguments of another. Thus, Augustine advocated the greatest of humility in all conversations. He praised his mother's humility and chastised young scholars who spent more time ornamenting their own speeches with jargon than listening to each other.[14] Those who want Truth rather than verisimilitude, or truthiness, must have an openness to being wrong that compels them not only to speak to others but also to listen.

Importantly, that humility and openness to others requires an incredible amount of confidence in the Truth and hope in Truth's accessibility. The foundation of Augustine's fearlessness in conversation and humility in debate was his bold certainty that Truth was seeking him, that his friendship with Truth was a mutual relationship. He believed that Truth is present, even when he could not see her, even when he was in a discussion with someone who did not believe she existed, and even when he was in a discussion with someone who wanted to do violence to him for his beliefs. This

---

13. Augustine went so far as to say that it is helpful to have heretics debate because it helps people shake off their sluggishness. See DGM I.i.2: "Sed ideo divina providentia multos diversi erroris haereticos esse permittit, ut cum insultant nobis, et interrogant nos ea quae nescimus, vel sic excutiamus pigritiam, et divinas Scripturas nosse cupiamus. Propterea et Apostolus dicit: Oportet multas haereses esse, ut probati manifesti fiant inter vos." (But divine providence permits many heretics with diverse errors so that when they insult us and ask us what we do not know, we may shake off our sluggishness and desire to know the divine Scriptures. Thus, the Apostle says, "It is necessary that there be many heresies in order that what is manifest be tested among you.")

14. For a discussion of Augustine's frustration with the arrogance of educated young men in comparison with the humility of his mother, see Conybeare, *Irrational Augustine*, 107–13.

meant he could hold conversations with Donatists even as they called him a dangerous seducer of souls and encouraged violence against him. This meant he answered back to the bishop of Rome even though this could have threatened his own position of power. But most of all it meant he spent a great deal of time reading Scripture, in prayer, and in worship, building his confidence in the Truth he believed loved him.

For Augustine, the only reason he had the strength and confidence to promote the liberal arts, to promote conversation with diverse peoples, to debate publically, and to listen with humility was because the Truth was helping him all the time. For Augustine, more important than any of the other pieces of advice he gave to philosophers was this one: trust the Truth who promises that those who seek will find. As such, Augustine's philosophy was completely built on faith—a faith that grew from his own lived experiences, certainly, but nonetheless faith.

Augustinian Concepts and Twenty-First-Century Professional Philosophy

The reader might wonder if a philosophy built on the faith of a fourth-century African catholic Christian can really be of help to twenty-first-century thinkers. And some aspects of Augustine's thought must surely be put aside by those who use his own criteria of not believing in things that are absurd,[15] such as his pre-Copernican cosmology,[16] his insistence on the existence of dragons,[17] and his advice that women ought to wear any fashions or jewelry that their husbands purchase.[18] But of course it is unlikely that the reader is concerned about these trifles. Rather, the reader might be more concerned that in order to hold Augustine's philosophical hope, she might be obligated to an "ancient metaphysics that tried to systematize" the movement of Truth

---

15. See DG12 I.xix.31: "Turpe est autem nimis et perniciosum ac maxime cavendum, ut christianum de his rebus quasi secundum christianas Litteras loquentem, ita delirare audiat, ut, quemadmodum dicitur, toto coelo errare conspiciens, risum tenere vix possit." (However, it is disgusting and dangerous, and a great thing to be wary of, that a Christian speaking about things that follow from the holy scriptures should presumably be heard to be delirious, so that something is said which is entirely nonsense and error so much so that no one can hold back from laughing.)

16. See DG viii.29.

17. See Conf. VII.xiii.19: "quoniam laudandum te ostendunt de terra dracones et omnes abyssi." (These things on earth show that I ought to praise you: dragons and all abysses.)

18. See Epis. 262, "To Ecdicia" (395).

in the world, an ancient metaphysics beyond which "we can do better."[19] Indeed, this concern, raised by contemporary philosopher and theologian Robert Neville, is a real concern. In the twenty-first century, when post ontological structuralism reigns at philosophical conferences, even traditional Christians like Jean-Luc Marion are writing books with provocative titles such as *God without Being*. Thoughtful philosophers no longer can assert the being of transcendent noetic concepts like "Beauty," "Goodness," and "Justice" in a culture where these terms no longer hold meaning as ontological realities that participate in the world; today, these are terms for human judgments made by humans interacting in the world. To be fair, arguments against Augustine's Platonic metaphysics have been made for centuries. Thomists have usually preferred Aristotelian metaphysics to what they consider Augustine's overreliance on Platonism; Lutherans have often preferred nominalism, existentialism, or process theology to what they see as Augustine's essentialism; and pragmatists have wondered why Augustine needed to talk so much about metaphysics at all.

But the central foundation for Augustine's hope, according to Augustine himself, is not found in the *being* of Platonic essences or even in the *being* of Truth herself but in the *friendly heartedness*, in the *misericordia*, of Truth. Augustine's metaphysics is not Platonic, it is relational. While he did claim that the Truth is eternal and unchangeable, the only Truth human beings know is the Truth for people, with people, in people, and in their world. For Augustine, the most important thing to know about Truth is not that it is transcendent but that it is immanent. Thus, whether a philosopher is convinced more by the metaphysical systems of Plotinus or Aristotle, the pragmatism of Quine or Neville, or the anti-metaphysical systems of Marion or Derrida, Augustine's central point is that the philosopher can trust that throughout her journey, the Truth is present and in loving relationship with her and all those she reads and teaches.

In the twenty-first century, there is good reason to suggest that philosophers need to create and embrace a radically new metaphysical understanding of themselves and the world. Cornel West has suggested that for nearly two hundred years, American philosophers have been making good arguments for embracing a *dynamic* understanding of both human selves and structures.[20] As such, perhaps the human might better be understood as a *becoming* than a *being*. A human person's identity does not appear to be isolated or fixed according to empirical evidence. A human person continually evolves into who she becomes as she is categorized, named, observed,

---

19. Neville, "Thanks and Conversation," 374.
20. West, *American Evasion of Philosophy*, 10.

and objectified by scientists, politicians, family members, friends, enemies, and clergy. At times, her material body seems to defy the names she is given, forcing observers to rethink their views. And other times, her body appears to be shaped in response to social pressures, psychotherapeutic drugs, surgeon's knives, and genetic therapy. Of course, despite all this constant, observable changing of labels and bodies, the most fundamental evidence experienced by each conscious human self is that she exists, she thinks, she doubts, she wills as an individual, even as she can recognize that how she exists, what she thinks, what she doubts, and what she wills is culturally and biologically influenced. In short, the human person can see herself as an individual who is so completely entangled in her physical and cultural environment that there are no clear boundaries to what is authentically her own. A person's merits, citizenship status, race, and gender are, in the present era, considered obviously fluid, determined by a complicated entanglement of physical data and competing cultural ideas, themselves in constant flux. Of course, the good that the person seeks is also a concept that changes, seemingly dependent on nature, nurture, chance, and perhaps choice. A philosopher today needs to take all the empirical evidence and cultural ideas into account. In the fourth century, Augustine found the books of the Platonists helpful because they expanded his ability to think abstractly. His advice in the twenty-first century would be to consider the writings and work that is being done by philosophers around the globe today.

Yet, given the incredible revolution in metaphysics that is happening in today's academy, Augustine would ask thinkers to consider his explanation for the ability of human beings to create a new metaphysical structure that better explains the reality they experience. His explanation is that Truth built human beings for relationship with Truth. Augustine might argue that the current revolution in philosophical metaphysics is evidence that philosophy is not at an end, the pursuit of truth is not pointless, and there is clearly the ability to recognize what works and what does not. Perhaps there is no other era in the history of philosophy where one might make a better argument that human beings can move beyond culturally accepted ideas that are not adequate or helpful to better ideas that are more adequate and more useful. The current burst of creativity among French and American philosophers on this front can be seen as evidence for the hope in philosophy.

Of course, Augustine used a particular kind of language to explain what he meant by Truth. In Augustine's language, Truth is the Being "in whom and by whom and through whom all things are true which are true" and "in whom and by whom and through whom all those are wise who are wise."[21] But his Platonic phrasing is less important than his relational phrasing. Truth is the one to whom Augustine cried,

> Hear, hear, hear me, my God, my master of my house, my king, my father, my cause, my hope, my thing, my honor, my house, my native land, my health, my light, my life. Hear hear, hear me. . . . Now you alone I love, you alone I follow, you alone I seek, you alone I am prepared to serve, you alone rule justly, I desire to be under your jurisdiction.[22]

Augustine's greatest message to philosophers is not to adopt an ancient systematic metaphysics but to open themselves to a relationship with Truth by opening their eyes and ears to the world and the people in it. Augustine's arguments for his hope are not metaphysical proofs, they are phenomenological arguments from his lived experience. He pointed to the observable facts that human beings can recognize logical statements and detect logical fallacies, that even small children can do simple arithmetic, that even in the most corrupt societies there are people who can articulate judgments against the authorities and work for different political structures that better treat human beings with kindness and dignity. Of course human beings make mistakes, but the remarkable thing, according to Augustine, is that human beings sometimes recognize those mistakes and correct them. These observable facts are a joy to acknowledge for human beings because, as Augustine witnessed from his own experience, human beings are built to seek wisdom. Humans are happy when they discover new knowledge, both because they can use that knowledge practically and because the knowledge itself gives them joy. Contemporary scientists agree, attesting biologically, neurologically, and psychologically that human beings are wisdom-seeking hominoids. Humans are passionately attracted to discovering new ideas; they are rewarded biologically with shots of dopamine when they hear something new to them. And while that passion might make them gullible to websites offering conspiracy theories and frantic to hold on to an idea even when it is proven wrong, that passion will not desist simply by being told that there is no possibility for knowing true things. How blessed, then,

---

21. See Sol. I.i.3: "in quo et a quo et per quem vera sunt, quae vera sunt Omnia . . . in quo et a quo et per quem sapiunt, quae sapiunt omnia."

22. Sol. I.i.4–5: "Exaudi, exaudi, exaudi me, Deus meus, Domine meus, rex meus, pater meus, causa mea, spes mea, res mea, honor meus, domus mea, patria mea, salus mea, lux mea, vita mea. Exaudi, exaudi, exaudi me. . . . Iam te solum amo, te solum sequor, te solum quaero, tibi soli servire paratus sum, quia tu solus iuste dominaris; tui iuris esse cupio."

said Augustine, that human beings can recognize that they certainly have moments when they do indeed find truths.

Certainly, Augustine's language is Christian, and this is more than a language game for him. Augustine put his trust in the words of Christian scripture. In moments of doubt and anxiety, he rested on the literal promise of Truth that tells people not to be afraid, that Truth is with them always, and that all who seek will find. Augustine put his trust in the Genesis creation story that the creator of the cosmos designed the world with an order that human minds can discover. Augustine put his trust in the Exodus story that the Being "who is what it is" speaks openly to people whether they are looking for truth or not. Augustine put his trust, most of all, in the gospel story that the Light who is the Truth came to seek human beings, to dwell with them, die with them, and rise with them so that they might know they are never without Truth's friendly presence. Therefore, Christian philosophers are the readers most likely to see the use of Augustine's account. Certainly, Augustine made a powerful argument to Christians that they should keep seeking understanding by observing their world and talking to their neighbors in it.

But Augustine wrote for non-Christians, too. Ultimately, he was not an evangelist for a specific religion but for Truth itself. He found that Christianity explained his experiences of a loving, friendly hearted, and personal God. He did not believe in Christianity and thus decide it seemed true; he found that Christianity seemed true and thus believed it. Moreover, he wrote the same message to both Christians and non-Christians: "Come with me to philosophy, here is whatever is needed to move you wonderfully, you who are often anxious or in doubt."[23]

Using Augustine's Method Today

To come to philosophy with Augustinian hope means to be open to the Truth as it moves through one's relationship with the world and other people. For Augustine, the most important part of philosophy is conversation. Thus, Augustine's invitation to philosophy is an invitation to conversation, certainly with the great books of philosophers from ages past and present, but also with nature and with people.

Certainly, finding the time to walk in nature and listen to the trees, the wind, and the animals is difficult enough. Moreover, finding the time to spend hours in long conversations, even with friends and family, might

---

23. CA II.ii.3: "Ergo aggredere mecum philosophiam: hic est quidquid te anxium saepe, atque dubitantem mirabiliter solet movere."

seem impossible given the frantic pace of work in the twenty-first century. After all, only illness, which prevented him from working, and a wealthy friend who became his benefactor allowed Augustine to secure the time for such walks and conversations in Cassiacum. But time and money aside, the real barrier to openness to conversation is likely fear. And fear is warranted. Sometimes conversations go badly, sometimes people deceive and are deceived. Sometimes people are physically and psychologically harmed. Cornel West once said that a love of truth requires love of other people, but "the love that I'm talking about is usually a love that leads toward crucifixion." The one who is the Light, the Love, and the Truth was tortured, crucified, and murdered. But Cornel West quickly followed this observation with the point that trying to avoid this pain by loving something smaller, such as a "love of power, love of pleasure, love of honor, love of king, love of queen, love of nation, love of race" is not going to be satisfying to the human heart. West asked rhetorically, "The other, narrow love, usually has the power to snuff you out. Augustine was fundamentally right—if you're going to love, why not have the broadest, deepest, self-emptying kind of love that embraces everybody?"[24] In other words, human beings are meant to love wisdom, and loving wisdom requires openness to relationship in the broadest sense. While this is dangerous, there is no other choice for human beings that want to have a happy life.

Moreover, while it is easy to name the errors of the twentieth and even twenty-first century—such as genocide, environmental harm, systemic racism, and specific scientific errors—it is also easy to name some of the advances in knowledge. Newborns with heart defects can be saved by surgeries, factories can be run on solar and wind power, human beings can walk in space, and researchers can find original Latin texts of a quote by Fulgentius in seconds on the world wide web. Suggesting that there are real advances in ethics is more complicated, of course. And Augustine, living at the end of late antiquity, when there was more decay in Roman society than flourishing, did not assume that human history was progressive in love, inclusivity, and kindness. And yet, he recognized that there were moments when people came together, when friendly heartedness was magnified.

In the news, there have been three remarkable stories that speak to the Augustinian hope for such friendly hearted relationships. These accounts neither prove the point nor do they suggest that there are minimal risks in such attempts. But they do speak to the possibility that in coming together in relationship, Truth's friendly heart is evident. All three involve people who were committed to the twenty-first-century's most dangerous kind of

24. West and Yancy, "Power Is Everywhere."

gnosticism, white supremacy, but who were opened to see more broadly through the friendship of others outside the group.

The first story begins with Pardeep Kaleka, whose father and five other people were massacred by a white supremacist during a service at the Sikh Temple in Oak Creek, Wisconsin, in 2012. Kaleka, whose Sikhism teaches optimism rooted in compassion, wanted to understand how and why someone would do this murderous act. In order that he might grow in his understanding, he contacted a former white supremacist named Arno Michaelis who had written a book about his experiences called *My Life After Hate*.[25] Michaelis was working as a motivational speaker to help people recover after leaving white supremacist groups. Michaelis had not just been a listener to white supremacy but a leader, a reverend in what he saw as a holy religious war and a lead singer in a popular white power metal band. He had in his past encouraged and trained the kind of killer who had murdered Kaleka's father. Kaleka's family asked him to reconsider the decision to meet with Michaelis, but Kaleka went ahead with their meeting. Michaelis was also concerned before the meeting. While he had become an anti-hate advocate, he wondered whether Kaleka wanted revenge. The two men met in a café and talked. Their conversation led to others. Together, they founded an organization called Serve2Unite and wrote a book, *The Gift of Our Wounds*.[26] Today, they continue to give lectures and lead discussions across the United States about the power of friendly conversation in increasing understanding and the power of forgiveness in healing traumatic wounds.

While Kaleka contacted Arno after he had become an anti-hate activist, the second story is about a Jewish student who sought friendship with a leader in a white supremacist group who was still an active member. Indeed, Derek Black was deep into the white nationalist movement when Matthew Stevenson invited him to dinner. Black's father started *Stormfront*, the first white supremacist hate website. Importantly, as Black has explained to reporters, he did not consider himself a racist or a member of a hate group. Those who come upon *Stormfront* are never told it is a hate group; they are not attracted to the group by racist hatred but by the promise that they are elite. They are given what they are told is simple and clear knowledge that has been withheld from them by the government and mainstream media. Black explained that as a child he was armed with statistics and rhetorical skill to argue for white separatism. Having grown up in a white supremacist family, he was given an upbringing that ensured his coherence to the group's beliefs. His father trained him to argue for the group. From the age

25. See Michaelis, *My Life after Hate*.
26. Michaelis and Kaleka, *Gifts of Our Wounds*.

of twelve, Black had appeared on talk shows and at rallies. When he went to college, he found himself surrounded by fellow students who were appalled at his active white supremacy. While the arguments and rage of other students did not at the time deter him from his beliefs, the arguments began to affect his views as he became friends with a Jewish student named Matthew Stevenson. Stevenson, a fellow dorm resident, invited Black to come to Shabbat dinner in his dorm room not only once but every Friday night for over two years. Black recounted that he came to the first dinner armed with arguments for his beliefs as he assumed that those attending would try to get him to renounce his views. However, he was unnerved to find that rather than arguments he was offered only friendship. For two years, Black continued to write and speak for white supremacy at the same time that he was attending weekly Shabbat dinners with Matthew Stevenson and others. Some students were angry with Stevenson for his friendship with someone who was working for dangerous policies. Stevenson said that because he was a Jew, a member of a group despised on *Stormfront*, he was able to convince others that he was not agreeing to Black's ideology but using another method to confront it. He said, "As far as hope, I think that the underlying spark of goodness that's within each and every one of us and within everybody in the world is ultimately going to win out; that this empathy that people can generate and feel—you can't stop it in the long run."[27] In the long run, this empathy did win out. Black found that he could not reconcile his friendship with a Jew with the tenets of white supremacy. Another mutual friend who had gone so far as to attend a seminar with Black on white supremacy asked him afterwards gently why, if the group really was only trying to support white people, the group spent so much time and energy making obviously false arguments against Jews, such as that the Holocaust did not happen. The friend asked how denying the Holocaust, when there was so much evidence of its reality, helped poor white people thrive. Black said he realized that this denouncing of the Holocaust was illogical, and the arguments he had trusted began to fall away. Black thus insisted it was not just friendship that made him renounce white supremacy, it was recognizing the untruth in the movement. But he said the logical arguments would not have landed without the friendship, and the friendship could not have endured without the logic. Importantly, Black would not say he came to a new opinion, he would say that he came to a new understanding. Today, he is pursuing a doctorate in history at the University of Chicago on the roots of racism.[28]

27. Stevenson interviewed in Tippet, "Befriending Radical Disagreement."
28. For more on Black's story, see Saslow, *Rising out of Hatred*.

While both Kaleka and Stevenson sought conversations with white supremacists, the third story is of an encounter of a white supremacist seeking friendship with an African American man. Daryl Davis, a jazz pianist, recounted how a white man asked if he could buy him a drink at a bar after a set. Davis, used to such invitations, agreed, but he was surprised when the man said that he had never heard a black person who could play like Jerry Lee Lewis. Davis was more surprised when the man admitted he had never actually talked to a black person before. Davis said he was wondering how this kind of ignorance and separation could be possible when the man suddenly confessed that he was a member of Ku Klux Klan. Davis immediately recognized the danger in the situation but continued the conversation. Over the next thirty years, Davis met with the man, his friends, and even a Grand Dragon. Every time he met with a new Klansman, he knew he could be in grave danger. But over the course of thirty years, he converted over two hundred Klansmen, including the Grand Dragon. As a symbol of this, he has kept a closet full of Klan robes that have been given to him by people leaving the movement.[29] He has written a book, *Klan-destine Relationships: A Black Man's Odyssey in the Ku Klux Klan*, about his experiences in order to encourage others to have the confidence to try to engage in friendly conversation with their most dangerous enemies. He explained,

> This book is by no means a how-to manual providing the solution to the racial plague on our planet. . . . Perhaps my experiences will shed more understanding and others will be inspired to seek out and eradicate racial prejudice with education, not only the academic type one receives in school, but the kind we attain when we learn about our fellow human beings from one-on-one, non-confrontational encounters. It is my dream, that through this new discourse, in a new millennium of brotherly love and friendship, we will overcome hatred and prejudice.[30]

These stories are hopeful. But of course they make the news because they are not the norm. More typically, people find it difficult to have conversations on subjects on which they disagree, even with those they love. This, however, is not a twenty-first-century problem; this is a human problem. Augustine was not a naïve thinker. He did not think that humans easily understood their world, each other, or even themselves. In his lifetime, he saw theological controversies tear apart the church, and he saw war and insurrection tear society apart. At the end of his life, he saw barbarous warriors destroy whole cities, slaughtering the inhabitants,

29. Brown, "How One Man Convinced 200."
30. Davis, *Klan-destine Relationships*, 312.

including the priests, nuns, monks, and teachers. He saw people lose their faith and lose their innocence as they endured this trauma.[31] He certainly understood the feeling of apocalyptic anxiety, the skeptical loss of hope, and the despair of nihilism. And yet, Augustine remained a hopeful friend of Wisdom until his death. As he watched the Vandals sacking Carthage, he wept, but he also went through each of his writings and explained better what he meant, making corrections where he realized he had erred. He knew his writings might be saved for later generations, and he wanted to be the best possible friend to later thinkers.

Augustine's tombstone, according to Possidius, had the following epigraph: "Do you know how the enthusiasm of the bard lives after death, Traveler? When you read, behold, I speak, and your voice is mine."[32] The hope of this book is to introduce the enthusiasm of Augustine to a new generation of people who are experiencing an old despair. Augustine's enthusiasm, his vim and vigor, came from his hope. His hope arose as a response to a promise, a promise his experience showed him was worth trusting. At the close of Augustine's *Soliloquies*, he wrote that his Reason told him, "Be of good spirit! God will support us, as we already know, in our quest. . . . He promises what is most blessed and the greatest fullness of Truth without any deception." Augustine ends the dialogue with the humble reply to Reason, "Let it be as we hope."[33]

Let it be as we hope as well. And let our hope allow us to be open to the world and our neighbors as we pursue a friendly relationship with Truth, who promises to always have a friendly heart.

31. See Possidius, *Vita* 28.

32. Possidius, *Vita* 31.8: "Vivere post obitum vates vis nosse viator? Quod legis ecce loquor, vox tua nempe mea est."

33. Sol. II.xix.36: "R.—Bono animo esto; Deus aderit, ut iam sentimus, quaerentibus nobis, qui beatissimum quiddam [post hoc corpus] et veritatis plenissimum sine ullo mendacio pollicetur. A.—Fiat ut speramus."

Bibliography

Abelson, Paul. *The Seven Liberal Arts: A Study in Medieval Culture.* New York: Russell and Russell, 1965.

Aristotle. *Metaphysics.* Edited by W. D. Ross. Oxford: Clarendon, 1924. *Perseus Digital Library.* Edited by Gregory R. Crane. Online. https://www.perseus.tufts.edu/hopper/text?doc=Perseus:text:1999.01.0051.

———. *Nicomachean Ethics.* Edited by J. Bywater. Oxford: Clarendon, 1894. *Perseus Digital Library.* Edited by Gregory R. Crane. Online. http://www.perseus.tufts.edu/hopper/text?doc=Perseus:text:1999.01.0053.

———. *Nicomachean Ethics.* Translated by Terrence Irwin. Indianapolis: Hackett, 2019.

Augustine. *Against the Academicians and the Teacher.* Translated by Peter King. Indianapolis: Hackett, 1995.

———. *Against Julian.* Vol. 16 of *Augstine's Works.* Edited by Roy Joseph Deferrari. Translated by Matthew A. Schumacher. The Fathers of the Church: A New Translation 35. New York: Fathers of the Church, 1957.

———. "Christian Doctrine." In Vol. 2 of *A Select Library of the Nicene and Post-Nicene Fathers of the Christian Church,* edited by Philip Schaff, 519–97. Translated by J. F. Shaw. Grand Rapids: Eerdmans, 1979.

———. *City of God.* Translated by Marcus Dods. New York: Modern Library, 1993.

———. *Confessiones.* Edited by J. J. O'Donnell. Oxford: Clarendon, 1992.

———. *Confessions.* Translated by Sarah Rudin. New York: Modern Library, 2017.

———. "Divine Providence and the Problem of Evil." In vol. 5 of *Writings of Saint Augustine,* edited by Ludwig Schopp, 239–334. Translated by Robert P. Russell. New York: Cima, 1948.

———. "The Happy Life." In vol. 1 of *Writings of Saint Augustine,* edited by Ludwig Schopp, 43–86. Translated by Ludwig Schopp. New York: Cima,1948.

———. *Letters.* Vols. 9–13 of *Writings of Saint Augustine.* Edited by Roy Joseph Defarrari. Translated by S. Wilfrid Parsons. The Fathers of the Church: A New Translation 12, 18, 20, 30, 32. New York: Fathers of the Church, 1956.

———. *The Lord's Sermon on the Mount.* Translated by John J. Jepson. Westminster, MD: Newman, 1948.

———. "The Nature of the Good." In *Augustine: Earlier Writings,* edited by John H. S. Burleigh, 326–48. Translated by John H. S. Burleigh. Philadelphia: Westminster, 1953.

———. "Of True Religion." In *Augustine: Earlier Writings,* edited by John H. S. Burleigh, 225–83. Translated by John H. S. Burleigh. Philadelphia: Westminster, 1953.

————. "On Free Will." In *Augustine: Earlier Writings*, edited by John H. S. Burleigh, 113–217. Translated by John H. S. Burleigh. Philadelphia: Westminster, 1953.

————. "On the Literal Interpretation of Genesis: An Unfinished Book." In *Saint Augustine on Genesis*, edited by Thomas P. Halton et al., 143–90. Translated by Roland J. Teske. The Fathers of the Church: A New Translation 84. Washington, DC: Catholic University of America Press, 1991.

————. "On the Morals of the Manichees." In *St. Augustine: The Writings against the Manicheans and against the Donatists*, edited by Philip Schaff, 69–89. Vol. 4 of *The Nicene and Post-Nicene Fathers*, Series 1. Translated by R. Stothert. Grand Rapids: Eerdmans, 1979.

————. *Opera Omnia: Patrologiae Latinae Elenchus*. Edited by J.-P. Migne. Vols. 32–47 of *Patrologia Latina*. Paris: n.p., 1841–1845. Online. http://www.augustinus.it/latino.

————. *Retractions*. Translated by Sister M. Inez Bogan. Washington DC: Catholic University Press, 1968.

————. *Sermons*. Vol. 3 of *The Works of St. Augustine: A Translation for the Twenty-First Century*. Edited by John E. Rotelle. Translated by Edmund Hill. Brooklyn: New City, 1990.

————. "The Soliloquies." In *Augustine: Earlier Writings*, edited by John H. S. Burleigh, 23–63. Translated by John H. S. Burleigh. Philadelphia: Westminster, 1953.

————. "Two Books on Genesis against the Manichees." In *Saint Augustine on Genesis*, edited by Thomas P. Halton et al., 45–142. Translated by Roland J. Teske. The Fathers of the Church: A New Translation 84. Washington, DC: Catholic University of America Press, 1991.

————. "The Usefulness of Belief." In *Augustine: Earlier Writings*, edited by John H. S. Burleigh, 291–323. Translated by John H. S. Burleigh. Philadelphia: Westminster, 1953.

Barron, Robert. "Thomas Aquinas and the Art of Making a Public Argument." *Word on Fire* (blog), June 21, 2016. Online. https://www.wordonfire.org/resources/article/thomas-aquinas-and-the-art-of-making-a-public-argument/5209.

Benedict XV. "The New Codex of Canon Law as Issued by Authority of Pope Benedict XV in 1917." In *The Summa Theologica of St. Thomas Aquinas*, viii–xxxv. Translated by the Fathers of the English Dominican Province. London: Burns Oates & Washbourne, 1920.

Bernard of Clairvaux. "Letter to Hildegard." In *Epistolae*, edited by J. Leclercq and H. Rochais, 323–24. Vol. 7 of *Sancti Bernardi, Opera*. Rome: Cistercians, 1974. Online. https://epistolae.ctl.columbia.edu/letter/1189.html.

Boulding, Maria. "Introduction." In *Saint Augustine: The Confessions*, edited by J. E. Rotelle, 9–33. Hyde Park: New City, 1997.

Bourke, Vernon. *Augustine's Question of Wisdom: The Life and Philosophy of the Bishop of Hippo*. 1945. Reprint, Providence: Cluny, 2019.

Brown, Dwane. "How One Man Convinced 200 Ku Klux Klan Members to Give up Their Robes." *All Things Considered*, August 20, 2017. Online. https://www.npr.org/2017/08/20/544861933/how-one-man-convinced-200-ku-klux-klan-members-to-give-up-their-robes.

Brown, Peter. *Augustine of Hippo*. Berkeley: University of California Press, 1967.

Burger, Ariel. *Witness: Lessons from Elie Wiesel's Classroom*. Boston: Houghton Mifflin Harcourt, 2018.

Butler, Judith. *Notes Toward a Performative Theory of Assembly*. Cambridge, MA: Harvard University Press, 2015.

———. *Subjects of Desire*. New York: Columbia University Press, 1987.

Cahoone, Lawrence. *The Ends of Philosophy*. Albany: State University of New York Press, 1995.

Calvin, Jean. *Institutes of the Christian Religion*. Edited by John T. Mcneill. Translated by Ford Lewis Battles. Library of Christian Classics. Philadelphia: Westminster, 1960.

———. *L'Institution Chrestienne*. Vol. 3 of *Ioannis Calvini Opera quae supersunt Omnia*. Edited by Guilielmus Baum et al. Brunsvigae: C. A. Schwetschike et Filium, 1865. Online. https://archive.org/details/ioanniscalvinioo1unkngoog/page/n70.

———. "Praedestinatione (1552)." In vol. 8 of *Ioannis Calvini Opera quae supersunt Omnia*, edited by Guilielmus Baum et al., 249–366. Brunsvigae: C. A. Schwetschike et Filium, 1870. Online. https://babel.hathitrust.org/cgi/pt?id=hvd.320440142107 28&view=1up&seq=5&size=125.

Cary, Phillip. *Augustine and the Invention of the Inner Self: The Legacy of a Christian Platonist*. Oxford: Oxford University Press, 2000.

———. *The Meaning of Protestant Theology: Luther, Augustine, and the Gospel the Gives Us Christ*. Grand Rapids: Baker, 2019.

Cicero. "Academica." In *De Natura Deorum*; *Academica*, edited by E. H. Warmington, 410–659. With a translation by H. Rackham. LCL. Cambridge, MA: Harvard University Press, 1957. Online. https://ryanfb.github.io/loebolus-data/L268.pdf.

———. *Tusculan Disputations*. With a translation by J. E. King. LCL. Cambridge, MA: Harvard University Press, 1960.

———. *Tusculanarum Disputationum*. *The Latin Library*. Edited by William L. Carey. Online. https://www.thelatinlibrary.com/cicero/tusc3.shtml.

Clifford, Anne. *Diary of Anne Clifford 1616–1619. A Critical Edition*. Edited by Katherine O. Acheson. London: Gartland, 1995.

Clinton, John, and Roush, Cary. "Persistent Partisan Divide Over 'Birther' Question." *NBC News*, August 10, 2016. Online. https://www.nbcnews.com/politics/2016-election/poll-persistent-partisan-divide-over-birther-question-n627446.

Colish, Marcia. *The Mirror of Language: A Study in the Medieval Theory of Knowledge*. New Haven: Yale University Press, 1968.

Conybeare, Catherine. *The Irrational Augustine*. Oxford: Oxford University Press, 2006.

Corbier, Mireille. "Family and Kinship in Roman Africa." In *The Roman Family in the Empire: Rome, Italy, and Beyond*, edited by Michele George, 255–85. Oxford University Press, 2005.

Dancy, R. M. *Two Studies in the Early Academy*. New York: State University of New York Press, 1991.

Davis, Cyprian. *The History of Black Catholics in the United States*. New York: Crossroads, 1990.

Davis, Daryl. *Klan-destine Relationships: A Black Man's Odyssey in the Ku Klux Klan*. Liberty Corner, NJ: New Horizon Press, 1998.

Descartes, Rene. *Meditatio*. 1641. *The Latin Library*. Edited by William L. Carey. Online. https://www.thelatinlibrary.com/descartes/des.med1.shtml.

———. *Meditations on First Philosophy*. 1641. Translated by Donald. A. Cress. Indianapolis: Hackett, 1993.

Emerson, Ralph Waldo. "The Method of Nature: An Oration before the Society of the Adelphi at Waterville College, Maine in 1841." In *The Complete Works of Ralph Waldo Emerson Comprising His Essays Lectures, Poems, and Orations*, 221. London: Bell & Daldy, 1866.

Epicurus. "Letter to Menoikos." With a translation by Peter Saint-Andre. *Monadnock Valley Press*, November 21, 2011. Online. http://monadnock.net/epicurus/letter. html.

Foucault, Michel. "Truth and Power." In *Power/Knowledge: Selected Interviews and Other Writings, 1972–1977*, edited by Colin Gordon, 109–33. Hertfordshire: Harvester, 1980.

Fredriksen, Paula. *Augustine and the Jews: A Christian Defense of Jews and Judaism.* New Haven: Yale University Press, 2010.

Frend, W. H. C. *The Donatist Church: A Movement of Protest in Roman North Africa.* Oxford: Oxford University Press, 1951.

Fulgentius Ruspensis. "Ad Monimum." In *Sancti Fulgentii Episcopi Ruspensis Opera*, edited by J. Fraipont, 1–64. CCL 91. Turnhout: Brepols, 1968.

Galilei, Galileo. "Letter to the Grand Duchess Christina of Tuscany." 1615. *Internet Modern History Sourcebook*, August 1997. Edited by Paul Halsall. Online. https:// web.stanford.edu/~jsabol/certainty/readings/Galileo-LetterDuchessChristina. pdf.

Gardiner, Anne Barbeau. "Entrusting Ourselves: *Fides et ration* and Augustine's *De Utilitate Credenti.*" In *Faith and Reason: The Notre Dame Symposium*, edited by Timothy Smith, 337–45. South Bend: St. Augustine's, 2001.

Garnet, H. H. *A Memorial Discourse.* Philadelphia, 1865.

Gilson, Étienne. *Philosophie et Incarnation selon Saint Augustin.* Montreal: Institute D'Etudes Medievales, 1947.

Goodwin, Deborah L. "Jews and Judaism." In vol. 2 of *The Oxford Guide to the Historical Reception of Augustine*, edited by Karla Pollmann et al., 1214–18. Oxford: Oxford University Press, 2013.

Hildegard of Bingen. "Letter to Elisabeth of Schoneau." In *Hildegard of Bingen, Epistolarium*, edited by L. Van Acker, 456–57. Corpus Christianorum, Continuatio Mediaevalis 91A. Turnholt: Brepols, 1993. Online. https://epistolae.ctl.columbia. edu/letter/125.html.

———. *Scivias.* Edited by A. Führkötter and A. Carlevaris. Corpus Christianorum 43–43A. Turnholt: Brepols, 2003.

Hoby, Margaret. *The Diary of Lady Margaret Hoby (1599–1605).* Edited by D. Meads. London: Routledge & Sons, 1930.

Hockenbery Dragseth, Jennifer. "The He, She, and It of God: Translating Saint Augustine's Gendered Latin God-Talk into English." *Augustinian Studies* 36.2 (2005) 433–44.

Hogenboom, Melissa. "The Enduring Appeal of Conspiracy Theories." *BBC*, January 24, 2018. Online. http://www.bbc.com/future/story/20180124-the-enduring-appeal-of-conspiracy-theories.

Hoitenga, Dewey H. *Plantinga: An Introduction to Reformed Epistemology.* Grand Rapids: Baker, 1997.

Hume, David. *Dialogues Concerning Natural Religion.* 1779. *Early Modern Texts*, 2017. Edited by Jonathan Bennett. Online. https://www.earlymoderntexts.com/assets/ pdfs/hume1779.pdf.

Irenaeas. *The Scandal of the Incarnation: Against the Heresies.* Translated by John Saward. San Francisco: Ignatius, 1981.

Isham, Elizabeth. *My Booke of Rememberance.* 1654. Princeton University Library, Robert H. Taylor Collection, RTCO 11639.

James, William. "Faith and the Right to Believe." In *William James: Writings 1902–1910*, edited by Bruce Kuklick, 1095–1101. New York: Penguin, 1987.

John Paul II. "Fides et Ratio." Encyclical given September 14, 1998. Online. http://w2.vatican.va/content/john-paul-ii/en/encyclicals/documents/hf_jp-ii_enc_14091998_fides-et-ratio.html.

Kajanto, Iiro. *Onomastic Studies in the Early Christian Inscriptions of Rome and Carthage*. Helsinki: Acta Instituti Romani Finlandiae, 1963.

Keneally, Meghan. "Parents Who Don't Vaccinate Kids Tend to Be Affluent, Better Educated, Experts Say." *ABC News*, January 29, 2019. Online. https://abcnews.go.com/Health/parents-vaccinate-kids-tend-affluent-educated-experts/story?id=60674519.

Konig, Daniel. "Augustine and Islam." In vol. 1 of *The Oxford Guide to the Historical Reception of Augustine*, edited by Karla Pollmann et al., 1214–18. Oxford: Oxford University Press, 2013.

Krause, John Godfrey. "The Rector and Public Assembly of Wittenberg University to the Kind Reader Render Public Greeting." In *Antonius Guilielmus Amo Afer of Axim in Ghana: Student Doctor of Philosophy, Master and Lecturer at the Universities of Halle-Wittenberg-Jena 1727–1747*, edited by Dorothea Siegmund-Schultze, 77–79. Halle, Germany: Martin Luther University Halle-Wittenberg, 1968.

Kuhn, Thomas. *The Structure of Scientific Revolutions*. Chicago: University of Chicago Press, 1962.

Lavin, Talia. "The Maddening, Baffling, Exhausting Endurance of Anti-semitism: In an Age of Conspiracy Theories, What Chance Do We Have against the Oldest Conspiracy Theory of All?" *The Nation*, February 13, 2019. Online. https://www.thenation.com/article/antisemitism-conspiracy-ilhan-omar.

Leo XIII. "Encyclical Letter on the Restoration of Christian Philosophy according to the Mind of St. Thomas Aquinas." In *The Summa Theologica of Saint Thomas Aquinas*, edited and translated by the Fathers of the English Dominican Province, ix–xxxiii. 2nd ed. London: Burns Oates and Washbourne, 1920.

Leyser, Conrad. "'Julianus' Pomerius." In vol. 3 of *The Oxford Guide to the Historical Reception of Augustine*, edited by Karla Pollmann et al., 1241–42. Oxford: Oxford University Press, 2013.

Luther, Martin. "Daß Jesus Christus ein geborner Jude sei (1523)" (That Jesus Christ Was Born a Jew). In *Predigten und Schriften 1523*, edited by Joachim Karl Friedrich Knaake et al., 307–36. Vol. 11 of *Weimarer Ausgabe*. Weimar: Hermann Böhlaus, 1900. Online. https://archive.org/details/werkekritischege11luthuoft.

———. "De Captivitate Babylonica Ecclesiae (1520)" (On the Babylonian Captivity of the Church). In *Schriften, Predigten, Disputationen 1519/20*, edited by Joachim Karl Friedrich Knaake et al., 484–573. Vol. 6 of *Weimarer Ausgabe*. Weimar: Hermann Böhlaus, 1888. Online. https://archive.org/details/werkekritischege06luthuoft.

———. "Die Disputation de Homine (1536)" (The Disputation on the Human Person). In *Disputationen 1533/38*, edited by Joachim Karl Friedrich Knaake et al., 174–80. Vol. 39.1 of *Weimarer Ausgabe*. Weimar: Hermann Böhlaus, 1926. Online. https://archive.org/details/werkekritischeg3901luthuoft.

———. "Die Disputation de Sententia: Verbum caro factum est (1539)" (The Disputation on the Sentence: The Word Was Made Flesh). In *Disputationen 1539/45*, edited by Joachim Karl Friedrich Knaake et al., 1–33. Vol. 39.2 of *Weimarer Ausgabe*. Weimar: Hermann Böhlaus, 1932. Online. https://archive.org/details/ab2werkekritisch39luth.

———. *Genesisvorlesung* (*Lectures on Genesis*). Vols. 42–44 of *Weimarer Ausgabe*. Edited by Joachim Karl Friedrich Knaake et al. Weimar: Hermann Böhlaus, 1911–1915. Online. https://archive.org/details/werkekritischege42luthuoft; https://archive.org/details/werkekritischege43luthuoft; https://archive.org/details/werkekritischege44luthuoft.

———. "Predigt am 2. Sonntag nach Epiphania 17. Januar 1546" (Sermon on the Second Sunday after Epiphany, January 17, 1546). In *Predigten 1545/46; Auslegung des 23. und 101. Psalms 1534/36; Schriften 1540/41; Sprichwörter-Sammlung*, edited by Joachim Karl Friedrich Knaake et al., 123–34. Vol. 51 of *Weimarer Ausgabe*. Weimar: Hermann Böhlaus, 1914. Online. https://archive.org/details/werkekritischege51luthuoft.

———. "Predigt am Sonntag Septuagesimä 24. Januar 1535" (Sermon on Septuagesima Sunday, January 24, 1535). In *Predigten 1535/36*, edited by Joachim Karl Friedrich Knaake et al., 17–33. Vol. 41 of *Weimarer Ausgabe*. Weimar: Hermann Böhlaus, 1910. Online. https://archive.org/details/werkekritischege41luthuoft.

———. "Sermon von dem Sacrament des Leibes und Blutes Christi, wider die Schwarmgeister (1526)" (Sermon on the Sacrament of the Body and Blood of Christ—Against the Fanatics). In *Schriften 1526*, edited by Joachim Karl Friedrich Knaake et al., 474–523. Vol. 19 of *Weimarer Ausgabe*. Weimar: Hermann Böhlaus, 1897. Online. http://www.archive.org/details/werkekritischege19luthuoft.

———. "Tractatus de libertate christiana (1520)" (On Christian Liberty). In *Schriften, Predigten, Disputationen 1520/21*, edited by Joachim Karl Friedrich Knaake et al., 39–73. Vol. 7 of *Weimarer Ausgabe*. Weimar: Hermann Böhlaus, 1897. Online. https://archive.org/details/werkekritischege07luthuoft.

———. "Von den Jüden und ihren Lügen (1543)" (On the Jews and Their Lies). In *Schriften 1542/43*, edited by Joachim Karl Friedrich Knaake et al., 406–11. Vol. 53 of *Weimarer Ausgabe*. Weimar: Hermann Böhlaus, 1920. Online. https://archive.org/details/werkekritischege53luthuoft.

———. "Vorrede zu Theodor Biblianders Koranausgabe (1543)" (Preface to Theodor Bibliander's Edition of the Qur'an). In *Schriften 1542/43*, edited by Joachim Karl Friedrich Knaake et al., 561–72. Vol. 53 of *Weimarer Ausgabe*. Weimar: Hermann Böhlaus, 1920. Online. https://archive.org/details/werkekritischege53luthuoft.

———. "Vorrede zum ersten Bande der Gesamtausgaben seiner lateinischen Schriften (1545)" (Preface to the First Volume of the Complete Latin Writings). In *Schriften 1543/46*, edited by Joachim Karl Friedrich Knaake et al., 179–87. Vol. 54 of *Weimarer Ausgabe*. Weimar: Hermann Böhlaus, 1928. Online. http://www.maartenluther.com/54_schriften_1543-46.pdf.

Mallard, William. *Language and Love*. University Park, PA: Pennsylvania State University Press, 1994.

Marion, Jean-Luc. *Dieu sans l'être*. Libraire Artheme Fayard, 1982.

———. *God Without Being*. Translated by Thomas A. Carlson. Chicago: University of Chicago Press, 1991.

Markus, R. A. *Saeculum: History and Society in the Theology of St. Augustine*. Cambridge: Cambridge University Press, 1970.

Marrou, A. *History of Education in Antiquity*. New York: Sheed and Ward, 1956.

Meeink, Frank, and Roy, Jody. *Autobiography of a Recovering Skinhead: The Frank Meeink Story as Told to Jody M. Roy*. Portland, OR: Hawthorne Books & Literary Arts, 2009.

Menn, Stephen. *Descartes and Augustine*. Cambridge: Cambridge University Press, 1998.

Michaelis, Arno. *My Life after Hate*. Milwaukee: Authentic Presence, 2010.

Michaelis, Arno, and Kaleka, Pardeep Singh. *The Gifts of Our Wounds: A Sikh and a Former White Supremacist Find Forgiveness after Hate*. New York: St. Martin's, 2018.

Miles, Margaret. *Desire and Delight*. New York: Crossroad, 1992.

Molekamp, Femke. "Women Readers (Early Modern)." In vol. 3 of *The Oxford Guide to the Historical Reception of Augustine*, edited by Karla Pollmann et al., 1920–22. Oxford: Oxford University Press, 2015.

Neville, Robert. "Thanks and Conversation." In *Theology in Global Context*, edited by Amos Yong and Peter Heltzel, 357–86. New York: T & T Clark, 2004.

Nietzsche, Friedrich. *Die fröhliche Wissenschaft*. Leipzig: E. W. Fritzsch, 1887. Online. http://www.nietzschesource.org/#eKGWB/FW.

———. *The Gay Science*. Translated by Walter Kaufmann. New York: Vintage, 1974.

———. *Jenseits von Gut und Bose*. 1886. Translated by Helen Zimmern. German-English Bilingual ed. N.p.: Wolf Pup, 2013.

Nussbaum, Martha. *The Therapy of Desire*. Princeton: Princeton University Press, 1994.

Nygren, Anders. *Agape and Eros*. Translated by Philip S Watson. Philadelphia: Westminster, 1953.

O'Connell, Robert J. *St. Augustine's Confessions: Odyssey of the Soul*. Cambridge, MA: Belknap Press of Harvard University Press, 1968.

O'Donnell, J. J. *Commentary on Books 1–7*. Vol. 2 of *Augustine: Confessions*. Oxford: Clarendon, 1992.

Ombretta, Chiara. "Fulgentius of Ruspe." In vol. 2 of *The Oxford Guide to the Historical Reception of Augustine*, edited by Karla Pollmann et al., 1022–23. Oxford: Oxford University Press, 2015.

Osiander, Andreas. "Ad Lectorem de Hypothesibus Huius Operis." In *De revolutionibus orbium coelestium*, by Nicolaus Copernicus, 10. Norimbergae: Apud Ioh. Petreium, 1543. Online. https://archive.org/details/nicolaicopernicioocope_1/page/n9.

Petri, Sara. "Facundus of Hermiane." In vol. 2 of *The Oxford Guide to the Historical Reception of Augustine*, edited by Karla Pollmann et al., 969–70. Oxford: Oxford University Press, 2015.

Pierce, Charles Sanders. "A Neglected Argument for the Reality of God 1908." In *Selected Philosophical Writings*, edited by Peirce Edition Project, 434–50. Vol. 2 of *The Essential Pierce*. Bloomington: Indiana University Press, 1998.

Plato. *Protagoras*. Edited by T. E. Page. With a translation by W. R. M. Lamb. LCL. Cambridge, MA: Harvard University Press, 1962.

Plotinus. *Enneads*. Edited by G. P. Goold. Translated by A. H. Armstrong. LCL. Cambridge, MA: Harvard University Press, 1967.

Pollmann, Karla, et al., eds. *The Oxford Guide to the Historical Reception of Augustine*. 3 vols. Oxford: Oxford University Press, 2015.

Porphery. "Προς Μαρκελλαν." In *Porphyre: Vie de Pythagore, Lettre a Marcella*, edited by Eduard des Places. Paris: Society D'Edition Les Belles Lettres, 1982.

Portalie, Eugene. *A Guide to the Thought of Saint Augustine*. Translated by Ralph J. Bastian. London: Burns & Oates, 1960.

Possidius. *The Life of Saint Augustine*. Translated by Matthew O'Connell. Villanova: Augustinian, 1988.

———. *Vita Sancti Augustini.* S. Aurelii Augustini Opera Omnia: Patrologiae Latinae Elenchus. Online. https://www.augustinus.it/latino/vita_possidio/index.htm.

Rorty, Richard. *Contingency, Irony, and Solidarity.* Cambridge: Cambridge University Press, 1989.

Rosen, Stanley. *Plato's Sophist.* New Haven: Yale University Press, 1983.

———. *Plato's Statesman: The Web of Politics.* New Haven: Yale University Press, 1995.

———. *Plato's Symposium.* New Haven: Yale University Press, 1968.

Santayana, George. *Character & Opinion in the United States with Reminiscences of William James and Josiah Royce & Academic Life in America.* New York: George Braziller, 1955.

Saslow, Eli. *Rising out of Hatred: The Awakening of a Former White Nationalist.* New York: Anchor, 2018.

Sextus Empiricus. *Against the Ethicists.* With a translation by R. G. Bury. LCL. Cambridge, MA: Harvard University Press, 1936.

———. *Against the Logicians.* Translated by Richard Bett. Cambridge Texts in the History of Philosophy. Cambridge: Cambridge University Press, 2005.

Shapiro, Hermann, and Edwin M. Curley, eds. *Hellenistic Philosophy: Selected Readings in Epicureanism, Stoicism, Skepticism, and Neo-Platonism.* New York: Modern Library, 1965.

Stowe, Harriet Beecher. "Sojourner Truth, The Libyan Sibyl." *Atlantic,* April 1863. Online. https://www.theatlantic.com/magazine/archive/1863/04/sojourner-truth-the -libyan-sibyl/308775.

Strauss, Leo. *On Plato's Symposium.* Edited by Seth Benardete. Chicago: University of Chicago Press, 2001.

———. *Studies in Plato's Political Philosophy.* Chicago: University of Chicago Press, 1983.

———. *What is Political Philosophy? And Other Studies.* 1959. Reprint, Chicago: University of Chicago Press, 1988.

Thomas Aquinas. "Hymn 98." In *One Hundred Latin Humns: Ambrose to Aquinas,* edited by Peter G. Walsch and Christopher Husch, 353–70. Cambridge, MA: Harvard University Press, 2012.

———. *Sententia Metaphysicae.* Textum Taurini, 1950 ed. *Corpus Thomisticum.* Online. http://www.corpusthomisticum.org/cmp02.html.

———. *The Summa Theologiæ of St. Thomas Aquinas.* Edited by Kevin Knight. Translated by Fathers of the English Dominican Province. *New Advent,* 2017. Online. http://www.newadvent.org/summa/3030.htm.

———. *Summa Theologica.* Textum Leoninum, Romae 1888 ed. *Corpus Thomisticum.* Online. https://www.corpusthomisticum.org/sth0000.html.

Tippet, Krista. "Befriending Radical Disagreement: An Interview with Derek Black and Matthew Stevenson." *On Being,* May 17, 2018. Online. https://onbeing. org/programs/derek-black-and-matthew-stevenson-befriending-radical- disagreement.

Troeger, Thomas H. "Praise the Source of Faith and Learning." *Hymnary.* Online. https://hymnary.org/text/praise_the_source_of_faith_and_learning.

Truth, Sojourner, and Olive Gilbert. *Narrative of Sojourner Truth: A Bondswoman of Olden Time.* Edited by Nell Irvin Painter. New York: Penguin, 1998.

Weinschenk, Susan. "Why We're All Addicted to Texts, Twitter, and Google: Dopamine Makes You Addicted to Seeking Information in an Endless Loop." *Psychology Today*, September 11, 2012. Online. https://www.psychologytoday.com/us/blog/brain-wise/201209/why-were-all-addicted-texts-twitter-and-google.

West, Cornel. *The American Evasion of Philosophy: A Genealogy of Pragmatism*. London: Macmillan, 1989.

West, Cornel, and Yancy, George. "Power Is Everywhere, but Love Is Supreme." *New York Times*, May 29, 2010. Online. https://www.nytimes.com/2019/05/29/opinion/cornel-west-power-love.html.

"Why We're Susceptible to Fake News, How to Defend Against It." *American Psychological Association*, August 10, 2018. Online. https://www.apa.org/news/press/releases/2018/08/fake-news.

Wilhite, David E. *Ancient African Christianity*. New York: Routledge, 2017.

———. "Augustine the African: Post-colonial, Postcolonial, and Post-postcolonial Readings." *Journal of Post-colonial Theory and Theology* 5.1 (2014) 1–34. Online. http://www.postcolonialjournal.com/Resources/Wilhite%205%201.pdf.

———. "Augustine in Black and African Theology." In vol. 1 of *The Oxford Guide to the Historical Reception of Augustine*, edited by Karla Pollmann et al., 126–34. Oxford: Oxford University Press, 2013.

Williams, Preston N. "Christian Realism and the Ephesian Suggestion." *Journal of Religious Ethics* 25.2 (1997) 233–42.

Wittgenstein, Ludwig. *Culture and Value*. With a translation by Peter Winch. Chicago: University of Chicago Press, 1980.

———. *Tractatus-Logico-Philosophicus*. With a translation by D. F. Pears. New York: Humanities, 1961.

Name/Subject Index